PENGUIN BOOKS

WHERE IT ALL BEGAN

Ann Cornelisen was born in Cleveland, Ohio, and educated at Vassar College. Her first book, published in 1965, was *Torregreca* ("deserves to be an all-time classic" — Sean O'Faolain). Her subsequent books include *Women of the Shadows, Strangers and Pilgrims*, and *Any Four Women Could Rob the Bank of Italy*. In 1974 she received a special award from the National Institute of Arts and Letters. She now lives in a thirteenth-century house in the Tuscan countryside.

ANN CORNELISEN

WHERE IT ALL BEGAN

ITALY 1954

BEGAN

PENGUIN BOOKS

PENGUIN BOOKS
Published by the Penguin Group
Viking Penguin, a division of Penguin Books USA Inc.,
375 Hudson Street, New York, New York 10014, U.S.A.
Penguin Books Ltd, 27 Wrights Lane,
London W8 5TZ, England
Penguin Books Australia Ltd, Ringwood,
Victoria, Australia
Penguin Books Canada Ltd, 2801 John Street,
Markham, Ontario, Canada L3R 1B4
Penguin Books (N.Z.) Ltd, 182–190 Wairau Road,
Auckland 10, New Zealand

Penguin Books Ltd, Registered Offices:
Harmondsworth, Middlesex, England

First published in the United States of America by
Dutton, an imprint of New American Library, a division of
Penguin Books USA Inc., 1990
Published in Penguin Books 1991

10   9   8   7   6   5   4   3   2   1

THE LIBRARY OF CONGRESS HAS CATALOGUED THE HARDCOVER AS FOLLOWS:
Cornelisen, Ann, 1926–
Where it all began: Italy, 1954 / Ann Cornelisen. —1st ed.
p.   cm.
"A William Abrahams book."
ISBN 0 525 24829 3 (hc.)
ISBN 0 14 01.4783 7 (pbk.)
1. Cornelisen, Ann, 1926–   —Homes and haunts—Italy.
2. Authors, American—20th century—Homes and haunts—Italy.
3. Italy—Social life and customs—20th century.   I. Title.
PS3553.0658Z464   1990
818'.5403—dc20   89–34457

Printed in the United States of America

WHERE IT ALL
BEGAN

One

Start at the beginning, they say. All else will fall into place. *They*, whoever they are, perceive dreams and chance meetings and whole lives as clearly organized, like a recipe for meringues. "Take the whites of four eggs . . ." If each step is followed, the result is apt to be meringues (and a quart of mayonnaise. *They* are cavalier about the four innocent yolks, probably feeling that nature, sooner or later, will adapt to the commercial credo of "return the unused portion and your money will be cheerfully refunded"). On the other hand, take a young American woman in 1954, put her down in Italy, follow her steps, and the result is apt to be the wife of a stockbroker in Greenwich, Connecticut, who, if she thinks of Italy at all, confuses it with a general nostalgia for her youth.

But it is thirty-five years later and I am still here. Any beginning would be arbitrary, would leave out the imponderables—my vision of Beatrice Cenci and Lucrezia, and the visions of half-forgotten teachers, who intrigued me with Catullus, Ovid, Galileo—and archaeology, which seemed a real, grown-up treasure hunt. The Italy we invented was a country of a thousand mysteries. It still is, only now for me the mysteries are different. Or perhaps after all these years the Italy I know is simply another invention. I test my resolution of the mysteries in the only way I can, by going back to the first encounters, when, yes, the mind and eye were ignorant, but so eager. The approach may be too empirical, but Italy, more than most countries, is everything and nothing that it seems to be. There is only one certainty: its mysteries never end.

Unfortunately what I remember best about the early morning of April 15, 1954, when I crossed the border from France into Italy, is another surge of panic, which had, anyway, been boiling around the emotional sluices of my mind ever since the night before in Paris. At the station my mother had struggled through our abortive platform conversation. Over the years of boarding school and college there had been so many, always the same, details already discussed, repeated, half heard, half misunderstood, and repeated again, a verbal treading of water.

"You will remember to write? Your father worries. . . . I'll send summer clothes as soon as I get back." She was to sail on the *Ile de France* a day or so later. "About money . . . Your father . . ." She stopped, looking up and down the platform for some distraction from the end of that sentence. (Her dilemma was perennial: how to explain to my father.) Now, the decisions made, about to get on the train, with my luggage already in my compartment, I suddenly did not want to go back to Italy and study archaeology. The world off out there beyond the smoky sheds was immense and lonely, and I, at twenty-seven and recently divorced, had run out of courage.

"Mother, maybe I shouldn't . . ." She was not listening.

Instead, like everyone near us, she had turned to stare at and then make way for a tall, very beautiful, blonde woman, dressed in black (even to a large cartwheel hat) who swept along the platform at such speed that the sable coat, draped over her shoulders, undulated voluptuously in her slipstream. She was pursued by a scurrying, stumbling cortege of porters and what might have been friends or secretaries. Or newspapermen. People around us murmured: she gave the impression we should recognize her. She paused, glanced at a ticket she held in one hand, and then, by some prodigy of muscle and determination, levitated up the stairs and disappeared into my sleeping car. Her attendants jostled along behind her and the engine began to shriek and tootle in the way European films had made so familiar. There was no time for doubts. Only a quick good-bye.

To reach my compartment I had to push against the current of late-staying friends and the more casual porters, now determined to escape. From my window I watched them tumble out onto the platform almost at my mother's feet. She waved wistfully, probably torn between the certainty that she would never again see her only child and that other horrible certainty, that my father would never forgive her for leaving me. With a low, moaning whistle the train pulled out.

The dingy Paris suburbs, at their best in the dark, were twinkling by when the *Wagon Restaurant* steward came to my door. One cursory look and he spoke English: Would I dine? Which sitting? I chose the first. Soon, he assured me, I would hear the chimes. Now, at least, I had something definite to do. The light from small brass side lamps, whose crystal drops shimmered and tinkled with the movement of the train, shrouded the compartment in somber, Victorian opulence. Dark paneling and bombé protuberances elaborately inlaid concealed all that was utilitarian, even the handles to what must be cupboards. A groping inspection revealed a basin, a mirror illuminated by the faintest glow and a short-snouted china pitcher, fitted into a chute-drawer, which hid it until it was needed (obviously by a gentleman) and also dumped it after use, presumably out onto the tracks. Official interest in sanitation ended there. Woman's place was in the home. If travel she must, the lavatory at the end of the corridor would do.

The compartment doors were all closed. No sound even hinted at who might be within. Behind one was the beautiful blonde. On my return a waiter swayed along in front of me, his loaded tray held high, dipping slightly with the rhythm of the train. No doubt she would dine in her compartment. He disappeared around a corner. A rush of wheels, a door slammed and he had gone on to the next car. Minutes later the chimes sounded far off, again closer and then were drowned out by another rush of wheels.

At my table two Frenchmen, neither young nor old, were already sitting in the aisle chairs, talking. They stood up immediately. Handing me to my seat by the window was a stately pavane. I looked out. The glass was a perfect black ground, mirroring the interior of the car back to me. The Frenchmen watched me, eyes half closed, intent on the traditional inventory. (That is, evaluation of my flaws and possible mitigating features and speculation on probable terms of concession.) It meant nothing. It was in the pattern of Why do men climb mountains? Because they are there. If need be, my French could slump from its rather approximate fluency back to fragmentary. Again the men stood up, figures blurred in my window view, chairs were moved and a woman in black slipped into the place opposite me. My window reflected a slender back and shoulders, a long neck and a chignon of hair. She had twisted around to discuss wine with the waiter. Next he asked for my order. I had to give up the anonymity of my mirror vision and face my dinner companions. There, staring at me with a slight smile and lifted, questioning eyebrows, was the beautiful blonde. Without the enormous hat she looked younger (she was, as came out later, only a few years older than I) but in no way more vulnerable.

"Do you prefer red or white?" she asked in English, American English.

"Red," I murmured, too startled to think her officious. Besides, her voice was casual, kind. I might have been a friend.

"Ah, then you must try the . . ." I no longer remember what. She and the waiter squabbled amiably, equal authorities, over which year would do until she was allowed to win. With that settled she turned back to us, ready to consider our petitions. The wine list she held up over her shoulder, expecting it to be taken. That simple gesture, like all her others really, had a flourish about it that was utterly natural. She was not trying to attract attention. She knew she would. She was serenely convinced of her beauty, of its importance and of her own to the people around her. There was nothing brittle about her manner, nor did ego have much to do with it: certain things about herself she accepted as fact and expected others to do the same.

The Frenchmen, far too impressed to bother about their inventories, leaned toward her, ready to charm. She listened absently, her answers to their questions as automatic as her quick glances at the people who moved back and forth in the aisle. Yes, she traveled a great deal. Indeed, wasn't the *Wagon Restaurant* food extraordinary? No, she lived in Florence and Rome. Her husband was Italian. She asked nothing of them, and when a waiter presented a tray of hors d'oeuvres for our admiration, she used it as an excuse to switch to English.

"You're American? Where are you from? Where are you going? What's your name? All those things— tell me." She prodded me along, listening and nibbling at her food with such concentration the men could find no excuse to reclaim her attention. By the end of the first course we had discovered a mutual friend. She told me something of herself, her American self. I explained I would study Italian in Florence, later in Rome, archaeology and was surprised to find the plan sounded quite reasonable to both of us.

The men watched us frowning, bemused by the idea that two young women preferred talking to each other rather than to them. Nor were they satisfied with the cheerful résumés of our conversation that she offered in the ceremonial pauses between courses. Isn't it nice, we have a mutual friend? Or, we've been talking

about New York. Do you know it well? They countered
with Paris, London. She explored their subjects with
neutral courtesy that tended to cauterize them. When
the inevitable silence came and she turned back to me,
I, following what seemed to be the rules of this peculiar
conversation, pitched us back into res americana.

Such meals have their own leisurely pace. By the
time checks were presented and we were to make way
for the second sitting, I had lapsed into semi-lucid som-
nambulism. Wine and food and uncertainty had taken
their toll. Nothing seemed quite real. My new friend
shed the Frenchmen and insisted I come to her compartment for a brandy. She instructed the sleeping-car
attendant at length about that, about our breakfasts,
hers and mine, and about our passports. My first night
alone in a foreign country and she expected me to break
the tourist's cardinal law—never let your passport out
of your sight.

"Don't be ridiculous. Give him your passport, tip
him well and you'll probably never even see a border
guard. If they want to know anything, they can ask me."
My feeble objections were lost in her further orders to
the attendant. Did he understand? He was to come to
her, not bother me. I went to bed feeling the world off
out there beyond the smoky sheds was not so immense
and lonely after all.

Banging on my door woke me up. It felt like the middle
of the night and was. The compartment was very cold
and very dark. Outside voices were screaming, the
loudest and shrillest that of my new friend. I groped for
the light switch and could not find it, nor could I remember where my robe was. Had I unpacked it? Louder

bangs were followed by shouted orders, which even before my first Italian lesson, I understood: open the door. How could I explain that I had no passport? Suddenly there were howls of rage from the corridor. The men at the door screamed something about "insults." The car attendant, who for the duration of the crisis spoke only French, mumbled placatingly and my protectress screamed even louder, presumably more colorful insults. I did the only thing I could; I pulled the blankets up around my shoulders and opened the door. Two small, dark men in rumpled uniforms peered at me, their dark, liquid eyes suggesting anything but an official visit. One flashed a light in my face, then leaned out into the corridor to study a booklet in the better light and my friend, somewhere behind the guards, launched into what sounded like the last act of *Medea*. The guards wheeled around to shout at her and the porter stuck his head in the door.

"Is all right. They say 'What the fuss about?' " And he closed the door, leaving me again in the dark. By then other passengers were up, out in the corridor. Footsteps came and went. Distance or good humor had softened the rumble of voices. Several minutes later my fretting about whether to get up and dress or not was interrupted by a knock at my door, which was immediately flung open. A guard appeared, or actually his face appeared, lighted by the full glare of his flashlight held just under his chin. The eyes gazed fondly, dementedly at me.

"Dank you!" And he gave me my passport.

For better or worse, I was in Italy.

The next morning the Tower of Pisa tilted by, glistening in the clear, clear sun of a false summer day. For

some reason no one could explain, we were very late
and rapidly became more so, shunting around on the
braided rails of a vast freight yard. Happy even with
that view, I leaned out my window. Off to the side of
the train a young boy, wearing a soutane and a surplice
of ragged filet lace and carrying a silver pot by its hoop
handle, followed a priest on his slow passage from car
to car. At each, be it boxcar, gondola or flatcar, the
priest raised his arm and waved a silver wand three
quick flicks. After every two or three cars he lowered
the wand behind him and, without looking, waggled it
until it found the boy's pot. Once satisfied that his as-
pergillum was again filled with holy water, he raised it
and paced on, flicking it rhythmically. He hesitated over
the rusty skeletons of two burned-out passenger carriages. On second thought he blessed them too.

In the years since I have seen a bit of everything
blessed—houses, excavations, mules, tractors, wells,
operating rooms—always in the weeks immediately before Easter, but that morning it seemed so strange that,
as our train jerked back and forth, maneuvering, I went
from my window to the corridor windows, trying for
glimpses of the priest and his acolyte. They moved me-
thodically from track to track, while we wandered about
erratically, lurching and bumping, always ending up exactly where we had started. I was craning out a corridor window when my friend appeared, dressed for the
new climate in navy linen and pearls. Oh yes, her house
was always blessed at Easter and in the country the
acolyte dragged along a burlap bag because not all of-
ferings were in money.

She had been on her way, she said, to tell me
that her husband was meeting her and they would take
me wherever I was staying. No need to fuss with por-

ters and taxis. And so I was caught. There had been no space on the train for Thursday night. I was arriving one day earlier than expected and hoped to find a hotel room. On Easter weekend! In Florence? I must be mad. But never mind, she would solve this problem too. Nothing was ever impossible to her. They would find me a room, or at the worst I could spend the night with them. They would bring me back to Florence—there were guests to pick up.

Her husband, as dark and handsome as he should be, met us in a dashing red convertible. He accepted me as the entirely normal by-product of his wife's train trip and rocketed away from the station and up and down narrow streets, chattering gaily, until we swept up to the door of the Grand Hotel. What she told the manager, I never knew, but I was given a comfortable single room and bath—on Maundy Thursday.

That settled, they got back into the bright red convertible, the motor snarled menacingly and they took off, waving back at me. That was the last I ever saw of Consuelo Crespi. The rest I read in magazines. She was already then one of the celebrated beauties of Europe, one, naturally, of the best dressed as well, and would become editor of the Italian *Vogue*. Why she adopted me, I do not know, but she convinced me that in Italy anything is possible and I am grateful.

Two

On the far side of the Ponte Vecchio, behind Palazzo Pitti, the Boboli Gardens form a secret island, which is, in turn, the secret view from the higher apartments in the buildings along the near side of the main street *and* from the few houses that line one narrow cul-de-sac. Passersby suspect nothing. They are distracted by the shops and bustle and then move quickly on, disconcerted by the shadowy medieval privacy of the alley. It does not invite intruders. Along one side is a blank brick wall, on the other, a row of well-polished front doors, each flanked by a window and its bowed-out iron grille. The room behind it, condemned to almost perpetual darkness, is inevitably the kitchen. The rest of life takes place at the back. Half a flight up, the drawing room runs the depth of the house and opens onto a fenced garden, perhaps twice the length of the room itself. And there, beyond the rose beds, the birdbath and the lawn chairs, are the Boboli Gardens.

With each successive flight up the view is more intriguing.

In 1954 one such house belonged to a Miss Child, a Bostonian of advanced years and failing health, who had, before the war, run her own "finishing school" in Florence. She was small, had very white hair and sharp blue eyes that disapproved of much they saw. A lifetime spent with spoiled, headstrong girls had taught her to express her displeasure in a hundred ways and degrees, and now that everyone seemed very young indeed to her, she seldom troubled herself with tact, except for the occasional person she, for her own reasons, considered Eminent. Many evenings by the time coffee was served at the far end of the drawing room, her guests, their egos in disarray, were reduced to murmurs about the weather. That year, like most, the weather was a subject of inexhaustible wonder.

Out of habit and some slight financial distress, Miss Child still "took in" three young women who came to Florence to "study." The subjects were vague and suitably elastic. She knew of schools for almost everything, but her first concern was the respectability and solvency of the parents. Diplomats were favored. Industrialists would do, if prewar. For her part she promised pleasant quarters, good food and careful chaperonage.

That year there were two blonde Viking sisters who giggled a great deal and spent much of their time on research into the mores and tastes of young Florentine men. They also must have had a stable of ladies who were willing to telephone Miss Child with faultlessly dull-sounding invitations, because, while she thought of them as enjoying the Bach B-Minor Mass or a Sunday outing *en famille*, they were actually at a night

club or zooming along the Firenze-Mare on their latest
conquests' motorcycles. No one could deny that they
learned Italian. They also had a season of thrilling adventures, which, not understanding the strict limitations put on well-brought-up Florentine girls, they
credited entirely to their own charms.

They shared the large front bedroom on the third
floor, the one that faced the street and so had no view,
with a serious American girl, named Angelica, a fine
artist and musician, who had won a grant for a year of
study. Miss Child was very pleased with the foundation
(and her director-friend) in loco parentis, but paid little
attention to the girl. Fortunately Angelica was too busy
with her work and her friends to mind. She was invisible, except at meals, where she sat, wide eyed, looking
from one guest to the next, as though searching for the
feature that would, forever, irrevocably establish the
difference between them. There were few clues in what
they said. They were Americans—relatively prosperous, well-educated Americans—who were smitten anew
with everything European and disparaged all things
American. They gloried in the monuments, in the custom of dining, as against eating, and in the cheapness
of their comforts. Americans were crass, cultureless, they
insisted, unaware that they were offering ample proof
to the two Vikings, who were only too happy to chime
in with snide remarks about our monstrous cars, our
food, our divorce rate and our loud voices. What puzzled her, Angelica finally admitted, was that these
Americans without ever consciously seeing the people
of the countries they visited, despised them. Then the
next day she sat at the table wide eyed, looking from
face to face, still searching.

Also on the third floor, at the back, overlooking

the Boboli Gardens, was a bedroom and bath reserved for The Eminent. A dear friend of my mother's, my favorite "pretend" aunt, was definitely one such, though she never realized it. She had urged us to call on Miss Child, had even written her a note, so one cold March afternoon we had gone for tea. Tea and questions. It was Eminence by association, but it was enough for me to be awarded the third-floor bedroom with bath and view for two weeks while "arrangements" were made for more permanent quarters and Italian lessons. By coincidence my term would end with the arrival of my pretend aunt.

Above us lived Maria and Mario, the middle-aged couple who looked after this unlikely menagerie. Exactly how the space was divided I never knew. There was a bathroom with a sitz bath and a laundry room and drying loft. The rest, however much or little, was their quarters. Sometimes in the evening after dinner we heard the cavernous sloshing of water in a tub. Probably sheets put in to soak. The soft padding of slippers and a muted radio were the only other sounds. They never seemed to go out, except for the daily shopping and Mass on Sunday. Maria was a sort of phantom. Very early in the morning you might catch a glimpse of her sturdy form weaving down the stairs under a load of fresh linen. Otherwise she was either in the kitchen cooking or in her attic washing and ironing the endless sheets, towels and napkins the household produced.

Mario, on the other hand, was omnipresent. He was a friendly, square little man with grizzled hair and moustache, who smiled easily and was always ready to help newcomers in Italian simplified to the exact level of their comprehension. In the mornings he could be found in his black-and-red striped jacket, dusting and sweeping or setting the table. At meals, now changed into a white jacket with brass buttons, he served. The rest of his time was spent in the kitchen, helping Maria while he waited for Miss Child, whom he always addressed as "Madama," to ring for morning coffee, or the post or afternoon tea or sometimes just for a good grumble.

Miss Child, who believed in keeping everyone busy, could in the right humor grumble a great deal. Her day's pleasures began with her breakfast tray and her interview with Joan and Jim, a young American couple who lived in the minute guest house at the bottom of the garden. Joan, tall, slender and blonde, did Miss Child's letters and bookkeeping. Jim, tall, slender and dark, chased plumbers, electricians and coal merchants for her and would at the right fee act as a guide to Florence or Siena. In their free time, which was limited to the sleepy hours of the afternoon, he was writing a book and she typed manuscripts. They were anything but omnipresent. They were charming at meals, answered a thousand questions about Florence and dodged hundreds of little favors asked of them by the American visitors who arrived at Miss Child's table. Afterward Jim would hand the coffee cups around very gracefully and explain the noon news broadcasts. Joan would sympathize with the newest confused visitor. For half an hour. Then they had engagements or work that took them, regretfully, away. Escape must have felt like rescue from a school of piranhas.

At lunch on Good Friday I became a member, a very silent member, of this odd mélange. There were ten of us at table, which meant that some were guests

for that meal, but I could not tell which. Easter Monday
being a holiday too, it was Tuesday before I was sure
who actually lived in the house. The Vikings disappeared for the entire weekend, on what sounded a very
cultural junket, although I did notice that Joan and Jim
quizzed them about the details and were not impressed.
Angelica was at some meals and not at others. About
the time I decided Joan and Jim were permanent they
vanished for all of Monday. Still, there were always
ten of us at table. Easter, spring, is a busy time in
Florence.

During the months I was around Miss Child's
house (as it turned out, I had my meals there even after
I moved) those gaggles of guests were as educational as
my Italian lessons. From listening to them I worked out
a formula, a sort of personal *jus gentium*, which, even
after thirty years' practice, I do not always manage to
follow, but which is still valid.

The American suffering from Europaphilia usually has a worse case of Americaphobia. With time, and
only with time, comes a sense of proportion, so twit him
or change the subject. Handle Italophobes with care.
All Italians are thieves. Are filthy. Look at their streets.
Do *not* say, "If you'd left your purse on an American
bus . . ." or "Have you looked at the streets of New
York recently?" Your defense will only prove you have
gone native, a state despised above all others.

The Europeans who make wild pronouncements
about the United States are another matter. Your choices
are more complex. If your temper is well under control,
deny, calmly, each point that is wrong. Or gibe mildly
at the other's country. None is invulnerable. Remember
the Germans' ubiquitous wurstels, the French's inevi-

table rudeness, the Italians' chaotic traffic, the bedlam of the streets. If you are willing to insult, try "Oh, do you know America well?" Thirty years ago, few did. Now is another matter.

The English are a question apart. The common language lulls us. We generalize about each other with learned abandon. So Winston Churchill was the savior of Britain, according to us, as Franklin Roosevelt was the savior of America, according to them. That about half the people in both countries opposed their savior is a detail we ignore. We press on with our assumptions right through boiled cabbage and chewing gum, until with luck we notice the dissenting squint. Maybe a few questions are in order. With time and tact the muddle can be straightened out.

My last rule was Remember, they, Europeans and English, will persist in thinking that all Americans, 160 million of us, are rich and ignorant.

I was not very talented at the verbal soft shoe my regime required, especially with other Americans, who irritated me most, but I learned. Slowly. Just as I learned Italian. That struggle began at 8:30 the Tuesday morning after Easter. Already the hints of summer had been swept away by a cold, driving wind and rain, which kept up with slight variations of violence for the next six weeks and eventually mildewed my only practical coat, a garment called a storm coat with a heavy twill shell, a fur collar and a furry-plushy lining. I had not yet solved the puzzle of Florentine transportation, so I slogged along past Palazzo Pitti, over the Ponte Vecchio and into Piazza della Repubblica, angling my umbrella in what I thought would be, and usually was not, the direction of the next gust of wind. Then there

was a choice, either the arcades that offered protection
from the rain, but funneled the wind at gale force, or
the café maze, through, around, between chairs and tables and impenetrable hedges of potted plants in waist-
high iron troughs. Whichever, I arrived cold and wet at
the corner of the short street where my teacher lived.

That first morning, like every other, anxiety and
my chronic pre-noon stupor made me early, so I became
a habitué among habitués of a corner bar with steamed-
up windows. From the outside it looked empty. Inside
it was an uproar. The air was so heavy with the acrid-
sweet smell of cheap Italian cigarettes, wet wool and
sodden leather that it was hard to breathe. Metal chairs
shrieked as they were dragged around on the marble-
chip floor, the coffee machine, like an upended antique
locomotive with its tank, its loops and swirls of tubing
and its knobs, snorted and hissed on the counter, and
the customers shouted at each other. They were all men
from the neighborhood. Young men, electricians, me-
chanics or plumbers, in sky-blue coveralls and bicycle
clips. Men slightly older and plumper, clerks in stores
and banks, judging from their neat but well-worn suits
and their pointed black shoes that too much rain had
left dull and inclined to curl. For them overcoats were
out of season. With umbrellas looped over one arm,
dripping wherever they might, they pushed up to the
bar and called out their orders to no one in particular.

Behind the counter a young boy, bundled in
sweaters and a dirty white jacket that was too tight,
never looked up. He seemed mesmerized by his own
hands. He watched them, red and swollen with chilblains, as they went round and round the rim of a cup,
as they gouged out the sugar in the bottom, as they

rinsed the cup under the cold water trickling from the tap, and then took another. He did little else all day long except swab off the counter with a stringy dishrag.

The rest of the customers were older men, probably pensioners, who were enveloped, almost swallowed up by long, bulky overcoats that made them seem clothes trees with human heads. Each had a newspaper folded in his pocket and each had a favorite place at a favorite table. It took me several weeks to realize they sat huddled there all morning and much of the afternoon, watching the street through peepholes they smeared on the steamy glass of the windows and complaining to each other in shaky, querulous voices.

No one ever paid any attention to me in that café. I was another tourist. We were not interesting, so after my coffee I could loiter by the door with the other habitués, squinting at the street through my very own spy hole on the steamy glass. When finally it was 8:25, I ducked out into the street, down a few doors and in again.

The hall was dark and dank, especially, I discovered, in the morning, when the miasma of cats and garbage pails, waiting to be emptied, was thickest. The stairs were steep and marble. An elaborate iron banister was reassuringly solid on the straight runs, but too inclined to wobble on the switchbacks for comfort. Up I went, stopping on each landing to lean close to the doors, which meant over the garbage pails, and decipher the brass plaques. I prayed no one would open a door and find me poised there on tiptoe, unable to explain my problem. I need not have worried. It was one of the oddities of the building that I never met anyone. I heard voices behind the doors and footsteps on the stairs. A door would open below me, another close above me. Still, I never actually saw even one of the neighbors. Finally on the fifth floor a well-polished plaque said CAVALCA.

At my ring a radio was switched off, firm steps echoed along a corridor and the door was flung open with the kind of brio that seemed unlikely so early in the morning. She was Bianca Cavalca and I . . . She whirled me off down the corridor. Some of the beige and red tiles were loose and clinked in protest at our speed. Through a sparsely furnished room to a table by a window with two chairs facing each other. She had decided, she informed me, indicating the left-hand chair, that rather than the two hours in the morning originally suggested, we would get on faster if the time were split, an hour in the morning, an hour in the afternoon, 3:30 to 4:30. *D'accordo?* I would have time for two sets of homework, two discussions of it and . . . She left that to my imagination, switching instead to a workbook on the table in front of me. We would begin with vowel sounds. Very important, vowel sounds. Vowel sounds alone, with accents, with certain consonants—vowel sounds. And this was her last word in English, very clear, only slightly accented English. Twenty minutes of my own grunts and grimaces and brays left me breathless and ashamed. From the mouth, tongue behind the teeth, so! Not from the throat. Again, please.

Suddenly she leapt up and dashed out of the room, apologizing. Several minutes later somewhere in the distance there was a bubbling hiss, followed almost immediately by hurried footsteps. Coffee would revive me. Five minutes to relax and back to those wretched sounds that were so beguiling in the mouths of others. I gulped the coffee, expecting the tray with the fine porcelain cups and sugar bowl to be whisked away before I could get the cup to my lips. Just in time. It was consigned to an end table, and we plunged into auxiliary verb forms. We would return to vowel sounds later and see what I remembered. Now for *essere* and *avere*. Did I realize that "whodunit" would be translated as *chi fu*? Never mind. I would not have to worry about that verb form for a week or so. The present tense . . .

By the time I knew about the past definite of *chi fu* I also knew that Bianca Cavalca did everything— movement, speech and thought—at double speed. It took slightly longer to realize that she was kind, patient and inclined more to quick irony than to rage. Certainly my first impression was of almost overpowering energy and determination. Physically she was less forbidding. She was of average height and had an average figure for a woman in her early fifties, tending a bit toward the matronly, though the layers of sweaters required to survive in a Florentine flat with wood-burning stoves probably accounted for the solid look. She had firmly waved, dark hair with here and there strands of gray, and she wore glasses, which at the time were anathema to Italian women. They preferred to grope around, just as she said, to stumble, shove papers right up under their noses rather than disfigure themselves. To her irritation she was often mistaken for a foreigner. The glasses again, she insisted, and there was no diplomatic way to tell her that more than the glasses, it was the black cord, looping down from the earpieces, always tangled with the clattery chains and beads she wore around her neck, that betrayed her. Until very recently that gadget was strictly American.

She admired all things American and English, even the Anglo-American colony's church bazaars and benefit card parties, which were surely acquired tastes.

She had traveled in England. Twice Canadian friends
had included her ticket with their invitation to visit. She
read our novels, plays and mysteries. She longed for
British cashmeres, and, if she must be ill, for American
medicine, and our easy inclination to democratic process. She was so partial, she almost forgot to be critical,
but to be labeled Italo-American was too much. She was
from Parma, and after her objections and remarks, in
her clipped, concise Italian, about the general density
of the Florentine mind, the southern mind, for everything south of the Po was southern, no shopkeeper or
bar boy would doubt it.

She did not care for Florentines. She found most
of them smug and their much-vaunted language, minc-
ing. Not as bad as the Sienese. They, the other con-
tenders for the perfect accent, were mush-mouthed.
Couldn't I hear it? Her cruel imitation was my first lesson in the snobbery that runs the length of Italy, from
north to south. The Parmesans scoff at the Florentines,
just as the Florentines scoff at the Romans or as the
Calabrians scoff at those island people across the straits.
Not just about accents. About mentality too, which
is much more damning. She wanted all Italian to be
staccato, clean and forceful. She may have equated
sound with thought processes, for she was also a fairly
irrational champion of rational thought. In the years
that followed she must have hated the government-
controlled television, whose programs pumped out slurred
Roman speech (and mentality) until now it is the lingua
franca, correct Italian to millions of people who were
only really comfortable in dialect.

She would tolerate no solecisms from me. No
kitchen Italian. Infinitives were not substitutes for the

proper tense and person. In any case of doubt the subjunctive was required, and almost every statement in Italian seemed to imply *some* doubt, even the simplest, like I think it is red. Just because *I* think it, does not mean it is so, therefore the present subjunctive is mandatory. *Io penso che* sia *rosso*. The foreign habit of tutoyer was absolutely unacceptable. The correct courteous forms of address would be used at all times, which, now that Fascism had been swept away and with it the *Voi* form Mussolini had borrowed from French, meant the old court usage of the third-person singular or plural. It made no difference that I might sound like a too-well-trained butler or a superior English salesclerk—If Madam could come back—. Indeed, since *Lei*, the proper formal pronoun, is feminine, I would in effect be calling men Madam too. She was so adamant about her rules that today in an absent-minded humor I am capable of using formal pronouns with a child, which makes everyone, including the child, giggle.

It takes awhile to get an Anglo-Saxon mind twisted into this sort of grammatical knot, and what the mind knows is not always what the tongue delivers. Months of stammering and open-mouthed *uh*ing were to be lived through before words, whole sentences tumbled casually out in something resembling coherent speech. Bianca Cavalca estimated a few weeks, at most a month and to push me along on her timetable thought up further exercises in torture. Each day I was to buy and read a newspaper. Morning and afternoon for fifteen minutes she had me read out loud to her from *Don Camillo*. The choice was not haphazard: Guareschi was from Parma too. Once I caught on to his passion for playful suffixes, I almost enjoyed it, and he was as close to a colloquial writer as Italy had, so any words that stuck in my memory were useful. I was also ordered to *talk* to people in shops and cafés. With my Italian locked at the pen-of-my-aunt stage and my timidity expanding to include English, I ignored that instruction. The last was to see as many films as I could endure.

In Italy, even then, most foreign films were dubbed, not as perfectly as they are now, but always with good actors and an approximation of synchronization. It may have started as a commercial necessity: Italians were passionate moviegoers, but many were not quick readers, or at least not up to a steady stream of subtitles. Whatever the reason, dubbing was a tradition. Before the war, for instance, some manic genius dubbed Laurel and Hardy, renamed forever Stanlio and Olio, by having them babble their nonsense in piping Italian mangled by a heavy American accent, the emphasis always on the wrong syllable, every vowel flat. The films still convulse audiences and are, in a way that defies definition, funnier than the originals.

American films, I reasoned, offered one advantage: the situations and characters were identifiable. I would know where we started. Old were as good as new for my purposes and, having slipped down to the neighborhood theater level, would be a great deal less expensive. I worried constantly about my budget and took absurd measures to keep it under control. (One of the most futile involved a smiling recommendation of Mario's, a streetcar a block away from Miss Child's, in Via de' Serragli, that went *in* town. I never discovered its return route, which, because of the narrow streets, was quite different, but I did discover that if I took it before 7:30, I was entitled to a second trip, logically a return, for an additional ten lire. Instead of the return, I used

it for going *to* both my lessons. The rain and fog must
have rusted my brain cells. Taking that streetcar by
7:30 became an obsession. Never mind that in the morning I arrived in Piazza della Repubblica before *anything*
opened. Never mind that I had to loiter for forty-five
minutes. I saved four cents!) So the cheaper cinemas
had an appeal of their own. There were a number of
them within easy distance of the house, and they opened
in midafternoon. The second showing began about five,
which suited my schedule neatly; I could get there after
my lesson and would be home well before dinner. After
careful inspection of my financial position, I decided the
capital drain—at least thirty-two cents, often forty-
eight—was justified as an investment, as long as I did
not actually enjoy it too much. The Puritan ethic is ir-
repressible! I allowed myself two films a week, three if
it poured rain.

   A cinema is a cinema, or so I thought. The first
surprise was revealed by the usher's flashlight, her hand
opened in the universal gesture that cannot be misunderstood: she expected a tip. Add another eight cents
to expenses. But it was a one-time-only expense. I
adopted what seemed to be the accepted local technique
and lurked around at the back of the theater until the
usher was busy, or outflanked her and took a side aisle.
The second and third surprises arrived together: the seats
were plywood, and so many people were smoking the
screen was fuzzy. (To my astonishment during intermis-
sions the fire doors were flung open to let the smoke
out—and the cold air in. There was no heat anyway. In
more modern theaters, at intermission the ceiling rum-
bled open, offering a double treat of cold air *and* rain.)
The fourth surprise, which should not have been one,
was Gary Cooper, his mouth pursed, his eyes twinkling,

mumbling something meaningful—in Italian. He had no trouble at all. He kept it up. He even laughed in Italian.

My ears were beginning to believe what they heard, without understanding very much of it, when the fifth surprise arrived from quite another quarter: a hand was crawling along my shoulder. I flung it off, glared at the man sitting next to me and turned resolutely back to the screen. Now Richard Widmark was fluently bilingual. And the hand crept along my shoulder again. I moved down a seat. The man moved down a seat. I did not wait to find out if he had joined me to apologize. I stood up, moved back two rows and took an aisle seat flanked by two empty seats. Now Grace Kelly was in the act, her voice uncharacteristically breathless and hysterical. Her Italian was perfect too. A man excused himself, stepped in front of me and sat down in the next seat. He folded his raincoat in his lap and put his hands on top of it. Very soon one of them dropped down to explore my knee and I was on the move again.

For two hours I played hopscotch around the theater. My average tenure was about ten minutes, certainly no more than fifteen. When the lights came up for the first intermission (and the doors were flung open), I saw that I was the only woman in a theater full of quite young men. It dawned on me that women did not go to the cinema alone. One who did was expected to be *compiacente*—obliging. That evening after dinner Jim explained the audience. They were unemployed men (and there were so many then), who killed long afternoons in the cheaper cinemas. He thought it would be easier to do battle with one, right down to blows, rather than be eternally on the move. Bianca Cavalca worked out a few pungent phrases I could use—*Giù con le mani! Basta! La smetta, per favore!*—and if they did not discourage my Don Giovannis, then we had a speech I was to deliver to the usher. For months it was my surest performance in Italian, other than "May I have a glass of water," a sentence which, in trying to quench my perpetual thirst, had acquired the pure *Italianità* of desperation.

Jimmy Stewart spoke Italian. So did Alan Ladd and, even more improbably, so did Vivian Leigh, Olivia De Havilland *and* Katharine Hepburn. And each time I saw them, I understood more of what they said and caught more of the curious anomalies of the Italian they spoke, which reflected the snobbery and the prudish public, if not private, morals of Fascism. There was a linguistic caste system. The hero could use the familiar *tu* with the lower orders, male or female, but in his own class he could only use it with a woman to whom he was married or related. The results were bizarre. Cary Grant, for all his charm, was not very convincing when he whispered *"Vi amo"* passionately into the ear of the lady of his choice. Of course in the newly revived court form, he would have lapsed into pure farce. Those pronouns! Treacherous pronouns! From every sentence they flung down their gauntlets, all because Bianca Cavalca had an idée fixe. Still, she and the movies taught me to listen, which is half the battle.

For the next weeks the rhythm of my life was decidedly pendular: from my room to my lesson, from my lesson to my room, again to my lesson and back to my room. There were hours in between when I did not have to conjugate verbs or write schoolgirl compositions, and a whole city to discover. Just to divine the time a museum or church or shop would be open took ingenuity. Each category had a general schedule, which was sub-

ject to quixotic variations. The State was the worst of-
fender. Not that I minded. Walking the streets provided endless amusement. Everything was new,
unfamiliar.

The simplest shopping was an odyssey to be un-
dertaken with a string bag. There were no paper sacks.
Women rushed from shop to shop, accumulating the
staples needed for that day. In the markets they were
handed their vegetables wrapped in newspaper. Almost
everything could be bought *sfuso*—loose. Codfish, wine,
oil, milk, anchovies, cigarettes. Bottles were precious.
The customer brought his own to be filled or exchanged
for another already filled. Tobacconists, who also sold
stamps and legal, franked paper, dispensed five, ten
cigarettes in pocket-sized tissue-paper bags. The extravagant customer who wanted a pack was offered
three, which he kneaded to discover the exact softness
or firmness that suited his taste. Material was for sale
at one shop, thread and buttons at another. Different
kinds of meat were sold in separate shops—pork in one,
beef, veal and lamb in another, chicken in still another
and, most startling to me, horsemeat in another. There
was a woman in a narrow, dark closet of a shop who sat
all day in the window, mending, reweaving runs in ny-
lon stockings. Other trades had window people—gild-
ers, leather workers and tailors' apprentices, who sat
cross-legged basting. Cabinetmakers, busy remaking the
antiques lost in the war, glued and clamped elaborately
curved frames in the street and then, if it happened not
to be raining, left them to dry, propped up against a
wall. If a museum was closed, it was enough to wander
the narrow streets to find a substitute.

Three

With my battle for Italian reduced to a schedule of perseverance, there remained one problem: my quarters. The first suggestion seemed nothing short of miraculous—a countess who would be charmed to rent me a room in her large, pretentious apartment, crowded with "antiques." As a recommendation, I think, though I was never sure, I was told she had been the mistress of an American colonel. Perhaps it was merely proof that she spoke English. I was sent off to discuss matters with her. She was fortyish, chic in the brittle, slightly shabby fashion of postwar Italy and very rude to the slovenly servant girl who opened the door to me. They showed me a sunny room muffled in dusty damask. Right across the hall was the bathroom. Water was scarce and the heating of it expensive, so one bath a week was offered. We agreed on terms (I had my reservations about that one bath, but had already learned that the offer of slightly more money

later would probably produce another, if not two more.)
She assured me I would have much in common with
her other "guests" and was positively effusive about
what close friends *we*, she and I, would become. I
had my reservations about that too. Nevertheless the
next morning I piled my bags in a taxi and moved
across town.

For some reason that day the countess and I were
alone at lunch. While she reminisced about the attractions and complications of life with an American colonel,
the first being food, I suspect, and the second, a wife in
the States, I puzzled over the silver. There was a standard amount, each piece with its crest, and each the
weight and size for Goliath. Then off to the right of my
wineglass was a gadget I had never seen before, silver
or otherwise. It was two large silver *X*'s, with knobs
where the points might have been, joined by a silver
crossbar. What could its function be? The maid, who at
least was not serving in her bedroom slippers, presented the solution very forcefully. When she came to
remove the pasta plates, she picked up my fork and
thumped it down on the silver bar, its tines facing the
tablecloth. It immediately began to dribble sauce.

That evening at dinner I met the other guests,
two German men in their mid-twenties and two Japanese men of an age no more identifiable than young.
They too were studying Italian along with courses in
their specific fields. The countess sent me to preside over
the foot of the table, where I could see my sauce spot,
now consigned to the man on my right. The countess
spoke excellent German, which may or may not have
implied a German colonel. The Japanese, left with me,
tried a few words of Italian. I could not understand them,
though they did understand me.

After the first course, when five forks (our hostess carefully licked hers clean) were dripping little blobs on the cloth, the countess reverted to English. It was our common language and remained such for the duration of my stay, or rather the duration of hostilities. The Germans and the Japanese had only one thing in common—their dislike of Americans, which, if unpleasant, was understandable. Or so I tried to tell myself. Still, a free English teacher was too good to miss. As the cloth became a chronicle of meals consumed, and the guests improved their English in pre–Third World War skirmishes, I became more frustrated. When for the fourth morning in a row I could not get into the bathroom and for the fourth morning in a row enjoyed the dubious comforts of the central station, I gave up and moved out.

In retrospect I do not understand why I expected people to help me nor why, when they disposed of me as they chose, I accepted it so docilely. Perhaps both are failings of the relatively young. There were still several days before my aunt was to arrive, and I knew what Miss Child did not, that she would let me have the other twin bed in her room for a few days if need be. My arrival with bags on Miss Child's doorstep caused some consternation and a flurry of conferences, which resulted two days later in an invitation to call on what might be my new landladies.

Indeed, they were ladies, gentlewomen anxious over the modern world and modern prices, and inclined to have as little to do with both as possible. Given their reluctance, the negotiations must have been complex. They had never had an outsider in the house. And a foreigner, at that. Foreigners were—well, they didn't hold with them. My *serietà*, that vague quality of sinlessness, past and future, required of "decent women," was, I am sure, discussed at length. Miss Child could say I came well recommended, Joan and Jim that, with my schedule, depravity was unlikely. Eventually the arrangement was presented as a fait accompli, or almost. They had invited me for afternoon coffee. If we took to each other, then . . . But that was rather indefinite. I was warned that *le signorine*—the neighbors and tradespeople had discarded the surname as though there could be no other maiden ladies—were very shy and very sensitive. In the event we came to an agreement, I would have my meals at Miss Child's, pay her the very nominal rent for my room as well, and the illusion that I was a guest would be maintained. Oh yes, and they spoke no English.

They lived in the last building of the cul-de-sac, a large palazzo, most, if not all, of which the family had at one time owned. It had been divided into two tiers of apartments, and from conversations I later overheard I learned that the signorine still owned and rented several apartments other than the one in which they lived. Theirs was, like all the others I had to do with in Florence, on the top floor. I arrived at their door breathless from the stairs and my own trepidations and was swept into a dim entrance hall by two white-haired, chattering women, who, though very different one from the other, had the faces of blonde, wide-eyed three-year-olds. They must have been in their sixties. Their names were so alike—Lina and Tina, or Rina and Rita, I no longer remember—that I always addressed them simply as "signorina," but in my mind they were Giggles and Toothy. Giggles was small and slight with large, innocent, pale blue eyes and an odd habit of speaking to her breastbone. After each phrase she giggled softly, apologizing in case she had said something silly, which she seldom did. Toothy was larger, heavier, had the same defenseless eyes and blustered mildly to prove she was shrewd. Actually she was as naive as her sister, but took her position as head of the household very seriously, which I thought explained the determined clamp of her lips over a luminous set of false teeth. For this very special occasion they wore dark wool dresses covered by layer upon layer of crocheted shawls that swayed and rippled around their bodies like limp plumage. Only one other time did I see them in such finery, which was also the only other time Toothy wore her false teeth.

They fluttered around, herding me into the drawing room, which was also dim. The draperies were drawn and the tiny bulbs of the light fixtures, well masked by deep red shades, but I did make out clusters of settees and scroll-backed chairs, all upholstered in dull damask, and at the center of one a spindly-legged coffee table with cups, saucers and pot already waiting for us. Knee-high tuffets of books and others of prints channeled traffic along fixed routes, which had the labyrinthine fault of leading as often as not to a dead end. Toothy finally issued clear left, right orders and I arrived at a chair.

When, at last, we were settled bolt upright on stiff, springless seats, I realized we were surrounded by tall vitrines that did not display so much as store a jumble of bibelots, stacked one on top of the other, shelf after shelf. The ritual of pouring coffee and passing cups, spoons, then sugar requires concentration and for comfort a table. One by my chair was indicated, a glass-topped table, chock-full of cameos. There were glass-topped tables at either end of the settee where the sisters perched. One was a depository for coins, the other for medals, with their gaudy ribbons tangled in a rainbow. Obviously someone in the family was a collector of just about anything. Maybe someday I could ask, but for the moment conversation was urgent. My mind was blank.

"You are American?" Giggles asked, her head bowed. A second later came the purling sound.

"Sì, *sono americana*," I intoned solemnly. "*Di Chicago.*"

"The city of Al Capone," they chorused. It was the standard reaction that as usual caught me off balance. While I rummaged around in my Italian for a countervirtue that was also pronounceable, the conversation went on without me. The signorine were bickering affably about a young airman they had hidden briefly during the war. Wasn't he from Chicago? No, Canada. But I remember distinctly he talked about a lake. No, Canada, I tell you. There are lakes there too. We went on that way for half an hour: a question to me and then a quiet natter between the sisters. Of the room, not even a hint. Obviously I would not do for some reason, so I must find a graceful excuse to leave. I had about decided on a lesson that required my presence, when Giggles came to my rescue.

"But we haven't shown you the room. It has its own bath, you know." She rose to her feet very slowly, as though lifted by a small electric motor, and led us carefully back through the tuffets and into the front hall again, where we stood for several minutes while she explained the bathroom. It was a remarkable prize *and* had no hot water. They were beginning to sense whether

I understood or not and supplied gestured clues if I seemed totally lost. Too expensive, we agreed. Then after some pantomime we established there was no man to bring up the coal, coke or wood, we never straightened out which, for the boiler. Finally a door was thrown open and we started into a cavern which, once a knobbly porcelain light switch was turned, proved to be a very long, narrow corridor, rather spooky in the penumbra supplied by the minute bulb, like going down a mine shaft, except that there at the end was a door. The sisters, pushing, twisting and lifting together, managed to get it open. In spite of our various stratagems later, it retained its difficult personality and could, especially in the middle of the night, screech out in a wild animal protest.

They motioned me inside: I was to view the fixtures—a gigantic tub high off the floor on ball-and-claw feet and a basin and toilet of doll's-house proportions. Well above the basin was a mirror and above that, surrounded by a large ruffle of milk glass, was a dim glow. Their combined efforts showed the top of my head as a blurry shadow.

I hurried along to catch up with the signorine, wondering where the bedroom could be. There were no doors leading off the corridor. From the entrance hall we followed a jog away from the living room and were again deep in a narrow corridor, which ran parallel to my bathroom corridor. At some time the two must have been one stately passage. We stopped at the first door. This would be my room. It had been their father's. He collected pictures, Toothy commented, a warning somehow implicit in her tone, and bustled off in the dark to open the shutters. Light revealed a large, rectangular room with a dado of ochreous simulated marble and, above it, red damask, much of which was hidden by paintings, all handsomely framed, of the gorier saints. A Victorian Saint Agatha in chiffon veils and misty smile proffered her breasts on a plate. Saint Sebastian was more bleeding holes than protruding arrows, and a smug Salome gazed down at a platter where John the Baptist's head trailed lifelike arteries and nerves and shreds of meat toward the foreground. Crucifixions abounded.

The furniture, imposing enough in itself, was eclipsed by all this gaudy iconography. Along the walls a towering wardrobe and a chest of drawers with a polished marble top shrank to attention, while in a corner a high brass bedstead, twinkling softly, seemed a misplaced bauble. In another corner near the large window a low armchair, upholstered in red plush, hid in the shadows, its back reclining at an angle that announced it hors de combat. Only an inlaid prie-dieu in the middle of the floor held its own. Proudly. It was also the one "work surface" in sight. The next morning I moved in, prepared for subliminal adventures in piety and some discomfort.

During the day I tiptoed in and out of the apartment on my errands, never seeing anyone, though I heard the sisters chattering away at the far end of the hall. Immediately after dinner I came back again, planning to study propped up in bed (already that afternoon the prie-dieu had defeated me, dumping books and papers in my lap and over the floor. Only an octopus could have used it as a desk, a curious picture at that). The sisters were still chattering, so I went along the hall, thinking they would be reassured to know I would not be going out again and had locked the door with all its various bolts and chains. Also I thought they might enjoy seeing the newspaper.

The corridor light switches eluded me, so I came from total darkness into the total light of a large room made small by an oval oak dining-room table and eight chairs. The sisters looked incongruous and uncomfortable sitting at it, knitting, and now it turned out that part of the twittering, chirping conversation I had heard earlier was a parrot, who was still chirping and twittering alternately in Toothy's and Giggles's voices. He (or she, I never knew. Sex, even of a parrot, did not seem an appropriate subject with the signorine.) was gabbling along. They were silent. It was a pleasant, digestive sort of silence. Two other bird cages, hooded in black, stood in the far corners of the room, flanking a row of windows. There had been trills and peepings too that morning, probably canaries. Opposite, where it was not immediately visible from the door, was a floor-to-ceiling bookcase filled with uniformly bound tomes. To my right a doorway led into what looked to be a pantry.

The signorine might almost have been waiting for me. They fluttered up, offering chairs, coffee or better, they insisted, camomile tea. It would help me sleep. I explained I really must work. They launched into apologies for the odd arrangements they had made at the back of the apartment. This room was the old kitchen, their kitchen had been a pantry and beyond was the real dining room, which connected with the drawing room. They liked the view from the kitchen. I would see in the morning. For now the shutters must stay closed. It was never wise to invite Peeping Toms, who, though I did not say so, would have needed grappling hooks and ropes to lower themselves from the roof. Perhaps the newspaper . . . ?

The offer brought squeals of pleasure. A newspaper! What a treat! These days they seldom saw one. Too expensive. That was odd: they only cost thirty lire (five cents). Did I realize that before the war thirty lire had been a month's salary for some people? My mathematics in Italian were not up to explaining the inflation of the lira, but I could promise them a newspaper every day. We would read it together, they suggested, and so began a daily ritual. Each afternoon, after I had read it and before I went to my lesson, I put it on their big, all-purpose table. They squabbled over it and chose articles they wanted me to read aloud. The discussions that followed were free-for-alls both psychologically and linguistically. Out of total ignorance I had chosen the right paper, a Roman paper I later discovered was known as the "newspaper of the servant girls." The signorine's tastes ran to crimes of passion and "human-interest" stories. National and international news bored them. They half-listened to it on their little plastic radio and dismissed it.

Only once did I succeed in starting on the first page. The main headline, some four inches high across the top of the paper, seemed provocative: CHURCHILL IN THE LAVATORY FOR 14 HOURS! They looked confused. I repeated *gabinetto* with some emphasis. They stared at me, uncomprehending. There was something about Italian journalistic tradition I obviously did not know. I still insisted. *Gabinetto?* Suddenly their eyes opened wide and they clapped their hands over their mouths, like little children, to stifle the squeaky, gurgling, hysterical giggles. No, no, they started time and again, then gulped and choked off into more giggles. It was contagious. Without knowing why, I was strangling and panting too. Eventually the meeting came to order and the honor of Italian journalism was saved. Churchill had spent fourteen hours in a cabinet meeting, not in a water closet, which was my only association with the word *gabinetto*.

That first evening I left them hunched over the newspaper and went off to study, sitting in the middle of the high brass bed, tailor fashion, which did not improve my handwriting or my back. The next morning at seven there was a knock on the door, followed a few minutes later by a second knock. Very wisely they did not trust me, nor were they familiar with the galloping toilette that got me out on the street in time for my tram. In my dash to the bathroom I almost collided with a tall, white enamel pitcher that sat just outside my door. Hot water! Just enough to be tempting, not quite enough to give more than an illusion of cleanliness and very hard to carry down the long corridor. By the time I came back there was a silver tray at my door with an enormous cup, a porcelain pot and a plate of sweet biscuits. In the pot was very hot, *very* rich, very, very sweet chocolate. The sisters had decided I was too thin. A young woman to be attractive must be plump. The tray slipped ever so slowly down the slope of the priedieu. It would not quite stay balanced at the top. Afraid that a split-second miscalculation would send it crashing to the floor, I took it to the chest of drawers and was standing there, by it, in the shadows when the mime, which often in the next weeks made me late for my economy transportation, began.

Across from my window, too high up in the brick wall to be noticeable from the street, was a large, shut-

tered window, which was suddenly thrown open by a
dark young man in a tan work smock. He leaned his
arms on the sill and bent forward to light a cigarette. A
moment later a girl with the golden red coloring usually
called Titian joined him, leaning on the sill almost in
parody of the young man. Her smock was black. As soon
as he sensed she had come, and without looking at her,
he started talking very quietly, very earnestly. He was
trying to convince her of something. She nodded,
watching his face, seeming to inspect it feature by feature, but never saying anything. If he stopped to glance
at her, she looked down at her hands.

There must have been steps up to the window.
People came in the room behind them. I could hear their
voices, but never saw anyone unless their heads and
shoulders slowly rose up in the window, which for the
most part was left as the private rendezvous of the young
couple. Apparently it was a workroom that had to do,
judging from the smell, with leather—purses or book-
bindings or even harness. Officially the day began at
eight. Lunch hour was from noon to two. Closing time
varied. It could be as early as six or as late as eight,
which was probably a reflection of rush orders. Jobs were
hard to find: no one complained of long hours.

During work hours there were the irregular
thumps of hand-operated machinery and the drone of
voices, which at times rose to good-natured laughter,
and, regular as clockwork, just before the lunch break,
the proprietor looked in on them. A scraping of chairs
and a rumble of good mornings announced his arrival.
His voice was so clear and the silence so absolute when
he spoke that I could hear his praise or upon occasion
his irritation, as he reported on the work in hand and

the deliveries expected. Then, after wishing them "good appetite," he vanished for another day and the conversations somewhat cautiously started up again.

My couple were as regular in their meetings. The young man must have had the keys, because they arrived long before work began and took their places by the window. After lunch they were back early and at the window, and again at the mid-afternoon break, always the young man talked, always she listened, shaking her head at times, whispering answers at times, smiling down into the street at what I imagined were his open compliments. There were mornings when they seemed to quarrel, and his voice would rise in irritation. *Babbo*, "Daddy," was the only word I ever actually heard. Her father, no doubt, who did not approve . . . of what? The young man? His daughter going out alone with a man?

Unseen by them, back in the shadows at the side of my chest of drawers, I enjoyed my breakfast, watching them, inventing stories about them. One Sunday I met them strolling in the Cascine, Florence's large park, and was afraid for a moment that they would recognize me and be embarrassed. But, of course, they had never seen me. He wore a cheap, tight suit and pointed shoes. She had the tiny-waisted, full-hipped figure much admired at the time and minced along in very, very high heeled shoes, which were clearly a size too small. He had bought her a flower. One red carnation, which all things considered was practical of him: before she went home, she would have to throw it away or explain to Daddy. Next morning they were back at their window, whispering, tempting me to leave later and later.

The sisters spent their days in that back dining-sitting room. The world came to their windows, as I discovered on my return the first morning. Toothy was shouting angrily at someone, but not in a tone she would ever have used with her sister. I went back, thinking that I might be of help. They were both leaning out windows, gesticulating at someone below. I leaned out too. There was a burly man in a duster, standing surrounded by rosebushes, looking into a basket that dangled from a rope in Toothy's hand.

"Those apples have been lying around lo these six months. If you can't give us anything better than that, we'll have to try Stefano."

The burly man looked contrite, said he would be back and disappeared. They were right about their view. Their garden, three or four times as wide as those of the single houses, had a once-upon-a-time topiary look gone ragged with blooming plants, which had not yet bloomed, and nonblooming plants, which, through some hormonal confusion, *had* bloomed. No uniform plan was at work, just lots of different green thumbs. And as always in that neighborhood, beyond stretched the manicured vistas of the Boboli Gardens.

From this higher, broader view the garden next door, which from Miss Child's house had appeared normal enough, was revealed as a corridor bricked in on both sides by a very high, solid wall. Looking out each morning, the signorine took a grim delight at the sight of it, the punishment meted out by the neighborhood's own war crimes commission.

During Fascism the woman who owned the house had served as the street spy. In each street there was someone who reported every slightest deviation to the police and was presumably rewarded with favors, or at

the very least immunity. Usually the neighbors knew
exactly who provided this service and took precautions
against real damage. False information and rumors, both
in quantity, could disqualify the spy *and* keep the authorities busy on false scents. In relatively normal times
our spy had been an amusing irritation, but in the last
years of the war—with the Germans ever more prone
to brutal reprisals and Allied flyers and soldiers, cut off
from their units and often wounded, needing more and
more help—she became a deadly danger.

The street was uniquely quiet for being so central, an excellent place to hide a soldier for a day or two
while contacts were made. Everyone, except the spy,
at one time or another had an Allied soldier in his attic.
The spy snooped in her neighbors' shopping, in their
garbage. By day she scanned their gardens with binoc-
ulars. By night she watched the street from the window
of her dark kitchen.

Ingenious ways to deceive her were invented—
and worked. Even Toothy, chosen as the least likely to
attract the spy's interest, or anyone else's in the area
because of her known innocence and probity, had played
her part one rainy spring night. Just before curfew she
set out to walk with an English officer to Porta Romana, which was only a few blocks away. She was to
turn him over to some young men of the neighborhood,
in hiding for the moment, who would start him on his
way through the underground, and take charge of another soldier. He had a slight leg injury, so the Englishman was to limp. It was vital that the man who returned with her appear to be the same man who had
left with her. They had only gone a few steps when the
spy's shutters clattered open.

"Out for a bit of air?" she asked, eyeing the young man suspiciously.

"My nephew," Toothy whispered, pretending she did not want to hurt his feelings. "Shock, you know. He's been invalided out. Hardly talks at all. Has terrible dreams and then sometimes, like tonight, he can't stand being shut in the house. We're desperate. We thought maybe a little walk.—I must go. So sad! War is so sad!" They shuffled off, the not very athletic older woman and the sham-lame English officer. When, twenty minutes later, they shuffled back into the street, Toothy lost her balance and bumped against the door of the first house. It was a signal that set off the siren of a homemade burglar alarm. The spy hurried past Toothy and her new nephew, too intent on the prospect of theft down the street to give them more than a glance.

Once the war was over, the Allies had too many real problems to take our spy seriously, so the neighbors banded together and did the only thing they could: they built the high brick walls on either side of her garden and ignored her.

The greengrocer shouted word that he had found some more respectable apples. They were reeled up and approved. He suggested asparagus, which was rejected as too expensive. But would he send the fishmonger along, if he met him? In due course the baker arrived with bread. The grocer's boy took and then delivered their order. The fishmonger appeared. The mailman too. Conversations were shouted down five stories and the basket, filled with goods, jerked up five stories and allowed to plummet back down again with the account book initialed. There was time for comments about the weather and the latest gossip, new cures for arthritis were exchanged and recipes. All in all they had a very busy, social morning putting the affairs of the day in order. Lunch and a rest would follow.

Afternoons were quieter, the hours for reminiscences. They talked of the balls and picnics of their youth, which must have straddled the First World War—and been muted by it. The tales had been told so often they had taken on the vitality of the very recent past. The signorine relived those outings daily, reminding each other of details—lawn dresses, a game of croquet, the carriage Father rented—as though it were all only yesterday. Until their mother died—and the date was one they never quite agreed on because they had been too young to remember it really—it had been a gay, congenial family, always within the limits acceptable to Queen Victoria. Even Italy abided by her dictates, only slightly modified to suit the Mediterranean temperament. There was a prosperous business and two sons. Their father went to some lengths in arranging suitable marriages for them. His daughters were another matter. He wished them to stay with him. Their every whim, every other, that is, was catered to: carriages ordered up for church on Sunday, drives in the park, outings in the country. He could not be long away from his business, so they were not encouraged to travel. One winter he sent them with an aunt to Forte dei Marmi. Over a holiday he came to visit them, disapproved of the other guests in the hotel and forced his daughters to pack and return to Florence with him. They traveled no more. Not to Rome, or to Venice, and certainly not to that wicked city Paris.

Their father had a ready excuse. These were dangerous times. Fascism had brought rule by hood-

lums. He was a pure Monarchist. A king not only sat
on his throne, he disposed of his subjects as he saw fit
without concern for Parliament, even less for a provincial journalist. His daughters must be protected
against the crudeness that prevailed. And they had not
been unhappy. They still talked of those early days as
times of gaiety. Really they were the only ones they
ever had.

Father tried to interest them in his collections.
Those tuffets in the drawing room, the objets in the
vitrines. The columns of loose papers stacked there were
prints of every Italian city at every age in history. The
books piled up were his stamp collection. When *Life* came
out with a cover showing hundreds of the world's most
valuable stamps, which were presumed to be buried and
forgotten in people's attics, we went through his albums
one by one. I would leave them poring over their pages
with magnifying glasses and return to find them in a
high state of excitement. They had found one! They were
quite sure this time! But, alas, their sight was not too
good and what they had chosen was close, only close,
not close enough. Next day they searched through more
pages and the story repeated itself. They were not discouraged: their hunt was as near to adventure as they
had come in recent years and had some of its truest
elements—it cost nothing and might garner a fortune.

They were only mildly curious about what I might
be up to in my hours away from their apartment. My
trials in the cinemas would not have amused them. The
concerts, they thought, sounded very nice. I did not dare
admit how much time I spent working out baths. My
aunt had proposed taking me to I Tatti for tea, and when
I regretted on the basis that I was probably too high

for polite society, she made *her* bathtub available, which
solved my problem for the duration of her visit. But she
did leave, and I had my first experience of that fine Italian institution the "day hotel," where almost anything
of a personal nature—a bath, shave, manicure, pedicure
or clothes cleaned and pressed—could be achieved in
depressingly austere and sanitary conditions. In my innocence I equated the day hotel with the ill-famed
Turkish baths of my childhood in Chicago. Not that I
had ever been near one. Also I had just discovered that
the Italian government ran the legal houses of prostitution, in the sense that it leased the concessions. The
day hotel seemed a probable recruiting ground. Prudish
and unrealistic as I was, I would rather have given up
bathing than patronize the public baths with all their
rampant dangers. (Six months later they had become
my idea of bliss.)

As a last resort I threw myself on Mario's mercy.
Much of one Sunday morning he, Maria and I sat in
Miss Child's kitchen, discussing possible alternatives.
Finally with some reluctance they offered to smuggle
me up to the top floor on quiet afternoons. About three,
they thought, would be the safest hour to use their sitz
bath. Twice a week I tiptoed past Miss Child's door with
my bundle of fresh clothes, and then, pink and steaming, I tiptoed back down with a bundle of dirty clothes.
One ill-fated afternoon Mario caught me just at the foot
of the stairs, on my way down. Unexpected visitors. I
would have to stay for tea and be casual. He spirited
my clothes off to the kitchen and reappeared with the
tea tray, shaking so hard the cups rattled and skated
about and the milk spilled over. Had Miss Child been
less taken with her guests, this sudden epidemic of palsy

in her household would not have gone unnoticed and un-punished.

There were so many things I did not understand. I rushed home one morning convinced I had narrowly escaped a riot. Under the arcades, near the post office. Crowds of men had milled around, shouting angrily at each other, and I had fled. The signorine were terribly upset and would have locked me in my room, had they dared. Bianca Cavalca, instead, roared with laughter. I had been caught up in the used-car market!

Bianca Cavalca had followed my peregrinations with interest and a good deal of amusement, which did not, for some reason, include the signorine. One remark that smacked of nineteenth-century novels dismissed them: "Oh yes, a commercial family." They were almost less curious about her, feeling apparently that if one wanted to learn Italian, a teacher was needed. She rendered a service—for a fee—but that implied no person-ality that required acknowledgment and, worse, no so-cial existence. So, when I noticed they were fighting at long distance over control of my mind, I was amused.

The signorine urged me to read the one Italian classic, Manzoni's *I Promessi Sposi*. "Probably never read it themselves," Cavalca grumbled and made a case in-stead for the study of Italian history and politics. If she suggested Siena for a Sunday junket, the sisters in-sisted Fiesole would be much nicer. The weather had gone right on displaying its full range of horrors until, after weeks of a damp, clinging coat and sodden shoes, I caught a miserable cold and even *it* became a bone of contention. Cavalca insisted I must see an American doctor who might have access to antibiotics. The signo-rine advocated a chest poultice of unknown ingredients.

For several days I barked and stumbled through my rounds, then, groggy with fever, collapsed in my bed for several more. Miss Child sent word that young women were best treated with a good purge. The sisters plied me with hot tea and gruelish concoctions. What in the end cured me was waking up one morning more or less without fever and looking up above my bed. I had always known he was there, but had never enjoyed quite that perspective of the crucifixion of Saint Peter upside down on the cross. We were head to head and slightly cross-eyed. That morning I got up, dressed and, still barking, stumbled through my rounds.

Convalescence set in, with its own local obstacles. Miss Child decreed I should not be allowed wine: it was bad for some aspect of the healing process. She was countermanded by the signorine, who force-fed me an inedibly rich and strong *zabaione* every afternoon, and by Cavalca, who replaced our coffees with hot Rhum Punches. And so I lurched drunkenly through my last weeks in Florence.

As a farewell party I invited the signorine into Florence for tea. They must choose their favorite café. We would order a taxi. They were pleased, then diffident. Clothes. Would they have anything to wear? Several afternoons were spent reviewing their wardrobes. Although it was mid-June, spring had not yet come, and they had seen no reason to think it would. Did I mind if they went to one shop and also saw their banker? They so seldom had a chance to go downtown. We could take a tram. Taxis were too expensive. I would not hear of it. One afternoon, coming home from lunch, at our door I met a hairdresser, who had lugged a drain board on a stand, a dryer and her curlers and combs up the five flights of stairs to do the sisters' hair. Rigidly crimped they looked quite unlike themselves.

Finally the day came. The taxi had been ordered through the out-the-window chain of command and was by their specific instruction to meet us in Via Romana, the main street. Forty-five minutes ahead of time they were already waiting for me, dressed in black-and-white silk print dresses, gloves, kid shoes, the special, shapeless bunion-comforting kind, and black straw sailor hats with pert feather ornaments. We must leave right away. They would not be convinced we were much too early. Oh no, they smiled sweetly. I would see. I did. They had planned a royal progress.

The shops were just opening. The proprietors came out and celebrated the official coming of spring. They teased and complimented the signorine. We stopped and talked to half-grown children, and old friends. Complaints about the winter were exchanged and prospects for the summer discussed, and finally, only a few minutes late, we met our taxi driver, who also seemed to be an old friend.

At the café we were claimed by an elderly waiter with Charlie Chaplin paddle feet. He too was a friend from another era. They lamented the demise of the string ensemble that used to supply a gentle, genteel background and had now been replaced by a band and a brassy chanteuse, who belted out songs for the evening crowd. That, of course, was the problem, they agreed: the custom, even here, was not what it had been. Our neighbors did not seem to confirm that. They were older, conservatively dressed and quiet, but the tea hour has never been for office workers and businessmen. People who had never before patronized such locales, they insisted, had taken over, treating it as a sort of club. Mercifully we would not be subjected to them or the band. And the prices! Oh, the prices . . .

It took a long time to arrive at our order and many trips by the slue-footed old man before we had what he considered a proper assortment of pastries with nauseous harlequin icing, but the fidgeting, fussing care added to the signorine's pleasure, almost convinced them the past was not gone forever. In an effort to move them along into the present, I told them that I had ordered the paper sent to the house for a year. Unfortunately surprise and delight soon gave way to worry about the expense I had incurred. It was less than twenty dollars, but— It seemed wise to send them on to the bank before our check was presented and they visualized me in debtors' prison. I promised to join them.

I was let in the side door of the bank and taken by the "usher" with many courtly If you pleases and Just through heres to the vice-director's office. A leatherette armchair was found and placed in the middle of the corridor, where I sat, enthroned, in dim emptiness. But only for a few minutes. The sisters were very quick about their business affairs, which seemed to be satisfactorily arranged. At least they came out smiling, almost bridling at a dark, middle-aged, immaculately dressed man. He suggested I might be more comfortable if I waited there for them. Five minutes and their errand would be accomplished. He performed the duties of usher and saw them out. When he came back, speaking flawless English, he invited me into his office.

"Perhaps you can help us." Improbable, I thought, following him into what might have been the interrogation room of the Spanish Inquisitor. Every surface, except the top of his long writing table, was carved and the high-backed chairs were of bone-bruising discomfort. "You see, there is no reason for them to live in that cold flat without heat or hot water. Their brothers, their nephews too, are worried, but they cannot reason with them." He was very discreet. Where details would have embarrassed, he found half phrases that told me what he wanted me to know. The signorine were well off, rich by normal standards. There was no reason to scrimp or worry. The family wished them to get away from the damp Florentine winters, the Riviera perhaps, wished them to hire a maid, wished . . . They owned the finest draper's business in Florence. It supplied damask and raw silk to the noble houses of Europe and trousseaus to their daughters. Could *I* talk to them? They seemed very fond of me. They were lonely. I had brought contact with the outside world.

I tried to explain my refusal. The differences in our ages, the impertinence an intrusion into their private affairs would be and the jumbles I inadvertently could make in Italian.

"Let's hope the nephews can influence them. They were waiting for them, you know, at the shop. Twice a year, spring and fall, when they come to see me, they stop by the shop—just to look. They are very upset if there are few customers." So that was their errand.

It must have been a busy day. They came back, murmuring happily to each other, and the vice-director saw us to our taxi.

"Such a lovely day, *mia cara!*" Giggles said to her breastbone and to me, as we crossed the Ponte Vecchio.

"Una vera gita," added Toothy, who for this public appearance had worn her dentures and enunciated so clearly that the mildest comment seemed a proclamation. "But much too expensive. You really shouldn't have—oh, but we *did* enjoy it!" They prattled on about the things we had seen and the prices and the changes, while I wondered, probably for the first time, about the peculiar optics of aging. Their narrow world, made still narrower by spinsterhood, war and inexperience, was, to them, safe. As it was. We drew up to the front door. Toothy must have read my mind.

"It's been a lovely, lovely day," she said, helping her sister out of the taxi. "But to be back in one's own home, safe, is like finding paradise."

My departure from Florence, although very different from my arrival, had its own element of comedy. A young man had come to Miss Child's several times for dinner. He had taken delivery on a car for his mother, was on his way to Rome and would be glad to give me—and my imposing luggage—a ride. His only reason for the offer, I am sure, was that I spoke some Italian and knew more or less how to get into the city. Slightly nonplussed by the freight he was to carry, he packed it in the trunk *and* the back seat with the silent patience that is a sure sign of male fury. I tried to make amends by getting us out of town with as little confusion as possible. He was very concerned about his mother's car and handing it over to her in pristine condition. Once we were safely in the country on a two-lane road—there were no thruways yet—with heavy but reasonable traffic, I noticed we were going very slowly. So slowly, in fact, that we could not even pass a fast-moving scooter, much less a truck. In the outside world it was a hot, sunny day. Inside the car we enjoyed carbon-monoxide fug spewed at us by the vehicles eternally in front of us.

Finally I found a roundabout way to mention our speed, or lack thereof, and was referred to the handbook in the glove compartment. At best they are enigmatic, but this one did not quite match the car. For the first thousand miles, the owner was advised, the car should not be driven over forty miles an hour for long periods, which, given the condition of the roads and the traffic, would have allowed respectable speed. But the speedometer was in kilometers—forty kilometers an hour equals twenty-five miles. Nothing would convince the young man. The abbreviation *KM* was technical information that I would not understand. The omniscient male! It soon developed that he also approved of stopping once an hour for fifteen minutes to allow the motor to cool.

We sailed into Arezzo around lunchtime. Sixty miles. Hour after hour the kilometer markers along the side of the road crept by and it is nothing short of a miracle that we reached Terni by dark. An overobliging hotelkeeper insisted on giving us our single rooms with a connecting bath—this when we were hardly on speaking terms. The long and short of it was that it took us two days to go from Florence to Rome, time enough for me to realize how many things I had learned in Florence—the most important being that what is absolutely, irrefutably true in the United States does not necessarily have any relevance, let alone truth, in Europe.

Four

O r maybe it actually began in the Roman pension, which, off and on for the next eight years, was my substitute home, a place where I left my "good" clothes, where I always found friends to celebrate Christmas and Easter, and could always bathe and be warm and think the world civilized again. It had been a monastery and, outside the single rooms, still had the old cell numbers worked in mosaic tiles on the corridor floor. Nothing was "standard." Each room had its own, distinct personality and its own, distinct malfunctions as each season had its regular residents, who gave eager briefings on in-house gossip.

There were also certain idiosyncrasies of the place it was wise to know. Monday mornings could bring slight, or at times spectacular changes in decor—a life-size polychrome statue of Mary Magdalene come to weep over our aperitifs, or a small section of stained-glass window placed to mask the light on the landing and so make the stairs dimmer, or a bronze Cupid and Psyche, managing in the midst of their amorous contortions to support a column, a light socket and a pink silk shade, suddenly appeared on your bedside table—all because the proprietor could not resist the Sunday market at Porta Portese. His mother was inclined to take the pass keys and drift from room to room, watering her plants, making sure that taps and light switches were turned off and incidentally that her son's treasures were not being mistreated by the current occupant. She never knocked. The Patriarch of the Marian Order, who was also the landlord, took his lunch and dinner in the dining room, so the unseemly display of female flesh, be it bosom, back or arm, was discouraged. One Easter morning, when I had been given a room at the far end of a corridor, I decided to take a bath. As I sank into the hot water, I thought I heard chanting. But no, it couldn't be. I splashed around washing, then subsided to soak and read—more chanting! Up near the ceiling there was an air vent, which must have let out on the other side just above the altar of the Marian Church. Whether or not they heard me as clearly as I heard them, I never knew, but imagining how offensive the idea of a nude communicant would be to the Patriarch, I stayed very still until the Mass was over.

And of course the residents had *their* idiosyncrasies. A few were or would be fairly well known literary figures. One spent his winters in Rome because he loved horse races, especially betting on them. There were academics on sabbatical and Swedish opera buffs and middle-aged art students, living the Bohemian dream of a lifetime in comfort. Usually there was a solitary woman busy about mild self-mythology. One year it was an Englishwoman with an odd accent who claimed she was related to much of the nobility and spoke at length about candle-bras and e-peer-gnes and other even more indecipherable appurtenances of noble life. Another, it was a thoroughly middle-aged American of the sculptured hair and annealed make-up school, who babbled to anyone she could trap about her glamorous nights at the opera, night clubs and restaurants with her "young Italian beau," and about the passionate importunings of this same dashing "young Italian beau," a man famous along Via Veneto as an expensive gigolo. Several staid older ladies had their own dangerous little habits. Often after dinner they smuggled fruit for their breakfasts out of the dining room and, having wedged it down, out of sight between the arm and the cushion of an overstuffed chair in the drawing room, forgot it when they went off to bed. A slightly messier variation was soft-boiled eggs, saved this time from breakfast for lunch (after a bit more cooking in whatever water-heating apparatus they kept hidden in their wardrobes). The experienced guest never sat on the overstuffed furniture without first groping around, as nonchalantly as possible, in the crevices. But these were minor defects in an otherwise charming hotel and could be avoided with a little care and the help of an engrossing book, preferably in Italian.

From a diary, one of those intermittent flurries that have always been my antidote for loneliness and frustration, I know I spent long hours of my first week there brooding in my room. The world seemed a very perverse place indeed. In our correspondence the University of Rome had answered all my questions and could not really be blamed for not answering what I had never thought to ask, even less for not specifying what was common Italian custom. The university was closed from May to November.

What should I do until fall? Stay in Rome? Go back to Florence? I knew only two people in Rome—a priest important in the hierarchy of a large order, who instantly invited me, pressed me, to join him on a motorcycle holiday to be enjoyed without benefit of cassock or crucifix, and Mrs. Luce, who was not apt to have much time for me. I needed to find another Italian teacher, and I had already noticed that Romans, like most people in large cities, were in too much of a hurry to dawdle in idle conversation with stammering foreigners. Florence was more relaxed, more comfortable because it was now so familiar. Tempting. The easy way out, but a reservation in a pension was *not* a reason for staying in Rome. I wavered, almost convinced.

In my diary I give myself a long lecture about the folly of rigidity, of never doing anything on the spur of the moment, of always planning and always adhering to the plan. I must do the first interesting thing that offered—not, however, go a-rambling with a randy, incognito priest. In passing I mention that an acquaintance of my mother's has asked me for a drink to meet "an English widow, a social worker, who represents the British Save the Children Fund in Italy. . . . As one gets older," I remark, "social life seems to deteriorate. Acceptance of dreariness is probably what is meant by the phrase 'settling down.' "

Giovanna Guzzeloni Thompson (later Mrs. James Mourton, M.B.E.) was not at all the bulky, earnest lady in gaslight-blue lace and ground-grippers I had expected. She was the exact opposite—a dark, minute, easily amused woman in her early thirties, wearing a chic cotton damask suit of white on palest gray. Her feet were tiny, really hooves, she always claimed, and her hands, which could do the finest embroidery or lull any suffering child or animal to sleep, were small and stubby. She was birdlike in figure and in face; she had rather too long a nose and large, luminous, brown eyes, deep set under the smoothly defined brows and lids usually seen only on the silkiest of marble statues. When she talked about Italy, particularly Southern Italy, her eyes glowed with a mystic, almost fanatic passion. She cast a spell, which, quite beyond any conscious intention of hers, convinced those who heard her that they were in a saintly presence. Of course they never saw her try to feed *salame* to a donkey or crawl along the mansard roof of Zagreb's best hotel in a billowing white nightgown, nor did they ever understand one basic contradiction about her—her exterior was as completely, convincingly Italian as her interior was English.

Nature plays tricks. Gianna looked exactly like her English mother. Her father, the son of an old Milanese family, a graduate of the Naval Academy and a specialist in turbine engines, could easily have been mistaken for an English gentleman. After the First World War they had stayed in Italy—in Milan as much as necessary, in a house overlooking Lake Varese as much as possible. Gianna was born. There are pictures of a frail, winsome little girl on a pony held by her tall, slender, handsome father. Mother was tiny and frail too, steely-frail as later years would prove. Also her heart was a bit temperamental, so winters were spent in the sun of the Italian Riviera. School for Gianna meant the more rigid expectations of the Ursuline nuns and her grandmother and her aunts, who believed in drawing-room discipline and formality in all things.

Mussolini and his Fascists had settled in to govern. Her parents in their own different ways were adamantly anti-Fascist. He and the peasants who farmed the land near the house quietly smuggled people up the mountains and across the border. She took a more English and ultimately more troublesome tack. At the theater she refused to stand for the Fascist anthem. If she saw a little boy wearing a black shirt, it was hard to keep her from going up to him and sympathizing: How sad! Who had died in his family? To the locals she might be the eccentric *signora inglese*, but Fascist bureaucrats were confused by eccentrics and wary. (They could not be expected to take Violet Gibson's attack on Mussolini as a recommendation.) They allotted her a place on their suspect list. Her husband's name protected her from more drastic measures.

Until, when Gianna was twelve, her father died, very young, of cancer and her mother was promoted to the black list. They fled, taking what they could with them, to England. Gianna became an English schoolgirl, later went to university. At the first scare of invasion she and her friends rushed off to the south coast and helped drag farm carts and abandoned harrows into barricades they hoped would defend England. Her friends went to Dunkirk. She became an air-raid warden. School holidays she picked crops. She studied. Her subject was child development, which led finally to a job with the Ministry of Education in an experimental group for difficult children. Her résumé might almost have been invented to satisfy the Save the Children Fund's requirements for its representative in Italy.

In 1947, with a mock military kit and a bit of
money, she set off across the Continent headed for the
Abruzzo, an area she had never seen and knew relatively little about except the rosy bits of information
supplied by the Fund's foreign relief committee. The
villages had been fought over one by one, the destruc-
tion in some places was total. Water was scarce *and*
dangerous. Food about the same. Housing was impossible to find (the head of the Women's Catholic Action
Committee in a town high above the coast, on the first
ripple of mountains, had promised her lodging). Gianna
was to start feeding programs and nurseries in the rubble of villages farther back in those mountains. The
Catholic Action promised to help her. The Italian government promised its complete support. The Save the
Children Fund promised to send money and supplies as
soon as she was settled. Promises, promises! When I
met her seven years later, her knowledge of the Abruzzo
was encyclopedic. So, though less freely aired, was her
knowledge of the Catholic Action, the Italian government and the Save the Children Fund. Survival was an
accomplishment. She had done a great deal more and
showed no signs of giving up yet.

The conventions of a drink with an imperious dowager
do not leave much room for impressions or even information. Gianna and I listened dutifully to our hostess's
descriptions of shopping expeditions and the failings of
her maid, but only as we were leaving, at the end of the
prescribed hour, did we discover we were staying in the
same pension. We walked back together: dinner together seemed reasonable.
    Gianna's composure I found daunting. Every-

thing about her was so completely, effortlessly in order. She asked me the courteous questions about myself, listened to my answers—they might almost have been interesting—then asked others. Once started, like a breathless schoolchild who rattles off the glories and disappointments of her day, I seemed unable to stop talking. She had the same effect on the maids, who lingered or drifted back to our table more often than strictly necessary to tell her about their mothers' illnesses or their little boys' progress in school. I was appalled by her Italian. It was absolutely clear and perfect. The only un-Italian quality about it was its lack of *any* accent, and I noticed for the first time what has, over the years, become a conviction, that people, when they change languages, change personalities. In English she was clipped, almost tart. In Italian she was gentler, more openly sympathetic, without edges and slightly whimsical. Which was the real Gianna? Both, perhaps.

Questions about herself she answered in such a way that the next logical question might possibly be an intrusion and so was not asked. About anything else she talked easily. Our fellow guests amused her and she was amusing about them, even tolerant of their lopsided view of Italy as one vast museum with good restaurants. To her it was so much more, a country of people and problems and a present, not just a past. All of it fascinated her, infuriated her too. She was highly critical of it, unsentimental about it, and at the same time its besotted champion. She was as lucid and irrational as any woman talking about a man she loves in spite of his faults and her own better judgment, with the difference that the listener seldom falls in love with the man.

By the end of dinner I had impressions and little

else. Of an intelligent, carefully controlled woman with
a sense of humor and one not so controlled passion that
eluded her unconscious, or was it conscious, seclusion of
self. I might never have known more if a couple staying
in the pension, friends of hers, had not asked us to go
out for coffee.

That was just the excuse. From the first café we
wandered down through the back streets to Piazza Na-
vona and another café, where Gianna convinced us we
should have an Aurum, a dry, Cointreau-like liqueur,
the pride of the Abruzzo. The night was warm and the
sky, that royal blue that never darkens, one of Rome's
summer mysteries. No one wanted to go to bed. Instead we drifted through piazzas, deserted now except
for cats, and along the narrow, winding streets of Old
Rome, which were dank and lighted by a shadowy,
golden flush from stray lanterns and transoms. Gianna
and her friends knew the secret courtyards and where
one column and its capital had been set into a palace
wall or a Baroque fountain was almost invisible in its
niche. No one bothered us. We never thought of such
things then. It was a long time ago. Eventually, well
after midnight, we sauntered back to the pension, sing-
ing, or trying to sing, Gilbert and Sullivan patter songs.

The next evening we ended up in Largo Argentina, hanging over the railings above the excavations of
four Roman temples, watching the swarms of cats and
kittens that lived there. The more enterprising, or maybe
just the hungriest ones scaled the jagged humps and
ridges of the ruins to reach us and then yowled at us in
disgust. They had hoped for a greasy paper of fish carcasses or a blob of spaghetti. Gianna was determined
we should give them some milk. We searched the neigh-

borhood until we found a squalid combination café and milk shop still open. After we explained our problem, the sour old woman who ran it even gave us a bowl, badly chipped but not cracked.

We had just managed to climb over the low gate and feel our way down some snaggle-toothed brick steps, when a light was flashed on us. A surly watchman told us to get out. Again Gianna explained, easing closer and closer to his flashlight, holding out the bottle of milk and the bowl for him to see. Well, if that was all we wanted, he allowed grudgingly, not quite convinced. But if he let us do it, only certain ones deserved it, those with new litters. He would show us. Follow him.

Back under the arches he had a sort of lair with filthy blankets spread out on the dirt floor, an oil lamp, a stool, a plate, a cup and a fiasco of wine. Now that we could see him more clearly, he was revealed as almost as filthy as his blankets, unshaven, dressed in a scarecrow collection of clothes and wearing shoes that were held together, uppers to soles, by bindings of string. A self-appointed watchman, a squatter who had found a home. We must wait. He would bring his deserving mother cats.

They came bounding after him, leaving their wobbly kittens to tumble along behind as best they could. While we guarded the bowl, he patrolled the entrance to his grotto. The toms were aggressive and vicious, he warned. They sounded it. When our milk ran out, he lighted our way up the steps, helped us back over the gate and invited us, very much the grand seigneur, to come back any evening. He was always there after nine.

At first he seemed dazed by the trickle that grew to a small parade of midnight visitors, all foreigners, bearing bottles of milk and scraps from their dinner, but he adapted quickly, especially to their tips, which he accepted with a nice show of obsequious truculence that suggested they were courteous to remember what was, let's face it, his due. He preened. Soon it was obvious he considered himself as much of an attraction as "his" cats, and, like a visit to the Colosseum or St. Peter's Square, an appropriate finale to Roman evenings.

During the day Gianna was frantically busy with appointments and meetings, so I was surprised, late one afternoon, to run into her in Piazza di Spagna, idling along, looking in the shop windows. She explained, overexplained, that she had taken the afternoon off, that this time she absolutely had to fit a coat she was having made, that she had been trying since Easter to get a chance, that there might not be another until fall, that . . . Her guilt and the string of nervous excuses amused me: even if some omniscient spirit-monitor of the Fund were watching her every move, no one expected her to run around naked. I suggested, now that she had been caught out, we might have tea somewhere. Had I ever been to Babington's, across the Spanish Steps from Keats's house? No? Then we must go there.

For all its name, Babington's English Tea Room had a curiously ambivalent personality, not quite English, certainly not Italian, but with the nostalgia of both, of the exiles, whose memories were slightly bleached by time and distance, and of the Italians, who still cherished their own concept, slightly distorted, of the solidity and dignity of Victoria's empire. Fortunately the rooms, even the staff, had a chameleon quality, which, since the two distinctly different clienteles kept to their national schedules—for the English, tea late morning and four-thirty in the afternoon, for the Italians, *aper-itivi* before lunch, tea at six—satisfied each that all was right with their imagined world.

Gianna and I arrived at an interim moment. Through the tall front windows, well above the level of the piazza, the last shafts of sunlight streamed across the large front room, casting shadows of the window grilles over pastel dresses, linen jackets and pink faces. Back in relative gloom along the walls, single customers perched precariously on stiff banquettes at tiny tables intended for two. Lest they forget, ladder-back chairs, jammed in against their knees, reminded them of their solitary condition. They read or stared resolutely into the middle distance. The clink of cups, papers rustling, subdued conversations, even the creaking of the parquet floor as the elderly, stolid waitresses in their dark uniforms with voile collars, cuffs and aprons bustled about, straightening, fussing, restless, could not disturb the almost library hush. The English were linger-ing contentedly over a last cup of tea. The Italians had not yet come.

We threaded our way through to a broad corri-dor that led, ultimately, to the kitchen, but bulged out along its course into alcoves large enough for a table or two. We found one, pleasantly dark and presided over by two blotchy prints of anonymous Gothic cathedrals. The waitress, when she came, was an extension of the general atmosphere. She was prim and very formal, and, although Italian, had a faint English accent, which she sought to authenticate with the loony English construc-tion of her sentences. Others of her sisters in service were, or had been, English and spoke the same fluent, improbable Italian, complete to Roman accents. Long years together had wrought a parody of racial osmosis. Anglicized and Italianized, they were a race apart, by their manner a very superior race at that.

I remember it all so well because it was there, after our tea and cinnamon toast, that Gianna invited me to the Abruzzo. That is, if I decided to go back to Florence, I might find it an interesting stopover for three or four days. I seemed to be curious about Italy. This was a very different one from anything I had seen or was apt to see. For once she would have the car. Usually she took the train, but the car had some complaint that could only be cured at the dealer's garage. The driver would be there early Monday morning and ready to leave again right after lunch. Another exception: she was taking the weekend off. Normally, not to "waste" time, she traveled on weekends. By then I knew that was all of a piece with her character. The invitation seemed less so, but for me it was one more temptation to go back to Florence. There was no hurry about my decision, she reassured me. I knew there was.

Slowly the sounds from the other room had changed from rustlings to animation. The Italians had arrived, not that they were raucous. Waitresses thumped back and forth by us, busy with their trays. Ours judged we had taken up space long enough and placed our check firmly in the middle of the table. She did back off a couple of steps, sternly awaiting the only appropriate reaction. When we opened our purses, she nodded in icy approval and muttered something about the cashier at the cake counter by the door.

Back in the large room a series of family receptions was in progress. At the center of each was an older woman, perfectly groomed and dressed in the varia-

tions of black, navy, gray or lavender and white that
complied with the delicate usages and stages of mourn-
ing. They had wise faces, softened for the moment by
the presence of their grandchildren and the nonsense
they talked. They too were carefully proper in their
dress, but the rules had been established by the best
designers and tailors. The young men had longish hair
and immaculate high shirt collars, the young women wore
silk dresses, cunningly made, and gold jewelry that
clanked noisily. Slender, stiff older men in impossibly
perfect suits without a wrinkle, without a pucker, passed
from table to table, bowing, talking, smiling. While I
paid our bill, Gianna stopped to speak to one of the ma-
triarchs. Grandsons leapt to their feet, performed their
jerky bows and quick pecks toward her hand. It was all
very formal, every move, every comment repeated, no
doubt, every day, but about the formality there was
something so gay and spontaneous and precise that it
could not have been English. Idly I wondered what would
happen if the English imitated the Italians and then realized that, for so many reasons, they never would.

Several days later a hurried scrawl in my diary,
the last, announces that I *have* accepted the first interesting thing to come my way, that I am going to the
Abruzzo—without the faintest idea where it was, *what*
it was, or quite how to spell it. In preparation for this
adventure I had washed my hair and all my clothes. So
much for renouncing rigidity. My mother's training had
won out.

Five

That Monday, just after lunch at the hottest hour of a very hot day, we left Rome in an old English station wagon, a clumsy charabanc in the midst of buzzing scooters, *Topolino*s, and the occasional bulkier cars of the day. A young man, introduced as Sorino, the staff driver, edged through traffic with reverential care. He was almost maternal about his lumbering machine. He coaxed her on, encouraged her, stroked her. If a fender was threatened, he paralyzed the enemy driver with gestures and half phrases that were eloquent comments on his victim's ancestry, sexual abilities and probable future. About Sorino's skill there could be no question. His appearance was another matter.

Of medium height with swarthy skin and arched nostrils, he would have been striking in a burnoose. Instead he was a bit too muscular for the cotton suit and checked shirt that were his "city clothes," and his black hair, long and curly, was richly brilliantined and arranged in a careful, striated pompadour cum waves. Even discounting the pencil-thin moustache and the sideburns as national trademarks, he seemed to have a Samson-esque fixation about hair. More startling yet, when he talked, which he did with great animation in an Italian too accented for me to understand, front teeth of polished steel or aluminum glinted and glittered with sinister insinuations of appetites various.

At first Sorino made me very uneasy. The world was still to me a black-and-white place, where the unfamiliar did tend to be confused with wrong and black, just as familiar, white and right clung together in molecular affinity. I had not recognized gray as dominant. After solemn consideration of his exterior peculiarities, including sandals worn without socks (why male bare feet should be equivocal escapes me now), I classed Sorino as probably dishonest and/or dissolute. As I came to realize, after only a few days in Ortona, I was unfair and categorically wrong.

Beyond his title, which was honorary and in lieu of an appropriate salary, he was a man of all work—mechanic, shipping clerk, storekeeper, maintenance expert, bill payer and toy maker—the only general staff there was. He was a kind, dependable man who was a master trader, an artist at cutting corners, always to the Fund's advantage. Friends, a whole network of them, helped in his deals. So two defunct stoves became a new water heater, or four tissue-thin tires, one solid spare. He kept the Fund's jeep (a hybrid veteran) in combat form through the good offices of drivers for Italian government agencies. Discreet swaps—his fuel pump for theirs, his piston rings, his gaskets for theirs. After all, the government would replace them and pay. These informal debts were retired with new customers referred, or three days' work for an unemployed friend or a tip on a job that was going and a reference, which probably implied Gianna's support as well.

Out of the multitude of chores he performed and the skills he mastered, there was only one that he detested: his accounts. He lost track of nothing in his mental calculations, but putting them down on paper was his monthly trial by fire. The first few days were always wasted in evasions—all manner of emergencies, many of them problems postponed, a few outright inventions—that kept him from the office. Finally, when he sensed Gianna's patience was fraying toward irritation, he would come, armed with a bundle of crumpled, illegible receipts, and struggle, sweating as though at hard labor, until he finished his list: cash received, cash in hand and then the long, snaky trail of expenditures. He had gone through the fifth grade. His writing was phonetic, every distortion of his accent faithfully reproduced. *Conti* were *gondi*, and the headings that followed had to be read aloud to be understood. Addition and subtraction were the elaborate and not always accurate wigglings of fingers. His shame, his protests of innocence, when his mistakes of 1,000 lire here, 100 lire there were shown to him, were agony for him. He never understood that it was a question of keeping his cash-in-hand balance straight, not of suspicion. Still, his months always followed the same pattern, from mortification to cheerfulness to optimism to martyrdom again, never, however, at the expense of the Fund. So much for Sorino's honesty versus my first impression.

His personal life was as blameless. What free time

he had was devoted to his wife and two boys. He adored his wife, Maria, a tall young woman with a doll-like face and long, long black curls. He adored her before they were married, was so afraid of losing her that he married her in a civil ceremony and agreed that she should continue to live with her family, that he would only visit when a chaperone was available, until he had saved enough money for their *camera da letto*, the all-important bedroom suite without which a marriage cannot be. It took him two years. Then there was a religious ceremony and she was allowed to go and live with him in what was little more than a remodeled shed. One fair-sized room was kitchen, sitting room and bedroom. A half room, slightly larger than a closet, next to it may, at first, have been a storeroom. Later it was the only place for the boys. There was running water.

And he adored her after their official marriage. He was determined she should be a real signora. Very early every morning, before he came to work, he did the shopping. Maria was not to be seen until evening, when, lavishly made-up and dressed in the latest fashion, although simply, she sauntered along the *Corso* with a relative or a married friend. Sorino was seldom available for the evening promenade, called the *struscio* in imitation of the sound of shoes on the dusty street. He worked long hours and would have needed time to clean up. Besides his "subscription" with the barber was for two shaves a week, Sunday morning and Wednesday evening. Professional men might pay little attention to how shaggy they looked, but Sorino, who on the job went anywhere and everywhere in town, no matter how grimy his state, did not think it fitting to parade—with his wife—in less than perfect order. Sunday mornings he usually obliged.

He did many other things that would never have occurred to other local husbands. He took Maria to the cinema. They went on picnics. He met the fishing boats at the port and bought fish that they fried with friends (his, male). Eventually, perhaps ten years after they were married, they were assigned a decent apartment in public housing. The boys were handsome and bright. Ironically one wanted to study accounting. Sorino was more prosperous and happy. He still adored his wife. Not that he ever missed a pretty face or a voluptuous figure. He ogled with the best of them and his throw-away remarks convulsed his friends, but he had no real interest in other women. He was heartbroken when, before she was forty, Maria died of cancer.

Later I would know so much, but that first day, heading for the Abruzzo, nothing about Sorino was re-assuring except his obvious devotion to a clumsy car, and, on the outskirts of Rome, even that deserted him. Without warning we took off like a dud missile, swoop-ing around curves, dodging cars that trundled along at more rational speeds, nipping back just in time to avoid oncoming traffic, all with the horn bleating and bawling. We caromed through village markets and charged herds of sheep milling drowsily about in the middle of the road. Whenever it was logical to slow down, he accelerated, peering through the windshield with manic concentra-tion, determined apparently that we should take to the air.

Gianna seemed unperturbed, though later, when I knew her better, I suspected that at a certain point in the trip she regretted inviting me. It was very hot. The three of us had to sit in the front because the back was completely taken up by her luggage, my luggage and a kitten who had refused to let us leave the ruins of Largo

Argentina without her and who now cavorted from bag
to bag, howling. On this one trip Gianna could have
traveled without having to explain Italy to an official
visitor from the Save the Children Fund, who understood the hidden depths of Birmingham or Brisbane but
really thought there were none to be fathomed here.
Instead she chattered along to me about the towns we
passed, the customs, the *festas* or anything else that I
asked about, including the enormous DUX marked out
by trees on the bald rock face of a mountain. I had one
virtue over the official visitors. Clinging to the window
post, Mrs. Grundy ready to jump, I *did* listen and later
I *did* remember. Privately I tried to figure out if adventure is synonymous with early death.

Two and a half hours of this battle with gravity
left me praying for the sea. I expected it behind each
hillock and was always disappointed. Finally we wound
up an almost-mountain, through gates in a fortifying wall
that seemed very businesslike, as though it were still
kept up against modern eventualities, and along quiet,
arcaded streets. L'Aquila, they said, was a good place
to stop for coffee. There would also be the only decent
lavatory on our road. Obviously I had underestimated
the width of the peninsula.

The café was in the lobby of a large cinema, and
we happened to arrive just before the film started. Men
crowded three deep along the counter, bellowing good-
naturedly at each other, impervious to the boom of their
voices against the marble of the walls and floor. Suddenly they saw us and stopped in mid-sentence, mid-
gesture to stare. Unabashed they stared. Transfixed,
speechless, they stared.

"Pretend you don't see them," Gianna murmured

in English. "Ignore them and they'll go back to their
own business." Ignore them! Those sullen, stubbly faces,
those eyes that stared without blinking, without
expression, but still conveyed every possible reaction
from lust to disdain.

The coffee machine gave an impatient snort. The
men moved aside grudgingly, silently, and Sorino stepped
up to the counter. He said a few words to the waiter:
"Mineral water and coffee" was the whispered message
that passed from rank to rank. As Gianna and I took up
our assigned places in front of the glasses set out for
us, the men folded back around us, forming a circle, the
better to complete their inspection, and Gianna started
a long, very quiet explanation.

In Southern Italy women led extremely circumspect lives. Every conceivable situation had its code of
rules for them. Absolute compliance established respectability. The slightest deviation was proof of loose
morals; a second misstep led straight to whoredom. Again
serietà, this time a rigid formula, was the issue. Without it a woman forfeited every right to courtesy and
respect, so she must not go into a café, travel alone,
wear short sleeves, be seen on the streets or in public
places alone . . .

I listened with desperate, straining attention. If
even one brain cell strayed, I knew I would bolt for the
ignominious safety of the sidewalk. And still the men
stared.

. . . The custom of the country. We were outsiders. *We* had acted *un*conventionally. The men had
reacted conventionally. What else they did depended on
us. By our manner we would be known.

Perhaps subconsciously I had always known it. I

had never put it in so many words before: a woman can, should and does force the acceptance of her own evaluation of herself. Not always the same evaluation. It can be modified to fit the circumstances. She has that choice. Already the yes-buts were popping up in my head and would, for years to come, pop up, like targets in a shooting gallery, daring me to knock them down. At the moment the concept bothered me less than its practical application. How was I to accomplish this state of grace?

A cigarette seemed a soothing idea. It might help me think. I felt Gianna stiffen. And then I remembered—Southern women undoubtedly did not smoke, even in private. Retreat can become a way of life. The moral laxity of smoking . . . ? I glanced up to find a paling of lighted matches in front of my face. I raised my eyebrows in thanks, used my own lighter and then, peering blindly into my glass, treated Gianna to an exhaustive dissertation on The Heat in June.

"You're learning." She smiled, relieved and also amused. I was learning and would go on learning, but I was never comfortable with my choice of roles. Neither professional prude nor putative tart came naturally to me, and only one thoughtless gesture, a polite smile, accepting a lighted match, separated them.

Coffee was followed by our stroll to the much-touted bathroom. I followed Gianna, who led the way with processional dignity, and slowly, never more than a few steps in front of her and without apparent movement, an aisle oozed open. Not even I had expected separate gleaming facilities for us, but I was not quite prepared for a doorless Turkish toilet. One sacred and comforting Italian taboo was and is that no man would bother a woman in a public lavatory. Sometimes men

turn gallant and bow you in as they might into a ball-
room or a carriage, which is flustering enough. This
particular toilet was . . . well, rank, and I played the
novice to the hilt, pulling the chain before moving my
feet (and by some unfortunate chance there *was* water).
It was a lesson one must learn. That day presented a
bewildering number of them.

Sorino, his face very red, waited for us at the
counter. He was angry and in a hurry to leave. He did
not really want to explain, but did finally give us an
expurgated edition of what had happened. The men had
theorized on where he had "found" us, for what sort of
master, and to what mountain seraglio he was taking
us, for what sort of orgiastic delights. In the end he had
lost his temper. No other details were offered. Why, I
wondered and asked Gianna, couldn't we have been his
wife and sister-in-law? There was, of course, no pat answer. For Southerners two women in a place where
women did not go, doing things women did not do
(drinking coffee and mineral water in a café!) and still
insisting on their respectability were contradictions. We
had disrupted their social syntax. Yet, Gianna explained, Sorino could have no close, permanent relationship to us. They would not have it. Every Italian pos-
sesses, whether consciously or not, an innate sense of
class. He knows which mixtures are possible, which in-
conceivable, by signs so imperceptible to the naked eye
that their interpretation often seems magic. Instinct or
sleight of mind, they are seldom wrong. Many skills can
be acquired, but this remains one of the more elusive.

Our road crossed a wide plateau, fringed with towers
whose castles had long since crumbled and slithered down

the stony ridges, leaving behind only these austere sentinels. For the first time the Middle Ages were more to me than dates and the suit of armor that lurked at the end of a dark hall in the history department. The sieges and the plunderings and the forced marches seemed real. Muzzy from the heat and my own golden imaginings, I was startled by our plunge downward, three thousand feet in thirty hairpin curves, off the mountain range, and almost at once into a gorge of jagged, treeless crags that gloomed in the yellow-gray dust spewed out by a nearby munitions factory.

Perhaps it is the best entrance to the South. It is, at least, an honest one. No half measures, no blandishments, no slow dwindling away of cypress trees. There it is, bare and unfriendly. Anything that grows does so unwillingly: saplings must be bolstered against the wind, wheat must thrive in clay, vines burrow into shale hillsides. Everything is stunted, even the human beings who cluster together on high, rocky bluffs, convinced that their stone hovels will be safe there from floods and malaria, and, though they were wrong, from invasions.

That June the full blast of summer had come early to the Abruzzo. The wheat had been cut. The stubble was already singed to the raw umber of the dirt in which it had grown, and the scrub that hunkered down along dry streambeds was dusty and brittle. For all the sun, it was a dour landscape—and hotter than ever.

Eventually Chieti reared up over us, an angry red silhouette of spires and sharp, pitched roofs balanced on a butte of corrugated clay, and soon after we did reach the sea, a limpid, turquoise sea that was particularly torpid. Heavy, damp air stuck to us like cobwebs. The sirocco was blowing, a mild one, they told me. Swirls of dust danced about in the road and, sucked up by our passing, sifted into the car, into our eyes and our mouths. It picked at us, goaded us into an irritable stupor. It was, as Norman Douglas described it in *Old Calabria*, "the withering blast whose hot clammy touch hastens death and putrefaction," or at least thoughts of death and putrefaction. In such high spirits, toward twilight, we reached Ortona.

Six

We did not "approach" Ortona, we simply stumbled in at its back door, one of them, for there was no real front door. It was that sort of amoeboid town. Trussed up on one side by the sea, which lay, ignored, three hundred feet below, it sprawled, spilled out cube buildings in every other direction. Rubble was piled in neat dikes along both sides of the streets, and more rubble was an imposing monument in the center of a *piazzetta* lined with two- and three-story dolls' houses. They had three walls: their façades were missing. Each room was a stage on which a family played out its life for any who might care to watch. The more prosperous, certainly a relative term, had tarpaulins that could be unfurled at night as frail partitions against weather and neighbors. The others made do with the pretense of privacy that old wardrobes or chests of drawers, shoved into the gap, offered. Already a few candles flickered. Human shadows dove around them and banked up onto the walls like giant bats.

After several more twists the street petered out in a clearing, a sad parody of a piazza, where one tall, square edifice with fluted cornices and a clock high on its forehead had to be the seat of authority, the *Comune* and also the post office, temporarily (which meant ever since the war, with no end in sight—a fair definition of *temporary* in the South). Turn of the century in style and newly painted a bilious ochre with white icing for trim, it gloated over its battered neighbors, whose moldings were reduced to random outcroppings and whose scattered islands of plaster had been used for cryptic notations, many of them military, company numbers, tantalizing arrows and curfew notices, others, more domestic scrawls, logged the exterminators' zeal with dates and the inevitable three letters DDT. Shop windows reflected the glimmer of tiny neon signs. Behind the doors, in the dark, the owners dozed, waiting for a customer: a light would be flipped on, should he come.

Their prospects, to my inexperienced eye, seemed excellent. Men stood about in clumps, alone, in pairs, in threesomes, some talking, most frowning into space intent on some enigmatic vision. Already the evening promenade was overflowing from the Corso. Couples reached the square, hesitated and then turned slowly to retrace their steps. Any or all might be customers. The shopkeepers knew better. They knew what I did not, that the bargains of the *struscio* are social and that the men had stood in those same places since morning, penniless and glum.

They lacked even the energy to move. Sorino had

to maneuver the station wagon around them, twisting
and reeling back and lurching as though he were driving an oversized Dodg'em car. A few sensed the soft
brush of our rounded fenders and turned to scowl, then,
recognizing Sorino, nodded. It was a compliment. In the
piazza that night were men whose only hope for a bit of
money was to claim injury by a passing car. There was
one, as in every Italian town, known as The Jeep Man
(he could just as well have been The Tank Man or The
Truck Man), who had specialized in tempting military
transport to run him down. Lack of success had not discouraged him: any machine in motion was a good
prospect.

    While Sorino went for the mail, we waited in the
car, surrounded by men who stared at us, especially at
me since I was the novelty, with the same apathetic
disapproval as had our evaluators in L'Aquila. I was
beginning to understand why children stick their tongues
out at silent grown-ups. I longed to make a face and
shout "Boo!"

    Sorino's return saved me from disgrace. He nuz-
zled a path out through the crowd with the car radiator.
The men shuffled aside an inch at a time. Down a dark
lane and along barricades of piled stones. Behind them
the cathedral might have been in the last stages of de-
molition. Actually the reconstruction was almost finished. Soon it would again be a suitable resting place
for the upper half of Saint Thomas the Apostle—
"Doubting Thomas." In spite of howls from hagiogra-
phers and the denials of historians, local legend says
that when the ship bringing Saint Thomas's relics from
the East sank, the *upper half* of his body walked across
the water to safety. This happened in the thirteenth

century. Ever since Saint Thomas has protected Ortona. During the First World War, one of the favored examples, he "caught the bombs" and threw them back as oranges. During the Second World War he was apparently distracted. They say he "fell asleep."

And slept very soundly. In December 1943 Ortona was 90 percent destroyed in a battle between the Allied Eighth Army and the Germans. They fought for twenty-three days, the last from house to house, street by street, until finally the German Army turned and retreated 275 kilometers (172 miles) north to the Gothic Line. Of the twenty-five thousand inhabitants, two thousand were killed, thousands more refugeed, pushed south toward Allied lines to fend for themselves. Not a window or roof was left intact. Water mains were destroyed and sewers, the few there had been. There was no food and winters were hard. Epidemics would take their toll. Only Cassino was more completely battered: it was obliterated. Nine years after the war, eight after the establishment of a Republic and six after the election of a democratic government, Ortona had not recovered. Money was scarce, energy even more so, but there was enough for the kind of bitterness that would inspire a plaque on one of the breakwaters: FROM THIS PORT THE TRAITOR KING, VICTOR EMMANUEL III, FLED ON . . .

South of town, where buildings had dribbled away into vineyards, the road split, one branch wiggling down along the coast, the other heading off into the mountains. The pie-shaped wedge of land stranded between them had, during the war, been an emplacement for enormous guns that had chewed and blasted it into a pit. When the

mayor and town council members realized that Gianna
was too stubborn to give up her idea of a small demonstration center and that the town had a debt, which could
not gracefully be ignored, they went into Solomonic session. Their solution was the ideal of every administration, one that established their concern and cooperation
without cost or loss to anyone: they deeded the gun pit
to the Fund.

Countless loads of dirt and a series of retaining
walls with stairs leading from one level to the next and
lots of planting, which over the years threatened to turn
jungly, had changed desolation to a dream garden. At
the top, along the mountain road, there was a prefabricated wooden building, painted white with green shutters, known as the "Baby Hut," where ten children under three came by the day or could in drastic cases have
twenty-four-hour care. Down along the various levels
were the toys Sorino had made for them from scraps he
scavenged: an engine with a bell that rang and a whistle
that shrieked and an old oil drum for its boiler and two
Lilliputian passenger cars, a slide, a merry-go-round and
swings. Gianna hoped that the Swedish SCF would give
her another, much larger building, which would be put
on the sea-road side, for the three- to six-year-olds'
nursery school and staff quarters. (In the meantime the
nursery school functioned in an inconvenient, shell-pocked
little building in town.)

At the bottom of the garden was a small house,
a white North African box with a flat roof and shutters
painted the silvery gray-green of olives, that Gianna
rented from the peasant who owned the vineyard beyond. Sorino pulled into the side lane and on down to
the gate, honking furiously at two young women who

stood talking in a cluster of rosebushes. One wore a
nurse's uniform and held a baby whose peaked, monkey
face is one of the all too common bequests of war and
poverty. The other woman, in an apron, had a jack-o'-
lantern smile with more flashing metallic teeth. Backless slippers exposed lumpy red chilblains on her heels.
Several cats ambled out from under the hedges and
stretched. They or the sound of Gianna's voice made the
baby nicker with pleasure. Then he screwed up his face
in what wanted to be a smile, but went right on crum-
pling into a squall of tears. The confusion had been too
much for him. Waving, Elisa, the nurse, started back
across the garden jouncing the baby up and down in her
arms. He nickered again.

Bags were lugged up the outside staircase to the
second floor. Ida, the maid, presented Gianna with two
armloads of mail. The kitten from Rome arched its spiky
back and hissed at everyone, while the other cats ignored her and went right on twisting around and around
our legs with bland self-importance. Ida cleared her
throat apologetically. There was no water, had been none
for two days. The peasants farther up the line had bashed
holes in the conduits to irrigate their grapes. The water
company promised repairs. She had hauled several
buckets up from the landlord's well. They were in the
bathroom. Elisa needed to talk to Gianna: some problem about the babies. That woman on trial as a secretary seemed to think she should come for dinner. Ida
had put her off. She eyed me; I must have been the
excuse. The Old People's Committee had already announced their official visit for Gianna's name day (Saint
John the Baptist on June 24). Don Stella had called from
the Boys' Home: the new director had arrived and would

like to pay his respects. Should she order sweets or just cookies? And what did she need for all those people to drink? Coffee? Liqueurs? The Infant Welfare had a special case they wanted Gianna to consider for the next term at the Baby Hut. The mayor . . . The nursery teacher needed . . . Sorino urged the shipping of some of the supplies in the stores. The railway office had already sent up notices of crates in arrival. He was worried about space. Gianna answered their questions as she sorted the mail into three separate piles. These were the usual complications of homecoming. After she had arranged to meet Sorino in a mysterious place called the "Autopark" at 8:30 the next morning, she went off to the Baby Hut, and I was left to the comforts of a pail of water.

The house was a classic two-up, two-down—a kitchen and sitting room below, two bedrooms and a corridor partitioned off into a miniature bath above. Nothing else about it was classic. The furniture for sale locally was either junky or brass, velvet and polished simulated onyx that would have done well in the lobby of a fancy new cinema, but not in a peasant house by a vineyard. Patiently Gianna had collected things as she found them; others, just as patiently, she had made by a local carpenter from drawings she gave him, fighting with him about seasoned wood—"Oh, but, signora, it *is*! I left it in the sun *three* days!"—going by regularly to make sure he followed her measurements, did not embellish her design. The result was simple and attractive.

The sitting room had a long table with an L-shaped bench at one end and the length of one side that had a back and so was relatively comfortable. There was a divan-bed with cupboards, then a bookcase high behind it. Books and shelves were everywhere. Two tall ladder-back chairs with cane seats migrated about the room, according to the season: in winter they sat in front of the terra-cotta stove, which was the only heat, in summer they moved over to a low window that overlooked the vineyard and beyond, the sea. To hide the drab marble-chip tiles of the floor, Gianna had found thick jute matting. Upstairs giant wardrobes were painted white in hopes they would disappear, and they did, storing every form of personal possession—from suit-cases and blankets to slips and Wellington boots. The overcurtains she had made of tailor's canvas and narrow embroidered borders of faintly Tyrolean origin. Under-neath, attached to the actual window frames, were starched white curtains tied back. All that was visible was charming.

But, Gianna had warned me, the flaws were there, secret and treacherous. Water, obviously, was a some-time thing. Electricity was as capricious and so feeble that often light bulbs could achieve no more than a golden glow. In storms the windows leaked. And, worst of all, there was no privacy—pronounced in the British way so that the first syllable rhymed with *spiv*, which, like jagged glass on the top of a wall, endowed the word with an extra measure of inviolability. Her examples seemed picturesque to me, scenes from Verga.

One Sunday afternoon that spring she had been in the sitting room, at the window in one of the high-backed chairs, having a cup of tea and sewing, when she looked up to see a *Carabiniere* leading a group of people along the side of the house.

"You see," he said to what probably were relatives. "This is how the English live. Notice the tea tray all set out. . . ." A born tourist guide, he pressed on with his spiel, pointing out the curtains, the rug, the books, just as though Gianna were another stone monument to be annotated for visitors. He then wished her good day and left. On to the next site of interest.

Even her bedroom was not safe, especially very early in the morning on market days. Women, coming up from the valleys below, took a shortcut that brought them out at the gate, which was also the place they put on their shoes, low-heeled black pumps considered suitable, if uncomfortable, for "the city," or in winter changed from their rubber boots. They shrieked at each other as though they were deaf. The commercially aggressive shrieked at Gianna as well.

"*Allù padrò! Allù padrò!*" they bawled. Ooh mistress! Ooh mistress! "*Vulete na gallinna? Vulete na gallinna?*" Do you want a hen? Do you want a hen? They repeated everything. Presumably anyone still in bed was deaf *and* slow-witted. If there was no answering shout or rejection, they stomped up the stairs into her bedroom, brandishing live chickens held, head down, by their feet.

And the garden was subject to night visitors. People dumped their ailing or for some other reason undesirable cats there. A few even went in for a bit of midnight trading. In the morning Gianna would find a thin, mangy creature cowering at the front door and a quick nose count would show that a fat, purring one had vanished. No privacy, no privacy at all.

That evening it was certainly private enough and very peaceful. We had dinner outside at a stone table under

a grape arbor. Deep twilight that never quite darkened
into night brought cool dampness up from the sea and
with it the lazy rustle of water far below. Our Roman
kitten was distracted from her fears and aggressions by
an almond tree. She raced up its trunk, frolicked in its
branches and then meowed petulantly for help. Descent
was beyond her, but she allowed herself to be lowered
to the ground on a broom, a service Ida performed between dashes to the kitchen and rambling reports of the
latest gossip. Once she had gone and the kitten collapsed in Gianna's lap, there seemed little reason to go
to bed. We sat on, drinking wine. I asked about Ida and
the man she had been laughing with at the kitchen door
when I had come downstairs, a tall, sad-eyed peasant
with a gentle manner. Was he Ida's husband? Gianna
smiled.

Amedeo? No. Unfortunately. He had just pedaled
down the road to welcome Gianna back and bring a big
bottle of his wine, the wine we were drinking. He was
a tenant farmer for a large landowner and her recently
acquired *compare*, a quixotic relationship, almost an in-
denture for the beneficiary, who was obligated to show
respect and gratitude and tangible tokens thereof for
the rest of his life. Gianna had helped Amedeo elope.
At least she had loaned him a suitcase and promised to
intercede with his father-in-law, a visit, she slumped at
the thought, that she must make in the next few days.

Amedeo had aspired above his station, or so his
bride's father and brothers claimed. They were prosperous farmers, owned some land. He owned no land,
had no money, no prospects. At forty, he was not even
young. For that matter neither was the bride. None of
her many suitors had met her father's and brothers' re-

quirements. She had never objected until, suddenly in her thirties, blonde and still pretty, plump and placid, she asserted herself: she wanted to marry Amedeo; she was determined to marry him.

They must elope, compromise her virginity, which was, theoretically, her most valuable asset. After two or three days of presumably wanton pleasure, to save the honor and dignity of the family her father would have to agree to their marriage. They made their plans carefully. The bride snuck away from home. Amedeo with Gianna's suitcase conspicuously in hand met her and, more cautious than romantic, spirited her off to relatives of his, where three generations of chaperones were in constant, tittering attendance. Such decorous debauchery precluded accusations of kidnapping and rape.

Father had no choice: he agreed to their marriage. But—one final ploy—as far as he was concerned she had forfeited her right to her dowry. Amedeo made no objections. The wedding took place with all the legal-religious trimmings and none of the social ones.

Their good clothes had hardly been washed and stored away before Amedeo was, once again, seeking Gianna's good offices. The bride wanted the trousseau she had so painstakingly stitched together over the years—the bed and table linens, her nightgowns, slips and the required suits of underwear and handkerchiefs for her eventual groom. No fuss about the dowry, just the trousseau and the blankets, pillows and spreads that went with it. Would Gianna negotiate with his father-in-law?

Gianna sent a note by Sorino. The answer was verbal, a clumsy excuse. Another note, another excuse and finally, on the third round, capitulation: if Gianna chose to waste her time she might come along any Sunday afternoon. They had settled on the Sunday after I arrived.

At exactly five, dressed in our best, I even seem to remember white gloves, we pulled up on a dirt road near a square house of rough yellow brick, a derelict abandoned in a field of rubble and dirt so barren that a dozen somnolent chickens, rather than bother to peck at it, huddled in the shade of a rusty oil drum. The shutters were closed. The doors were closed. Over one hung a curtain of aluminum chains that tinkled faintly, more in reaction to the heat than to any stirring of air. At our knock an unsmiling, middle-aged woman opened the door a crack, peered out and without a word motioned to our right. She disappeared into the kitchen opposite.

We found a large, bleak room, lighted by a single bulb, and that partially eclipsed by a coil of over-crowded flypaper, with straight chairs lined around the walls and a long deal table, varnished and then tickled with a comb to look like walnut, at which sat a thin, hunched man in a blue shirt, staring down at his own folded hands. When he looked up, shadows accentuated the gaunt crabbedness of his face. Everything about him was meager—the wisps of red-blond hair, the few remaining, long teeth revealed by his welcoming grimace, the way he very slowly, reluctantly rose to his feet—everything, except his voice, which was loud, a boom without inflection, and echoing. A bully's voice. He bellowed for his sons, for coffee, for the women to get a move on and do their work.

The sons, three, appeared, beefy and inclined to sweat. The women, undoubtedly their wives but they

were never introduced, scurried around with coffee cups
and sugar and plates of gritty, stale biscuits, then, their
duties accomplished, withdrew, supposedly to the
kitchen, actually to the hall, where they eavesdropped
and whispered together loudly.

Father put on quite a show. Speaking to Gianna
he managed to bluster and fawn at the same time. When
his sons in belligerent confirmation repeated what he
said, he told them to shut up, they knew nothing, therefore should say nothing. He wheedled. He whined. He
fulminated. He implied that a matter so minor, a hum-
ble family matter of, as we could see, the humblest of
families, was beneath the notice of august personages
such as ourselves. In an abrupt about-face he maun-
dered over whether women were capable of understanding the importance and complexities of dowries.
He decided they were not.

After an hour of this ranting self-debate, without
preamble he decreed that, if Amedeo sent along a cart
within the week, they could have the trousseau. Within
the week, mind. And he must *send* the cart, not come
himself. Didn't want to see him—or his "wife"—around
the place. Could take her mattress too. Within the
week, mind.

With this concession, which had been the only
purpose of our embassy, and elaborate professions of
mutual appreciation, of pleasure, indeed enjoyment of
such a felicitous meeting, we escaped, Gianna still
mumbling to herself that Amedeo would have done much
better to marry Ida, except, of course, that had never
been a possibility.

Ida's story was very different, yet with crucial
similarities. Her father was a wheelwright, a profession

almost extinct even in Southern Italy, who had always
been convinced that fortune awaited him in America,
and who, luckier or more determined than so many others, actually got there, not once but several times. His
pilgrimages were cyclic and, like nature's interlocked
systems, fatal and immutable. Once started, his depar-
tures being the only events over which he seems to have
had any control, the sequence was beyond his power to
interrupt, each a repetition of every other.

As soon as he was settled with work and a place
to live, he sent for his wife, and she came, bringing Ida,
still a baby. In ten months she had another baby, a boy.
A few months more and she announced that they all
must go "home" to Ortona. She hated America. She did
not speak the language. She was isolated. She knew they
were being exploited. She would never be happy away
from Italy. The second trip, his wife's eventual arrival,
another baby, a boy, and again they must go "home."
The third trip, in 1935 or '36, she was even more miserable. She could not endure it. She dragged her husband and Ida, not quite a big girl, back before the baby
was born, leaving the older boys in America with relatives, which suggests that she was resigned, that she
expected to return.

But she had reckoned without Mussolini. Italy
needed its sons, and if they were so dissatisfied that
they must emigrate, there were, or there would be, the
glorious African colonies, with land and riches for all.
They could dream of America. Nothing more. So Ida
grew up in Ortona, two of her brothers grew up in
America, citizens by an accident of birth, and their parents, relieved of choices, at "home," could indulge in
little more than recriminations.

At the beginning of the war, Ida "eloped" with a young man from a nearby town whose family disapproved, not of Ida but of her nonexistent dowry. Again the infallible strategy, and again the desired result. They were married and in due, though not unseemly, course a little girl was born. The young father went off to the army, leaving Ida with his family, despised, half a servant, yet a daughter-in-law.

During the bombings and the confusion they were separated. Ida could not find her in-laws, could not find anyone she knew, nor could she get back to Ortona. Armies herded her with her baby and a ragtag collection of others like her back and forth through the mountains and across the lines, and finally south, from one feeding station to the next, along muddy roads, sleeping in ditches, until they came to a halt at the sea and Taranto.

There she learned to loathe lice and endless days without water and being hungry. No one wanted to help refugees. There were too many. Who knew where they came from, what they might do? With a new friend, another refugee, she rented a room in a tenement deep inside the casbah of the Old City. They both worked by the hour at whatever jobs they found. The rest of the time went to scrounging, maybe even stealing, food. Ida hoarded money, centesimo by centesimo, until she could buy a small bar of soap. Then she took the baby to the sea and they had a bath. No matter what, the lice thrived. Taranto was like that.

Eventually through the army, she found her husband. He came to Taranto on leave. The roommate moved out for a few days. The baby cried incessantly. Ida had nothing to cook. He accused her of not being *seria. Serietà*, always *serietà*! Nine months later—nine more months, eased slightly by her army allotment, of scant food, lice and typhoid—another little girl was born. Now with two children, all Ida could do was wait. She waited for the war to end, for refugees to be allowed to return home, for word of her husband, and, while she waited, his family set about the redemption of their son. In Southern Italy a mother does not surrender her son: he must be wrested from her. Father is her docile second. They appealed to his reason with a total lack of it themselves. The first little girl was obviously not his. He had been duped. He need not support this woman and the child of another man. His life must not be ruined . . .

By the time Ida reached Ortona, her husband, overwhelmed by self-righteousness and his mother, demanded the baby be given over to him and announced he had no intention of living with her, of supporting her and even less her child by some unknown father. He virtually kidnapped the baby. Ida heard later, and indirectly at that, that the baby died.

She might have been a good wife to Amedeo and happy as well, but there had never been any chance of that, and the one chance of escape she did have her husband ruined. Those two brothers, abandoned so many years before, had grown up to be solid, prosperous men in America. After the war, they begged her to join them with her little girl. They filed the proper papers, guaranteed a home for her, work and the payment of any debts she might incur. They were ready to send her the tickets. Only one thing was missing: the passport. Her husband refused to sign the application giving his consent. He would not suffer his wife, *his* daughter, so recently her bastard, to be removed from his jurisdiction. He had a new "wife," a new family, a new life in a northern city. Ida lived with her father, mother, brother, and her little girl. She was the only member of the family with work.

Other evenings, after dinner, under the grape arbor, Gianna and I sat on talking, drinking wine, not a lot, just enough to temper the shyness of two people who, suddenly alone, realize they do not know each other. Once local tales had, for the moment, been exhausted, we had too little in common for the conventional evasions, so we talked about ourselves—first about growing up and the war, college (to me), university (to her), and on tentatively toward the present. Nothing confessional, not even very personal really, merely pieces here, pieces there of the puzzles that had been our lives. Hers was the more intriguing, like a round puzzle that conceals its edges. One of the key pieces, her arrival in Italy and her early days, is inextricably part of those evenings at a stone table under a grape arbor.

Seven

Gianna was a devout real-ist with, like most of us, a few harmless, well-guarded self-delusions. The most dogged was that she was typi-cally English. Her school friends, who were not bilin-gual, had not spent holidays playing with the children of the Italian royal family and certainly had not fled from the Fascists, might not have been convinced, but I sus-pect that her aunts and uncles in Verona, where she stopped on that first long, slow trip across Europe to the South, may have been. To them she must have seemed very un-Italian: so independent, so resolute, so idealistic, not at all the jeune fille she *should* have been.

They were landowners with large, comfortable houses in the country. They set out to lure her from this mad project, back to the proper ways. Her cousins planned picnics and swimming parties and evenings of dancing with friends. After the austerity and dread of the war years in England, it was all so gay and normal, her first real taste of being young. And she had almost forgotten there could be such quantities of food. The aunts and uncles talked about her father, the little boy with the perfect manners and the perfect formal pronouns, who always wore his white gloves and never sat in his mother's presence unless invited to by her, but who resented every minute wasted on formality. In his secret heart he was rebellious, and they had, somehow, always sensed it. That once out of the naval academy he rejected his parents' rigid plan for his life had not surprised them. Gianna could imagine them saying to each other, "She's Guido's child all right."

He had run off. They were vague about where his adventures had taken him—France, Germany, Russia and finally England, they knew, but what exactly he did in such places they did not know. Obviously he prospered, and with his marriage they had expected him to settle down, always in that family a most desirable condition. But they had calculated without the Great War. He immediately became an officer in the British Navy, was wounded and invalided out, only to talk his way into the British Army as a liaison officer on the Italian front. At Caporetto, an inglorious battle where tactical retreat turned into mass desertion, he was operating a radio when it was hit by a shell and exploded, riddling his body with fragments of metal and wire. He was taken to a Milan hospital.

Gianna's mother was determined to join him. The authorities refused, quite logically, to issue the necessary papers. Undaunted, she started off across Europe and did, eventually, by the most circuitous of routes, reach Milan. *She* would see to it that her husband had expert care, by which she meant she would see to it

that the hospital staff was properly terrorized. She took
rooms in a respectable hotel, where of an evening, over
her dinner, she, the demure wife of a wounded hero,
could observe the behavior of a more flamboyant guest—
Mata Hari. The lady, she reported, was very *comme il
faut*.* If the aunts and uncles thought Gianna her father's own daughter, they could not deny that she was
very much her mother's too.

Still, they tried every argument to dissuade her
from going to Southern Italy. They, of course, had never
been there themselves, but everyone knew . . . There
followed a catalogue of northerners' prejudices, smat-
tered with the horror stories of friends' sons who had
fought there. She should stay with them. Who knew?
She might meet a nice young man. . . . She met a great
many and swam and danced and flirted with them,
but she did not change her mind. Promising to come
back for Christmas, she set out on the last leg of her
journey.

She never talked about her arrival. She had, she
thought, known what to expect: the poverty, the squa-
lor and the discomfort. Her miscalculation had been in
degree. Lanciano, as large as Ortona, ten miles from
the sea and high above it on a rocky plateau, had a dank,

*I never questioned the story, neither, I am sure, did Gianna; how-
ever, it is unlikely the lady in question was Mata Hari. She was
arrested in Paris on February 13, 1917, and finally executed on October 15, 1917. The battle of Caporetto was October and November
of 1917. Mata Hari's only documented visit to Milan was in the "season" of 1911–12, when, remarkably enough, she danced in two bal-
lets at La Scala. The mistake is symptomatic of the time. Mata Hari
was such an intriguing figure that any unaccompanied and unex-
plained young woman with a bit of dash near a war front must be
she, or at the very least a spy.

gloomy quality that neither summer nor sun could dispel. It was battered and somber and musty, all characteristics that seemed to have infected the people. On principle, they lowered at each other, at outsiders, and ruminated over every smallest gesture, every errand that had no obvious explanation in custom. Convinced of the misanthropy of others by their own, they sorted their facts to fit the new truths they were inventing and waited their chance to report them. It was, perhaps, the natural vice of people with no work, too little to do and too little to eat: they fed on each other.

Every year there was one moment of jubilation, well bounded: the festa in the fall. For those brief hours the town's, and therefore the people's supremacy over the neighbors was established by an arsenal of fireworks blown off, wave after wave after wave, across the valley. They watched with grim complacency. No one could equal that! No, no other town was that profligate. At any season life there was melancholy. In winter it was simply more so, colder, damper, drearier, and the people, if possible, more misanthropic.

Gianna's hostess, the perennial leader of the Catholic Action and the local representative of the Papal Assistance Committee, so known as La Pontificia, had all the right credentials for her positions, including the local disposition and a lumpy, low-slung figure. She was a widow of adequate means. She was pious and always wore a rusty black hat. She also had two daughters *da marito*, of marriageable age, or in truth a bit more. They were pious and lumpy too and rather over-endowed with facial hair. Gianna, it evolved, was to share a room with them. The rest of her life "at home" centered around the kitchen, where meals were eaten and

evenings spent and where, eventually, once a week she
was allowed to heat a pot of hot water and have a "serious" wash, which they deemed an affectation and dangerous as well. After several months of the communal
bedroom, tight-sealed at night, shuttered and dark by
day, she asked permission to put a cot in an unused
pantry. Her schedule was so different. She was up early
and often late going to bed. In the pantry she would not
disturb them. She would also be alone, or at least part
of her would be: from the knees down she and the cot
stuck out the door into the hall.

At first life "abroad" was almost as circum-
scribed. Gianna had no contacts other than those presented by La Pontificia, who expected more from her
boarder than a modest rent. She made no secret of it.
She *assumed* they agreed. To her *clientelismo* (patron-
age), a system as old as its Latin root, *client*, was, for
a just cause, entirely moral. The money, food and clothing, which would soon come flooding in from the Fund,
were for the relief of the poor but, she intended to see
to it, for the "right" poor, those who were religiously
and politically dependable. She saw nothing wrong in
the manipulation of people, for their own good, or in the
personal power that automatically was hers. Had there
ever been any discussion of it, she would have found
Gianna's and the Fund's point of view hopelessly naive.
How could they see children only as poor, ragged and
hungry, not as Catholic and Christian Democratic? How
could they say that membership in the proper party was
not a qualification for a teacher or nurse? That a Social-
ist or Republican mayor had as much claim to help
starting a nursery or feeding program as a priest? The
Fund had left Gianna to treat and dodge for herself,

preferably without offending. At first her great advantage was an accident of mismanagement: she had nothing to give except her own skill and experience, neither of which was exactly what the supplicants who besieged the signora had in mind.

For the most part they were an unctuous lot, intent on establishing their own satellite duchies. But there were exceptions—priests, nuns and a few teachers marooned in villages too desperate to be thought of even as potential fiefs. They had no time for fawning. They needed help. Now. From anyone. If this was the wrong place, they would move on to the next, even to the Communist party. Naturally they interested Gianna. Could she come to see them? Maybe . . . She left the word to dangle alone, promising no more than interest.

Plans had to be vague because transportation was, for her, a complex matter of luck and calculation. The buses plied leisurely ebb-and-flow routes as immutable as the tides, or so they were perceived by the bus owners and the Ministry of Transport, who with offhand benevolence had decreed that in the morning people were to be shuffled from smaller places to larger ones, where the buses sat in the station parking lot until, in the evening, people were to be shuffled back to their villages. (The long layover had one unpublicized advantage: the drivers had ample time to exploit their lucrative sidelines as village "fixers.") So buses tootled and bounced down to the sea and tootled and bounced back into the mountains on schedules the absolute reverse of Gianna's. She could reach Chieti, with stamina probably even Rome, but for all practical purposes she was cut off from the Sangro Valley. To have one working day in a village, she would have had to spend two nights. There were no charming Alpine inns, in fact nowhere to sleep *or* eat.

Every town worthy of such status boasted one driver who owned a car, however palsied, licensed for "public service," but even had Gianna been willing to put up with him, arrange somehow for him to have a full meal at noon and a comfortable nap, she had no money to pay him. Her only other choice was to beg lifts, a simple expedient rendered problematic by the rabid imaginations of her neighbors, who held that the first law of human nature is concupiscence. As protection against appetites vile, an unwritten code of moral behavior was in force. Abide by it or invite trial by slander and anonymous letter.

Gianna could accept a ride—*if* another woman was in the car, a rarity and a bore at that because they were always carsick; *if* there were two men (one would not do), respectable, of a certain age, not too young, not too old, *and if* they were not the same men too often. The field was limited. Those few who qualified were construction engineers, surveyors, housing officials and the various teams of government inspectors. Their destinations were not necessarily hers, and they had to account for every kilometer. Jobs were too precious to risk junketing. So they dropped Gianna at the nearest crossroads, promising to pick her up that evening—if they could. Usually they did. Sometimes they were held up, sometimes they were sent off to a different project altogether, and Gianna was left, stranded.

Before dark someone always came along. Any wheeled vehicle would do, a truck, a Topolino crammed with soap samples, the sidecar of a motorcycle, and if the driver misinterpreted the situation, became a bit impetuous, it was another lesson in the techniques of what became her implacable *serietà*. She got home safely, which was the point. Damn the neighbors! Let them talk.

They certainly would have if they had considered the obvious gaps in Gianna's itinerary. Once she had been put down and her chaperones of the day had chugged off about their own affairs, she was on foot. She was free. Happy to have escaped the claustral impositions of La Pontificia and her listless daughters, she set off up the narrow, stony roads and onto steep shortcuts toward the ridge and the single row of low houses, just visible against the sky, like crenelations of some mysteriously sunken castle. With each step it seemed to recede, ever so gently, in front of her and at the same time to rise, until she half-imagined it a Shangri-la never to be reached.

However bare and abandoned an Italian landscape may appear, someone is always around. If she went off on paths, she met shepherds and peasants, who already considered it late on and were busy about their mid-morning "snacks." They stuck their slabs of bread with peppers or rounds of *salame* toward her and urged *"Favorite!"* Such well-meant invitations could not be rejected, she felt, so she forced herself to take one large, symbolic bite, commented on the weather or the village she hoped to reach, then thanked them fulsomely and trudged on up the path. Later, when she knew better, she laughed at herself. *"Favorite!"* was merely a convention of hospitality, not to be taken literally. Courtesy required the peasant to offer, and courtesy required the passerby to answer *"Grazie. Buon appetito!"* The real courtesy was that no one ever bridled at her dutiful gobbling. Quite the contrary. They pressed her to have a swig of wine.

If she stayed on the road her encounters were few, but slightly more cosmopolitan. A government clerk wavering along on an old scooter bound for some out-lying settlement of his domain. His eyes might be sly and his thoughts lascivious, but Gianna's manner dis-couraged more than *"Buon giorno!"* He would watch her and speculate. No more. Occasionally she was sur-prised by a car. A doctor too busy or absent-minded to stop. Or the inevitable brace of Carabinieri patrolling the mountainside's scrub and boulders for nothing in particular. They always stopped. Who was she? Where was she going? Why? She had a well-edited précis of her life that rippled out like a patter song. They nod-ded. They would report this meeting. If they had a car, they insisted on taking her to her destination, which gave her arrival an impressive and not entirely desir-able aura of authority. If not, they walked with her, which gave them more time to explore the savagery of the local people, their backwardness, their villainy. Carabinieri always come from somewhere else, a place, according to them, conspicuously more civilized.

She listened without necessarily believing what she was told. Information was valuable. The best sources were the young midwives she met, on foot or pedaling rusty, high-wheeled bicycles between the villages and scattered houses of *their* domains. Of course they were curious about her. Again, Who was she? Where was she going? They were also lonely and longed to talk. Most were from the north. They were shocked by what they had found in these desolate, forgotten villages—the poverty, the filth, the fear of outsiders, of new ways, and perhaps worst of all the rancor that seemed to govern lives, to cripple. Brothers feuded with brothers, neighbors with neighbors, all over a patch of land, a few sticks of wood, or a pittance allotted for a sick child.

Nor were the midwives themselves immune, for every village had its entrenched *mammona*, the unofficial midwife, dirty, untrained and illiterate. (I never quite believed they could be illiterate until, one day, Ortona's preferred *mammona*, who was even allowed to work in the hospital, came to the house, asking to make a telephone call. She did not know the number. I gave her the book. She handed it back to me. Would I look up the number for her? Then would I dial it for her? She did not know how to read.) They had a double profession really. They delivered babies. They were also willing to try their hands at abortions, charms against the evil eye and love potions. To them these young, trained midwives, who would intrude on their monopolies, were natural enemies, and they fought them with the most vicious of natural weapons. Too often modern methods were no match for superstition, custom and slander.

For the outsiders the best, the only defense was encyclopedic knowledge of all that went on in their territory. Their work offered a special vantage. Common sense and ingenuity would decipher the rest. They could tell Gianna which was an absentee mayor who left administration (and the spoils) to his clerk, which was on the take himself, which was being blackmailed, which had been elected by promising that his uncle on the railway would get men jobs, and which of all these honestly wanted to do something for their villages. The same for the priests and the entrenched teachers, who were often the true tyrants of all they surveyed.

They gave Gianna clues about where to begin, who to be wary of and who might cooperate with whom. The rest took time and patience, endless patience. She called on the mayor. She called on the parish priest, on the town councilor for welfare, if there was one, and any other powers, declared or in petto. She explained herself again and what she hoped to do. A nursery-feeding center was not controversial. The need was obvious. Or if that was in doubt, a short walk through those narrow streets that served multiple uses from latrine and garbage dump to playpen, would convince. The streets swarmed with thin, potbellied, lethargic children, who showed textbook symptoms, again obvious, of poverty and malnutrition: impetigo, lice, worms, enteritis and rickets.

After she explained, she begged. If she could just have a room. Surely the priest had an unused store-room. Or the Comune? If the priest and the mayor were sworn enemies, as they so often were more through haggles over rights of command than ideological differences, then she played one against the other. The priest had found a room. Surely the mayor did not want him to take *all* the credit. Wasn't there an old clay stove somewhere? And some wood—not, after all, a lot—that could be spared? *Va bene?* Now about food. The priest . . . the Pontifical Aid Committee . . . Perhaps the province could help, if you approached them. The village qualified for aid in every conceivable sense—war damage, poverty, lack of the most basic services like water and sewers. Until her supplies arrived, Gianna could promise little, but she thought from the Americans she might have tinned goods, cheese, even powdered milk. If they got pasta, more milk . . . She had

asked the teacher about old furniture that might be
around, forgotten in some cellar . . . She had heard that
the priest in the next village was hoarding . . . Would
some sort of exchange be possible? And slowly, for all
the wrong reasons, people began to work together,
temporarily at least.

None of them knew much about running a nursery, but each had the ideal candidate for the teacher—
a sister, a niece, a cousin, almost always elementary-
school teachers who had ranked too low in their
competitive examinations to have any hope of an
assignment. Just exactly what Gianna did not want. She
stalled. It was too soon. There was still so much to be
done. Besides, the job was beneath a real teacher's dignity. The girls who trained for nursery school went
through the ninth grade, then did two years of "theo-
retical" work. The salary, if and when any money was
found, would be infinitesimal. A disgruntled signora,
enthroned behind a desk at the front of the room, keeping order, would not do. Gianna wanted a young girl,
willing to learn the simple mysteries of how to make
toys from nothing—earth colors and paste for paints,
spoons dressed as dolls, hand puppets of gloves with
papier-mâché heads—young enough to pretend with the
children and not so impressed with her own position that
she was above scrubbing the floor or cleaning up a child
who had dirtied himself. No, no, they must be much
further along with their plans before choosing a teacher.
Now, for instance, about the furniture . . .

Each morning on her hike up to a village she
planned her strategy. Step by step. There was no room
for mistakes. She must never hesitate, or seem to be in
doubt. Then, each afternoon, on her hike back down to

the road, she puzzled over her modest successes, an almoner without alms. Rooms *were* found and stoves and wood and food, even battered furniture, the flotsam and jetsam of ministerial projects, long since forgotten.

The rooms needed new windows, doors and floors: a coat of whitewash had to do. Cosmetic therapy was not enough for the chairs and tables, splintered, wobbly and three-legged as they were. A master craftsman might reclaim them.

In defiance of La Pontificia (who mistook pragmatism for free thinking and with inquisitional fervor suspected even priests of heresy, if they were determined to give the world plumbers, electricians and carpenters, rather than more priests), Gianna had made friends with the Salesian Fathers. They were a special ecclesiastical breed—energetic, ragged, nonsanctimonious and beset by shortages, most essentially money. They camped in any large, usually at that time bombed-out structure that no one else claimed, slowly rebuilding it, while they fed, clothed, taught and generally kept a hundred and fifty or two hundred boys out of trouble.

Chaos seemed to be the basis of the curriculum. At every hour of the day there were scrimmages in the halls, volleyball players and roller skaters, together, in the courtyards, basketball squads banging the walls in the most distant, and often windowless room, soccer teams rocketing around the rubble field in front and from somewhere in the background an obbligato of hammers, saws and Ping-Pong balls. The mortally wounded screamed. The convalescent haunted the kitchens. A line of boys, carrying hods of cement, snaked through the halls, disappeared into dark, cavernous places to snake back out, carrying hods of rubble. A priest blew a whis-

tle, bellowed instructions. Bells rang. A metal saw
screeched. It was chaos, but orderly, planned, intentional chaos, as much, that is, as anything can be orderly, planned and intentional with two hundred boys
under fifteen.

Each priest had his duties, but only the director's absolutely required a presentable cassock and a pair
of shoes, still black and with soles and uppers joined.
He was the financial wizard, the authority on welfare
laws and subsidies, who begged from office to office.
Pickings were thin, and his official budget—the government's purely symbolic contribution for each boy of forty
cents a day—left more to divine providence than even
the most optimistic could reasonably expect. With cun-
ning and perseverance he could add a teacher's salary
for each elementary and middle school section, war reparations for the building, special contributions for vo-
cational equipment, for war orphans, for children of
prisoners in Russia, of the disabled, of the dispersed
and, although it required mildly larcenous ingenuity, from
various funds—for the South, for the Italian Recovery,
for the Propagation of the Faith. So he blanketed Rome
with letters and canvassed the provincial offices, then
the regional ones, and still solvency depended on the
caprices of divine providence.

His assistant, with whom he shared, and so
squabbled over, the only available bicycle, was what the
formal world would have called the provisioner-bursar,
except that his provisioning was a glean-and-barter operation and his accounts, artful fictions. His capital was
mixed: the most dependable assets were, thanks to the
American government, powdered milk and "processed"
cheese, but nothing used, defective or unclaimed was

ever rejected. After all, someone, somewhere would
trade the canned eels or inner tubes he collected for
items more useful to him, like broken pasta, a haunch
of horsemeat or a gross of sweaters with mismatched
sleeves. He needed to be gregarious and shrewd. A sense
of the ridiculous helped. Perhaps as a direct result, most
of the men I knew in this position were talented racon-
teurs.

One such assistant, who came to the office whenever he realized he had more buttons in his pockets than
on his cassock and might soon be indecent, regaled us
with tales of his shady acquaintances and even shadier
deals, while we bent over him, sewing him back together. (Unorthodox as he was, he could not quite bring
himself to take off the cassock and await repairs in his
thick wool undershirt and trousers.) He also loved practical jokes. No one was safe. Once at a farewell dinner
for his director, he had him served his favorite dish,
rabbit stew, only, because no rabbit was available, he
had substituted the director's own beloved cat. The boys
cheered and giggled. The priests urged a second helping and giggled. The director, an earnest little man, was
touched by their gaiety, by their special gift. He waxed
sentimental about the years spent with them, their loy-
alty, and now at his departure had only *one* regret—his
cat seemed to be lost. No one ever dared tell him.

The third, and in some ways the most vital, figure in this crazy hierarchy was in charge of athletics.
His responsibility was to keep the boys, who had a natural bent for mutiny, semi-exhausted and tractable. He
was usually young, muscular and slightly manic, all
qualities that served him well in organizing the perpetual rounds of roller races, road races, soccer, basketball

and volleyball tournaments. His days were hectic and his nights only slightly less so: his cell was the dumping ground for the day's casualties—three-wheeled roller skates and floppy balls in need of cold patches—and the choice was fix them or prepare for anarchy. Waking or sleeping, equipment was his nightmare, a nightmare suddenly clear to me when Don Stella, the Ortona incumbent, fell into ecstasy over two crates of left-footed tennis shoes, sent to us, because of some invisible defect, by the manufacturer. The boys could practice in them, could save their "good" shoes! He fielded some very odd, kangaroo-gaited teams, but it was considered a stroke of genius, or more probably of divine providence again.

The other priests, never quite as many as needed, scurried from classroom to laundry room, from study halls to the playing fields, teaching, boiling, wringing, monitoring and refereeing, from the infirmary to the confessional and back to the kitchen with that expression of glazed concentration common to the marathon runner. Salesians are seldom fat.

For their part the boys were happy, always ragged, sometimes hungry, like their mentors, but as happy as boys are apt to be in an institution. Even the dullards learned enough about a trade to be valued helpers; they could get jobs. A few who took to books were helped on in school. Somehow, against all odds, the Salesians made chaos work.

At first Gianna must have confused them. If rumor was to be believed, she would have vast supplies of the very things they needed most, but she was not another languid lady bountiful and she was not waiting around, dreaming of marble-encrusted edifices with echoing halls for her feeding centers. She took what she could find, patched and pared, tried to get it started, to make it work, just as they did. Odd, unexpected. They suggested people who might be useful. They hinted at pitfalls. She was wary. She found they were right, and, unlike La Pontificia, they accepted politics as an everyday inconvenience, not a criterion. She felt slightly less isolated.

By early fall she was on the verge of opening rudimentary feeding centers in three villages. Furniture was still the problem. She had an imposing accumulation of shanks, planks and carcasses, but no master craftsman to accomplish their metamorphosis into chairs and tables and no transport to take them to him. The village bus that catered to a population of non-travelers and the occasional goat bound for sale at a market would shuttle them to the valley, where all forward progress stopped. The valley bus picked up passengers in twos and threes at each crossroad until its tires bulged and its tail pipe dragged. Freight was beyond its contract and its capacity. Gianna, imagining herself marooned on the roadside with her treasures, which each day looked more like firewood to her, went to the Salesians for advice.

They knew a man with a truck who hauled sand and gravel up into the valley. He owed them a favor, never specified, and agreed that on his return trip, empty, it would not be too much trouble to stop for her. Now there remained the question of the master craftsman, and the only offer of help did not quite meet that qualification. The Salesians proposed an exchange—the skills of their apprentice carpenters, aged ten to fifteen, for Gianna's prowess, and that of anyone she might recruit, at mending. They could provide needles, thread and an ancient pedal sewing machine. They were also on good terms with three or four women who might come of an afternoon for a chance to gossip, a cup of cocoa and a cookie.

An unlikely bargain that quiet desperation made attractive to both sides and, of course, Gianna had no choice. The boys went to work with noisy enthusiasm, the older ones nailing and gluing, the younger ones sawing and sanding. Their teacher, a young man only slightly more expert than they, tried to keep an eye on them and at the same time measure and shape new legs and rungs and backs. Then they watched, not quite believing what they saw, as Gianna stroked coat after coat of paint, and new dignity, onto their fairly approximate reconstructions. The results were hardly sets of furniture: no two chairs or tables were exactly alike. They certainly were not masterpieces of cabinetwork, but they were strong and serious looking and would do nicely for most everything except impressing the director of Infant Welfare.

Gianna's menders were less raucous and just as industrious. They also had a good time, the secret of success with such groups, and soon asked if they might bring friends. Would Gianna read to them? Cinderellas and Young Lochinvars charmed them (this was long before television tempted, or tried to tempt them with steamier situations). The next step was so natural, one that was later repeated by many other groups of women, that Gianna never understood why she was so surprised: Would she teach them to read? For that they moved on to innocuous *romanze rose*, popular romances, which were published in bewildering numbers

on spongy paper and cost pennies. Mending went on at
such a pace it progressed to hemming sheets and towels
and knitting sweaters, and reading progressed to
writing.

Finally the work was under way, not as she had
planned it, but she had begun to suspect that *that* was
the flaw—that she had planned it, as she would have
wanted it, the ideal, without enough margin for the conditions, the various climates and her own non-existent
means. Now her days were busy with the centers, born
and aborning, and the menders, and she was suddenly
wildly happy. There was no end to the possibilities—
until, at night, when she went "home" and had to face
all the negatives that nibbled away at her as persis-
tently as the covey of fleas that had adopted her.

La Pontificia stumped about the house, her steps
wordless reminders of her disapproval. Her private In-
dexes had been ignored and her aloof, barely sustained
courtesy was, Gianna knew, the prelude to reprisal,
probably some sort of lay anathema.

Other problems were more immediate. She still
had no money. The Fund regretted the situation in ful-
some prose and denied all fault: undoubtedly it was lost
in the labyrinthine bureaucracy of the Italian banking
system. She should take up the matter with her local
bank manager. He, in turn, had received no notification
of her existence. Since she was a non-customer with no
account and no money, he did not feel she had much
claim to his time and implied that she was in some way
attempting to fiddle the export-import restrictions.

The National Railways took the opposite tack.
With shipments of goods various in arrival she was decidedly a customer. It was their pleasure to warn her

that any delay of more than forty-eight hours in her acceptance of the above-listed consignments would incur penalties and fines as provided by law. They remained entirely at her service, awaiting instructions. Each week now several such prophetic notices arrived in the mail, each signifying another lot of goods, which would, presumably, in the not-too-distant future, come to rest in the freight yards. At Ortona, the nearest point served by the railroad! Impossible, but true. The Fund had stationed her in a town with no railhead. Even if the Salesians were again kind and gave her, temporarily, some unused cavern for storage, who would transport the crates and bales up to her? For that matter, how would she pay them?

And, if all that were not enough, she had picked up what was fast becoming a virulent case of crab lice, an affliction which, according to local wisdom, was *only* contracted through sexual promiscuity. At the best of times she could not have asked advice of La Pontificia. The doctors available were out of the question. They were medically ignorant and gossips as well. So she prescribed for herself—twice-daily dousing with pure Dettol, a caustic disinfectant which seems to have been the civilians' secret weapon in the Battle of Britain. It must have been a bracing way to begin and end her days, several weeks of them, but the vermin were eventually routed, and thoughts of plague, death and disgrace receded.

Meanwhile she wrote reassuring letters to her mother about her adventures, the glory of sunsets and friendly peasants. After years of writing such letters myself, I know they help the writer. The contretemps that seemed the first step toward disaster is suddenly funny, the sunset, muted at the time by exhaustion, *was* in retrospect glorious and recalcitrant peasants, recalcitrant for such good and millennial reasons, earn compassion. Still, this was the perfect moment—once more divine providence hovered attentively over the Abruzzo— for Gianna to meet the team of young men, English and American Friends, who lived, after a fashion, in one of Ortona's battered "palaces" and worked throughout the Sangro Valley, helping peasants rebuild their houses.

Their project was much like the old-fashioned "barn raising," except on a progressive, communal scale. Once the owner of a destroyed house, a peasant owner, had filed a request, accompanied by a veritable trousseau of documents, measurements and calculations, *and* once some approximate relationship between reality and fantasy had been established, the government contributed whatever quantity of cement, sand, gravel and stone it deemed appropriate to rebuild the house. It did not supply transport or labor. The Friends would—if neighbors banded together and agreed to help each other rebuild, which from an Anglo-Saxon point of view was to the obvious advantage of them all. A Southern Italian peasant's point of view was quite different. He did not trust his neighbors any more than his father and grandfather had trusted theirs. He knew how it would go. The first, Mario's—his house would be built. Then Giovanni's and Bruno's. And what about the men who had to wait longer for their supplies and work on all those other houses? When their time came, Mario would be too busy, Giovanni sick and Bruno, well, we all know about Bruno and his promises. To convince them in the first place was no mean task. To keep them together later was almost impossible. The young foreigners needed a variety of skills: driving and repairing trucks, of course; something of building methods; wheedling, persuading, even tricking; and how and, almost more important, when to bully. Patience and a strong back helped too.

Gianna had heard about them. Their good deeds, much embellished, were the stuff of local myth; so were their appetites and idiosyncrasies, which turned weddings, christenings and rooftree parties into epic celebrations that were followed by just as epic daredevil truck derbies back to Ortona, not always by the most conventional routes. To Gianna they sounded rowdy, which, given her faith in the absolute and unshakable propriety of British behavior, she probably credited to the unfortunate influence of the Americans in their midst. She had not exactly avoided them. Not exactly, but she had not sought them out either. Nor they her. Being La Pontificia's protégée suggested a prim, middle-aged worthy of less than elastic mind and body, not every young man's dream. They had, however, heard of her problems with transport and felt they should offer help. Once they met her a number of things were suddenly obvious. The places she went were on the way to places they went. They, whichever truck and crew happened to be going her direction, could stop and pick her up. Those evenings, on their way back, they reversed the process.

They also took her to Ortona to see their "palace," a once stately residence of many rooms and many windows, few with their glass intact, that had been loaned to them by a prominent local lawyer, who with his wife had retired to his country villa to avoid the Germans and the artillery shells and had wisely decided to stay there, free of the rubble and confusion that would

be Ortona in the next few years. "The Boys," as they
were inevitably known, moved in, plugged the more ob-
noxious holes, hired a woman to cook and rigged up a
shower on a terrace. It was a fairly crude arrangement
of a ladder and a small drum, originally an institutional-
size tin for tomato sauce, with holes punched in the bottom, supported on a giant-height framework. Water was
a twenty-four-hour problem. It had to be hauled from
fountains, which, if they ran at all, kept erratic schedules. Full buckets, cans, pots and basins lurked in the
halls and behind doors, waiting to trap the unwary, and
each candidate for a shower had a moral obligation to
replace, if he could, whatever he used. He also needed
an acolyte who would, at the proper moment, climb the
ladder, buckets in hand, and dump them into the drum.
To Gianna it all seemed a miracle, a reminder of a distant, perhaps imaginary world and in itself would have
been enough to allay any lingering doubts she had about
The Boys.

Restless and unsure of what they wanted to do
with their lives, they functioned as a group but had only
one real bond—the war and their reaction to its brutal-
ity. Otherwise they were dramatically different one from
the other. There were the brooders and the extroverts,
the solemn and the cavalier. Several sported spectacular beards, a fairly rare sight at the time. One wandered around with a pet monkey on his shoulder. The
official bookkeeper always found an excuse for not putting figures on paper. When, finally, the project was
disbanding and he could put it off no longer, he listed
an enormous amount, for which he had no receipts and
no shadowiest memory, as "Lost in Accounts," a bit of
bravado Gianna longed to imitate. She liked them all

and was more than grateful for their help and for the fun and company that twirled her life around toward a besieged normal. Occasionally now she was even clean.

Fall set in cold and drear. Outside the wind howled. Inside windows rattled and braziers smoked, giving only enough heat to singe shinbones. Layer upon layer of clothing helped. Gianna felt upholstered, like a child in a snowsuit, with her arms sticking out away from her body. She also found that each night she stripped off fewer layers. La Pontificia advised she gain weight. Look at her "girls." They didn't suffer. True. Placid at all times and now bundled to semi-immobility, they had subsided into hibernation. Gianna did not comment. No point in riling her hostess, in whom the arrival of the first supplies had inspired a domestic truce. Already it wavered between amnesty and blackmail and was occasionally strained almost to collapse by drunken midnight serenades from The Boys on their way home from celebrations farther back in the mountains. One more excuse to squabble would not help. Gianna had more important things to do.

One by one she had opened the centers amidst all the usual mix-ups, power struggles, screaming mothers and wailing children. The teacher wanted to bring her little nephew. The flue would not draw. The mothers threatened to riot unless *all* their children, no matter what age, could come. The mayor's wife would, if she were not squelched, play patroness. The three- to six-year-olds were frightened by the uproar and sobbed until they were sick or wet themselves or were beaten over the head by larger children who had come to enjoy the fracas. And above it all Gianna had to maintain her own unruffled calm. Authority is a prime ingredient in that baffling quality—*serietà*. All is lost without it. In the end she sorted out the birth certificates, sent the mothers and their strays home, sent the priest and the mayor's wife home, tactfully, helped the teacher comfort her exhausted charges, explained the mysteries of making chalky powder into milk to the cook, and somehow the first day came to an end with an approximate order. She went back the next and the next until she could chance a day away. There was another center to open.

Success does breed success. Suddenly Gianna was no longer begging for cooperation. She was beseeched by mayors and priests. Their villages were devastated, their children starving. They competed in horror stories. Through The Boys she met the first of the social workers assigned to new housing. Each had a unit that was to serve as a social center. They too hoped for nurseries—and after-school groups where the children could do their homework and maybe have something to eat. They were all hungry. All the time. Could she help?

As Christmas approached, she took inventory. In the stores she had enough warm clothing for each child to have a present. There was enough tinned meat and tuna fish. The supply of powdered milk was assured. Cadbury had promised a steady flow of cocoa. Jam had arrived. Both these last were vital in selling powdered milk to children who had never before had milk and were not enamored of the taste. The Friends would give her cheese in daunting quantities. All in all she seemed to be on her way. Modest expansion was in order. Indeed, she had only one complaint: no money had arrived.

She had none of her own left. She could not even pay for her train ticket to Verona. She was too proud

to admit it, to ask her aunts and uncles for help. She
did not tell The Boys either. They had their plans. She
did not want to interfere. Prospects for Christmas were
fairly grim: La Pontificia, her daughters, Mass and a
plate of spaghetti. Not the parties and presents and good
food she had looked forward to for months. Then the
Salesians invited her to "celebrate" with them. They had
commandeered from some secret source two barrels of
flour. The priests were out begging sugar. The boys were
out collecting wood for the ovens, which undoubtedly
meant pilfering wood, a stick here, a branch there. Did
Gianna know how to bake? So it was that she spent her
first Christmas up to her shoulders in dough and batter,
trying to keep up with the appetites of two hundred
boys—and twelve priests. She always said it was one of
the happiest of her life.

Eight

When, finally, we would go to bed, it was late, but in my room a squadron of listless flies still idled around, trolling under the shade of a hanging lamp, fizzing sleepily. At dawn they were still there, still fizzing sleepily. They joined what I learned were other early-morning constants. The pipes overhead bubbled and belched as the day's ration of water, greater or lesser, tried to reach the holding tank on the roof. Pigeons, kept there in a cote by the landlord, cooed and scratched and strutted in their courting maneuvers, and from the garden came the hiss of a hose. Pasquale, a pensioner who for the munificent sum of sixteen dollars a month spent twelve hours a day pottering around the flower beds or doing whatever chores Sorino and Ida could convince him were important, did not hold with baths. Gianna, barefoot, padded down the stairs, and after whispers and grumbles, and a clunk from the faucet, the hissing would stop. Pad, pad back upstairs, and

she turned on the radio, very low. It was one of the few
moments of the day when there was enough current to
produce sound. Otherwise the dial light flickered coyly,
nothing more. I could just hear the tweedlings and
chirpings of mechanical canaries, which, with chimes and
gongs between commercials, promised that sometime in
the not-too-distant future the Italian radio authority
would impart all the news the government judged fit for
its subjects.

Just after seven Ida clopped up the stairs in her
backless wooden sandals, bringing breakfast—a Spartan toast and tea—first to Gianna with further addenda
to the gossip of the night before. In small Southern towns
gossip and fresh vegetables in the market were both
dependent on the weather. If it was fine, supplies were
renewed hourly, if it rained, retailers stayed indoors,
sin and commerce ceased. Appetites too, presumably.
Ida's husky voice thickened consonants and broadened
vowels to confuse familiar words, then rushed on to
mysterious sounds I had never heard before nor imagined. People were intriguingly active—doing what escaped me.

My breakfast came with a strictly grammatical
summary of the weather. Ida strained to give me flawless Italian; I strained to guess at her juicier, more con-
voluted accounts of local lore to Gianna. Practice, free
association and the identification of dialectal corrup-
tions—inverted consonants, wayward *r*'s, the phonetic
vagaries of *d*'s, *b*'s and *t*'s—helped, especially if I came
in at the very beginning and knew what or who was
under discussion. Latin words flashed reassuringly by,
to be followed by some inscrutable local invention of unknown roots or a disguised activity like "guadambiare"

(guadagnare). Gianna was endlessly patient about re-
peating the key Italian word in hopes I would recognize
it and be able to follow. It was learn or vegetate. So,
slowly I learned.

Days in Ortona had a fixed pattern too. Gianna was at
the Baby Hut before eight, seeing the babies, listening
to the problems of the nurse, her assistant and the cook,
discussing special diets for particular babies with stubborn problems.

By eight-thirty we had walked along the road
toward town as far as the Autopark, which, it turned
out, was a dusty field enclosed by a variety of fencings,
including panels of the ubiquitous PSP (pierced-steel
planking) from military landing strips. Where the
Friends, English and American, had originally locked
up their trucks and supplies, now the Save the Children
Fund housed its modest relief goods and rolling stock.
A Quonset hut, "borrowed" from some passing army,
was stacked floor to ceiling with cases of canned goods
and dried milk, tea chests and wooden crates of clothes,
some waiting to be sorted, others serving as holding
bins for specific categories of clothes.

Outside, ready to take us to town, sat the other
"official vehicle," known from her bright blue paint job
as Celestina. She was a mechanical marvel achieved
through the marriage of a U.S. Army jeep that had survived the African and Italian campaigns and an English
Land-Rover, the gift of the Lord Mayor of London, which
had been disemboweled by the usual "persons unknown" while it sat on a Naples dock, waiting to clear
customs. Her top was a tattered piece of canvas, her
back seat, something lumpy covered with a blanket. None

of her gauges worked, and she crabbed on curves in a
headlong, distinguished way, like a hot-blooded horse,
an idiosyncrasy she had developed after Gianna, one day
that proved to be her swan song as a driver, sent Celestina swooping down off a hill toward a bridge. They
did not quite make the turn. Now only Sorino drove
her, and only he could diagnose her indispositions, which
were basically geriatric: mechanically and psychologically she was tired, therefore grumbly and chary with
her favors. The meditative whir of her starter warned
she might refuse to exert herself, just as her little sigh
when the ignition was switched off made it clear that
this time her exhaustion was terminal. She could be
wooed by a known, friendly hand. Sorino's in fact. Theirs
was a very particular relationship.

By the time we reached Porta Caldare, where
the town and the Corso officially started, Sorino had
coaxed her to a dignified, if rattling sprint. The gate no
longer existed, and, except for the Banco di Napoli on
one corner—with its new pink plaster vibrating in the
flat light—the buildings were battered, their yellow brick
and stone bared and pitted by the war. At the intersection the main road veered left to go around the back of
town. To the right another, narrower road wound off
down toward the sea. There was a littered triangle of
park, several gas pumps, one wall of a building with the
rubble of the rest piled against it and enough unclaimed
space for buses from outlying villages to stop. As a result knots of people stood about, semi-dazed, waiting.
To them, our approach seemed a wondrous event. They
stared, they pointed, they turned, expecting to see us
lunge into the Corso and scatter pedestrians like startled pigeons. We must have been a disappointment. Au-

tomatically Sorino slowed Celestina to a crawl. The hazards were too varied.

Ortona's general crumbling, aided almost daily by
the sand-laden sirocco, dusted the streets with a pow-
dery bloom. Tires slipped and slithered over it, polish-
ing the paving stones to a treacherous slickness that
made sudden stops uncertain and, in a drizzle, positively thrilling. Traffic was unaccountable. The young
men, nominally students, who spent their days ambling
in herds down the middle of the street, suffered from
either megalomania or preternatural deafness. They
moved for no one. Then those two or three men, whose
one ambition was to be run over by a "foreign" car, might
be skulking in the shadows of doorways, ready to fall,
stumble or just plain throw themselves under Celestina's wheels. Little boys on tricycles careened out of hidden alleys. The street sweepers, who should have known
better, were even more unpredictable. They were spi-
dery, pinch-faced little men, all members of one family,
all identical in their dirty smocks and their visored caps
with N.U. embroidered in dingy braid. Unfortunately they
also had minimal IQs and, what seemed to be a corol-
lary, gaggles of children. Theirs was a dynasty of sorts:
some town council had decided it was better to employ
them than have them on the welfare rolls. They performed their duties as whim took them, without fear of
reprimand, shuffling about from orange peel to cigarette butt, from sidewalk to the middle of the street,
flicking their pointed, sway-backed brooms, oblivious
of cars.

With so many potential victims, to attempt the
Corso in other than first gear would have smacked of
blood lust. But stately caution had a disadvantage too:

anyone who had a half-formed scheme brewing in his brain was reminded that Gianna might, just possibly, go along with it—especially the women of the make-do world, out on their morning circuit of chores. Just as their more prosperous sisters, whose husbands were employed and insured, had discovered the pleasures of regular visits to their doctors—a few mild symptoms were always good for a free prescription—so they devoted their free hours and ingenuity to winkling handouts from welfare agencies. They specialized in a sad tale and a tear or two. If that was the wrong note, they switched to screams and threats. At worst they got 500 lire or a sack of flour. It was their version of private enterprise.

And there was Gianna. They felt she could do something about a house, a blanket, an overcoat, a sponsorship—whatever at the moment seemed desirable. Nothing ventured, nothing gained, not that they would have bothered to hike all the way up to the office opposite the Autopark to ask. The chance of success was too frail.* Instead, they stalked her in town. "*Permet-*

---

*In an effort to eliminate the professional raiders *and* the most degrading, pernicious aspects of distributed goods and services, Gianna had established some set rules. It was generally accepted that the SCF food supplies went to nurseries and feeding centers in mountain villages. Places in the Ortona nursery and the Baby Hut were assigned strictly according to need. Families who wanted to send a child were asked to apply—the simplest letter, giving the child's name, address, and age, was enough—and could expect a visit from the teacher, the nurse and probably Gianna as well. For those who were accepted, all food and clothing needed at the centers, including shoes, would be supplied. In return, the mothers were expected to do the cleaning and laundry, which in practice worked out as two Saturday afternoons a term, in tandem with another mother, for each woman. Clothing was given out on just as strict a basis. It was

tete una parola!" They asked for just one word, which
cascaded into ten thousand and tears.

They knew about rules and fairness. The slo-
gans, they were, the shibboleths of this new, "democratic" welfare. The slow-witted might believe in them
and for their pains get a place on every waiting list. In
real life to the exceptions belonged the spoils. Gianna
seemed adamant about no exceptions. That was what
she said. Was it what she did? It was, but they could
not resist testing her. The right approach. That was what
was needed, so *"Permettete una parola . . . ,"* and instant inspiration produced a new tale of woe and hunger
garnished with threats and accusations and hopes for
eternal damnation. When, ultimately, they were convinced of their claim's futility, they went off good-
naturedly, sometimes with a sly little smile that seemed
to say, "You know how it is? The idea was good, worth
a try." Soon enough another idea would pop into their
minds and another morning it would be *"Permettete una
parola . . . ,"* followed somewhere down the line by that
other chilling phrase, anathema to Gianna, *"Se volete,
potete."* If you want to, you can.

They were young women, at least chronologi-

---

earned. Women who signed up to work three afternoons in the sewing room, where all manner of linens for the boys' home, the hospital, even the nursery were made, qualified for an overcoat or dresses
for themselves, or children's clothing, or a complete, new layette.
Men, who signed up to work three days on various projects that
Sorino supervised, including later much of the new nursery construction, had their choice of an overcoat, a suit, or new heavy-duty
shoes. Blankets, clothing, soap (and some food that came through a
special arrangement with the American Friends Service Committee)
were sent to small, usually forgotten orphanages in mountain villages.

cally, many with the local coloring of red-golden hair
and green eyes that could be so beautiful in extreme
youth. But youth for them had been short. They looked
ten years older than their birth certificates guaranteed.
War and childbearing and poor food and physical drudg-
ery had left their faces creased, their bodies prolapsed,
their teeth falling out and their backs stiff. Only their
tongues were agile—and their will to fight for their pound
of flesh, whatever flesh might be going, and for their
children.

They may have felt better for venting their de-
spair and rage. Each believed herself the victim of a
malicious plot. Who was behind it? Anyone, everyone.
The neighbors, the mayor, the children's teachers, their
sisters, the indigenous government minister, the nuns,
their mothers-in-law, the priest, and most obviously God.
They were paranoid, their vision too narrowed, their
minds too embittered to realize that their chronicles of
frustration were not the chronicles of a plot but of a
system strained and failing. The Abruzzo was *one* Re-
gion; three-quarters of the country was destroyed or
depressed or both. Their complaints were just: favorit-
ism was relentless in what had never been a democracy;
bureaucracy was blatantly incompetent, war pensions
not yet processed, idem for war reparations, new housing, new sewers, new aqueducts promised but not built;
health and welfare services functioned badly for everyone, not at all, it sometimes seemed, for the poor.
Promises had raveled into more corruption, unemploy-
ment and hunger. They had been cheated again.

When Gianna insisted on taking me around the market
that first morning, I did not realize the hazards nor quite

how much she begrudged the time. Visitors discombobulated her, pitting her rigid sense of courtesy against her equally rigid, compelling urge to get on with The Work. *It* was the important business of the day, not the impressions and information she might possibly funnel into a visitor's spongy brain. A priori all visitors had spongy brains, though secretly she expected more of the rare personal ones than she did of those "official" representatives sent by the Fund and its committees.

Still, she gave up the time with good grace, and only occasional twitches of urgency reminded the guest this was not, after all, a special treat for her. She bargained for bits of linen and lace and copper pots too large to ship, too large to carry though they would be. She explained that both lace and copper were sold by weight; that, as would have seemed self-evident, the war had left no antiques; that tools were still scarce, so while there might be hoes, there would be no decorative wrought iron; that no, the little tin boat with a covered prow and a handle at its stern was not, as everyone assumed, a toy, it was a small oil lamp. A sobering thought. How could people read by what would be a very dim light? Of course they did not read, and Gianna was patient about that too.

"Sanitary conditions" came in for an inordinate amount of tut-tutting. From swaddled babies to children with impetigo, who fingered every object their hands could reach, particularly food, to dried cod soaking in tubs of water on the ground, where anything could and often did fall in, guests found them deplorable. At the end of their market inspection, those same people insisted on stopping in a café for a cup of tea with milk or a cooling glass of fizzy "mineral water" from a siphon bottle and found it impossible to resist custard-filled pastries. Too often Gianna's firm warnings were ignored: she was overcautious, they objected. Minutes before in the market they had suspected her of "going native," a deplorable lapse. Guests were captious, willful, easily confused and tired, sentimental, confidential and captious again in predictable turns. Gianna always prayed they would move on before they were felled by a local bug.

She took me on the Express Tour—a bit of everything at a clip fast enough to fuddle the buying urge. Any round would do as long as it included just one copper stall. Water jugs and coffeepots were too tempting and too often, upon sober consideration, left behind to be mailed. I was unafraid, fascinated and a nonbuyer, so Gianna decided to leave me on my own. She would go to the nursery, Sorino to the bank; we would meet in forty-five minutes at the post office. Just as she was swirled away by the crowd she told me to look in any doorway that was open, that I would understand more from what I saw than I would from learned books and explanations. Already overwhelmed by the jumble of sights, sounds and smells, I was not at all sure I would *understand* much, but I was determined not to miss much either.

A bulky young woman with a large, flat basket on her head passed, backing me into a wall. Beaky little heads on long, scrawny, featherless necks peered over the edge at me, their eyes and bills working frantically. It was suffocating. The sun beat down on the narrow streets, now even narrower with the stalls, and the people, jammed against each other, seemed to wrestle for space. Vendors clamored the superiority of their

wares in voices hoarse from shouting and cheap to-
bacco. Children screamed, were slapped and screamed
the louder. Women huddled in clumps, whispering, their
eyes darting about, apparently on the watch for eaves-
droppers. The most likely suspects were only trying to
push by them. Country women, slightly shabbier than
their city cousins, wore strings of bulbous amber beads
around their necks and scarves on their heads. One, who
noticed me, pulled her scarf over across the bridge of
her nose and scurried away. We were farther east than
I had thought. Another ignored me to turn toward the
wall and delve around in the top of her dress. After a
complicated, elbow-lifting maneuver, she extracted a
wadded bundle of paper money that had been clamped
firmly in an armpit for safekeeping, which suggested an
explanation for the musky quality of the bills in local
circulation.

For a while I watched a fat crone who presided
over a tub of oversized orange butter beans set on a
fruit crate. A band of children, just tall enough to hook
their chins on the rim of the tub, also watched her with
extravagant innocence. If her eyes wandered, they
plunged their hands into the briny water and squiggled
them around. One little boy spit instead. At the arrival
of a customer offering a few coins, the woman twirled a
piece of coarse brown paper into a cone and dipped out
a ration of beans. Women she gave a bit of extra service. She held their baskets, while they twisted a towel
around a hand, making a doughnut-shaped pad, and
placed it carefully on their heads. Then they bent their
knees slightly, she helped them lift and settle their baskets firmly in place. They paced off with their peculiarly
graceful step-and-glide gait, already gnawing at the hard

shell of a bean, spitting it out and munching on the meat. The children had managed another quick swish or two.

Nearby a little man with a big, rough voice expounded the joys of his bunion cure to a knot of blank-faced people. As proof he pointed to the picture of a monstrous, gnarled foot, which he flipped to an "after" version of suspect smoothness. *If* it was the same foot, it had been treated to a full pedicure. He crooned that his miraculous liquid was even effective for snakebite and arthritis, which brought a murmur of interest, but no buyers.

A thin man in a checked shirt and with a tray hung from a strap around his neck drifted back and forth. Whenever he stopped men gathered and he went into the patter and quick hand movements of his shell game, always staying carefully on an axis with a pair of Carabinieri who sauntered about, "keeping order." If they more than glanced in his direction, he palmed his shells, the pea, settled the bets and slunk off in search of a safer base.

Finally, when several children stood and stared at me with unblinking curiosity, I eased back into the crowd and let myself be bumped along the rows of stalls. There were a bewildering number of doorways and many more open doors than I would have noticed without Gianna's prompting. Some let into black, semibasement caves that served commercial ventures—a plumber's storeroom, a mop and broom merchant's shop, the deposit for tanks of butane cooking gas. Others, guarded by small children sitting on the stoop or old women leaning against the jamb, let into one-room grotto-houses. Still others, similarly guarded and black, let onto two or three stairs with, above, a one-room house. And still others showed a steep, tunnel-like staircase disappearing upward to, probably, the third in the tier of one-room houses. By what plan the buildings had been laid out was hard to imagine. Or maybe the doors and rooms had been improvised from some more elegant whole.

However they came into being, those room-houses were much alike—perhaps twelve by fourteen feet, windowless, whitewashed. Two or three beds, one always a "matrimonial" bed, with shapeless mattresses, covered by immaculate white, fringed spreads and pillow shams, were pushed back along the walls. A scarred wooden table, complete with crocheted doily and ceramic something, and four spindly chairs more than filled what space was left in the center. Wedged in wherever it would fit was a metal stand for a hand basin and, off in a corner on a cabinet, a two-ring gas burner for cooking. The rooms were swept and clean, very orderly, as they had to be if anyone was to move around or work. Some had water, almost none had toilets. A tall, bellied, ceramic slop jar hid behind a makeshift curtain ready to serve. Decorations were modest, a few framed "studio" portraits, going to sepia, of stiff, pop-eyed relatives and, sometimes, a framed dollar bill. No wonder the men shuffled around the streets and stood in the piazzas at all hours. The comforts of home were meager, at best, and cramped. The nightmare of a long, cold, dank winter had not yet washed over me.

Off the main piazza I came upon a man with a small display of safety razors in an open suitcase and a canvas stool on which sat a potential customer, swathed in a towel, half of his face fluffy foam, the other half pink and smooth. A number of men, scattered around at a careful distance that did not quite commit them to interest, stood, gazing raptly into space. The vendor stopped his demonstration to explain the fine points of shaving oneself. Matters of grain and stroke, how not to burn or nick oneself. His audience shifted about restlessly. The vendor must have seen the reaction before: he went back to his shaving.

When he had patted the last of the soap from his client's sideburns, he released him with a flourish of the towel and started his pitch. The man sidled away, making excuses and little fluttery gestures with his hands. No, no! It was just to show . . . He hadn't promised . . . Thanks, but he couldn't afford it, and he was gone, neatly folded into the passing crowd, anonymous again. The others turned slowly about to ease off.

"Who's next? Free introduction to this . . ." The man brandished the razor. "Who . . . ?" The men looked at the ground, demure as young girls waiting to be asked for a dance. "Here, you . . ." He pointed at an emaciated young man, who came forward grinning. The others took up their stances, gazing raptly into space. Maybe next time.

Near the post office Gianna and Sorino sat in Celestina, waiting for me, absorbed by their own conversation. I had the uneasy feeling they were discussing me. Had I . . . ? Nothing good came to mind. Whatever it was, must be bad. Or was I too self-conscious? The men, who had moved unwillingly and not very much to let me pass, stared at me. Gianna and Sorino's nervous compliments abut my punctuality did not reassure. He sent Celestina threading her way around clusters of people; I threaded mine around through possible sins and gaffes. Gianna was explaining a change—The Work, I assumed, nothing to do with me. I slipped deeper into

my burrow of introspection. A silence brought me
scrambling back. "Of course, if you don't want to," Gianna
commented and shrugged. I admitted I had not been
listening.

　　I had been demoted, or promoted, depending on
the point of view, from my status as coddled houseguest
to impressed laborer. Bales and crates of clothing needed
to be sorted. Would I help? Then the girls at the Baby
Hut were having a hard time. Two babies, both frail,
both from outside Ortona so they were day-and-night
residents for the term, needed more help at lunch than
the girls could give them and still look after the others.
Would I feed them? In the afternoon . . . I had already
realized that Gianna could not bear the thought of idle-
ness. I was young, strong, intelligent enough: I should
be doing something. In the afternoon she wanted me to
look over translations of sponsored children's letters.
With the mail the night before had been an envelope of
the on-trial secretary's efforts. The English was inac-
curate, ungrammatical, the typing messy. The letters
could not be sent. We would see if I could do better.
And this, I suppose, is how it really began.

Nine

Now my days in Ortona had taken on a shape. I saw more used clothes than I had ever known existed. Or could have imagined. Now in the morning I drove Gianna to the nursery, did the errands and picked her up. Sorino, dressed in a dashing costume of his own undershirt and swimming trunks borrowed temporarily from a bin of oddments that defied classification, stayed at the Autopark, preparing bales for us to sort.

On our return he retired to the other end of the hut for a session of packing the lots to be shipped. The center of the hut was a torrid no-man's-land. Quick organizational trips were possible, but a stay of more than ten minutes was life threatening. At our end we changed to shorts and whatever shirt came to hand, my first being a soigné blue-and-white striped, collar-detached with the clearly stenciled laundry mark CLEMENT ATTLEE. He had failed to send collars, so it was not immediately placeable as relief goods. I became very fond of that shirt, but we were soon parted, by popular demand—Ida's, Sorino's and Gianna's. Even though it had belonged to a former prime minister, in wearing it I threatened the good name of the Fund. They sent it to an old people's home, where I hope it was appreciated, with or without collar.

Once we were properly suited down for the operation, we attacked a bale, which was literally that—a mass of jumbled clothing, compressed to about the size of a cotton bale, wrapped first in corrugated board, then in burlap and bound with metal bands. The shipper's bills that showed some as women's clothing, others as men's and children's were not infallible, and the packers were vague to the point of disorientation about sex. Sorino tried to find the category we needed most at the moment and laid those bales out, minus burlap and bands, like giant books open to a middle chapter, except that the pages were baby's faded corduroy playsuit with ominous brown stains on seat and crotch, followed by an unknown matron's dirty corset and a rubber diaper cover, now permanently molded into a linen-fold shingle. Overcoats with their crooked arms and bulging pockets looked as though the owners had been left in them by mistake. Trousers were woolly slabs. Dresses, blouses, shirts, sweaters and the like fared better. Shaken out, hung up or neatly folded, most would look at least decent. Some would not. Some brought on seismic waves of revulsion that were not to be quelled. We flipped those to the pending pile and pawed on, sorting for widows, women and girls, for newborns and under-threes, for men, boys and waiters (a special category and bin for men who found jobs and did not have the proper clothes.

No one ever sent a full suit of dinner clothes, but from a heterogeneous collection of bits a passable imitation could be put together). And of course each of those lots had to be divided into winter and summer *and* prepared for shipment or stored in the proper place.

The stout of heart could last two or three hours. No more. Even the most careful handling sent up heavy puffs of dust, a gritty accretion from the closets, the warehouses, ships' holds and customs sheds through which those clothes had been dragged. No air currents spun it about or sucked it away. It had to settle and did, in our hair, on our arms, in the creases of our necks and in our noses. We itched, we choked, our eyes were grainy. But worst of all was the smell. Firsthand the human being can be an attractive animal: secondhand he is *not*.

The individual Fund committees in England, Australia and Canada sent tons of new, lovingly assembled things—babies' layettes, blankets and quilts, hemmed diapers, bibs, sweaters, hundreds of small sacks for children at Christmas with simple toys and all manner of useful items. These same committees collected, sorted and packed other tons of used clothing. Sometimes the elbow of a sweater was patched or the hem of a coat unsuccessfully let down; they, however, were *clean* and wearable.

But there were also general clothing drives with collection barrels spotted around where they were most apt to attract casual givers. *They* were the unknown, faceless sources of all this human dross, who, beyond being pleased with their own generosity, apparently expected the desperately poor to be grateful for ragged, stinking garments that would have and should have been pitched out with the garbage.

Instead the worst of them ended up on the pending pile. What to do with them? They were "relief goods." The Italian government had waived duty fees and had paid the freight charges to ship them from the port of entry to Ortona, or any other place Gianna designated. She was bound not to sell them (not even as rags) or destroy them: they must be distributed. People who had accepted the idea of "work," of "earning clothes" rather than the indignity of the eternal handout and the obligation to toady, would not accept someone's grubby tatters no better than their own—if for no other reason because they had invested their time. (The question was hypothetical: they were not offered to them.) Pride is not always a sin. So—What to do with them?

Nuns who cared for the old were perpetually in need and patient. They would wash and mend and remake and never complain. Some of the horrid rejects were sent off to them—with apologies. In the fastnesses of little, lost towns other nuns ran orphanages without benefit of official largesse. They were patient too. Their children were never warm enough in winter, never had changes of anything to go round. Some were also sent off to them with apologies. Of course, the next time they had to be better treated. Still, the pile grew and our stomachs churned. My vague ideas of "giving" and social work began to change. For one thing I was on the other side now.

My hour at the Baby Hut was the ideal physic. At noon, as clean as a slosh in a basin of water and a hairbrushing could make me, I joined my charges, Carlo, the little boy who had nickered and grinned at our arrival, and, in the crib next to his, Mirella, a little girl with the same monkey face and dry, stand-up dark hair. They were not quite two years old and might have been twins.

Mirella came from a small village, an aerie really, on the very top of a bald mountain at the end of a track that was subject to landslides. Indeed, birds could reach it more easily than humans, who, anyway, seldom were tempted. (The Germans being the exceptions. They occupied it and before they left blew up a number of the sagging stone huts. A hundred more refugees to shove toward the Allied lines were the only possible military advantage.)

It was one of those places where no priest stayed more than a few months and government never arrived, which, for all the pluses its absence might offer, also meant services were at an absolute minimum. Gianna had started a nursery and convinced a young teacher from Ortona to live there and run it. She eventually married the son of the one semi-prosperous family. They owned the village mill and a truck. She had begged Gianna to take Mirella for a term at the Baby Hut. Otherwise . . . She had been very pessimistic. Mirella had a congenital heart defect, which, combined with poor food and not much of it, and haphazard, if loving care, suggested a bleak "otherwise."

When, at the end of a trip to see sponsored children, Gianna and Sorino arrived, Mirella had a bad bronchial cold. There was no doctor or pharmacy in the village and no car, either private or for hire. The family was on the official list of poor, as most were, and so entitled to free medical care by the *medico condotto*, who was shared with another, much lower village that made up the township. That is, had one ever accepted the appointment: none had.

The hospital in which Mirella had a right to care,

if her mother could impress the doctors with her need and then stayed to nurse her, was in Chieti, eighty miles and six hours away by bus. There was one bus a day. The pilgrimage started with a warning siren at 2:00 A.M. Departure was at 2:30. Assuming that the dilapidated, prewar vehicle did not break down and that more of the mountainside had not dribbled away during the night, it made connections with its cross-country double at the valley road. That bus followed a snake trail through the mountains, stopping all along the way to pick up other well-served citizens, until it delivered them to the main square of the provincial capital at 8:30, in good time to await the pleasure of government clerks. By midafternoon, after the closing of the vital government offices and the end of all hope, the bus was loaded and ready to reverse the route. In bad weather the round trip had been known to take twenty-four hours.

Gianna was not an alarmist, but she knew that nothing worked entirely as intended and what *almost* did attracted the attention of that mysterious force called unforeseen circumstances. She wrapped Mirella in a blanket and held her in her arms on the slow, twisty trip down to Ortona. At least she could be sure the baby had medical care and was well-fed and nursed. The next day the bronchial congestion threatened to become pneumonia. The day after Mirella also broke out in a rash: she had measles. She was isolated and, as a precaution, so was the little boy in the crib next to hers. Eight days later Carlo came down with measles too.

By the time I met them they were gurgling convalescents, happily sharing a room and the affections of every adult who came near the Baby Hut.

They were shy little mutts. They had adopted

Elisa and Vanda, her assistant, as mothers pro tem.
Every time they saw one of them or heard their voices,
they jiggled up and down in their cribs and nickered,
like overly realistic mechanical toys, thumping along as
hard as their batteries could drive them. I did not immediately qualify for their enthusiasm. I always appeared with food, which should have been in my favor,
but they were diffident. They lowered their heads and,
puckering up their faces ready for audible protest, pretended to ignore me. They watched, though, sneaking
peeks, then quickly slanting their eyes away again. They
missed nothing: the stool placed between their cribs, the
towel spread on my lap, their bowls with the separate
compartments, their cups of juice, their spoons, they
saw them all.

Carlo could be courted with food. He gobbled it
and long after he had swallowed it or let it ooze down
his chin, his mouth went on lapping and nibbling in an-
ticipation of the next spoonful. He resented any time
wasted in coaxing Mirella to taste her lunch. She was a
fretful eater. Two bites in reasonably quick succession
brought on seizures of choking and a deep pink flush
that darkened alarmingly to purple and seemed never
to fade. For long minutes she would gasp for breath,
while, with one hand, I rubbed and patted her back and
with the other stoked Carlo to avert outright rebellion.

Gentle, babbling sounds soothed them. Italian,
English or plain nonsense would do as long as it swayed
along toward lullaby. Carlo played absent-mindedly with
his toes or a toy or twisted my fingers, if he managed
to catch them, lapping and nibbling all the while in hopes
more lunch might come his way. Mirella watched me
with large, sad brown eyes, accepted another spoonful

of food, thought about it before she mouthed it a few times and finally swallowed it, and then, pleased with herself, giggled at me as though we were sharing a silly, private joke. When she decided she had had enough, and I found there was no point in arguing with her, she stuck out her arms. She wanted to be picked up. Instantly so did Carlo. They fussed and scrambled and crawled over me, clinging to my hair for balance, making their soft bleating sounds of pleasure, until slowly, very slowly their eyelids drooped. They struggled, but sleep surprised them. They collapsed, like puppies, where they were. I put them in their cribs and closed the shutters. Our hour together was over. There would be others; we had adopted each other.

The sponsored children, who now absorbed my afternoons, were encouraged to write for themselves. Most of them did, following the stylistic decrees of their teachers. The results had their own charm, a pompous naïveté, that defied flights of bilingual fancy, positively repulsed the well-turned phrase. Translation was verbal botching: lumps smoothed out, sentences turned when verbs were too doggedly passive to make sense in English.

The approved opening was: *"Venco a scriverti guesti poghi ricchi per farti sapere che io sto bene e spero anche di te."* (Even the phonetic misspellings were predictable.) "I come to write you these few lines to let you know that I am well and hope the same of you." More bureaucratic types, influenced, no doubt, by more bureaucratically minded teachers, took the legalistic approach. "The undersigned, ——, son/daughter of —— and ——, born the ——, at —— in the

province of ——— declares that on this day ——— of
——— he/she did receive 5,000 lire (five thousand lire)
from the English lady . . ." With that great blob of of-
ficialese out of the way, the tone became more domestic. "As soon as she left, mamma rushed out and paid
the grocer [the fruit vendor, the pharmacist, the baker]."
Or "Mamma rushed out and bought me a pair of white
shoes for the festa." From Gianna's point of view
"mamma" already had her nicely embroiled, but mamma
could, and often did, do worse. "As soon as she left,
mamma rushed out and bought my *little sister* a pair of
white shoes for the festa."

Mammas, and by association Gianna, had a penchant for breaking the rules. The sponsor expected his
money to be spent for the child he sponsored and only
for that child, which was hardly a sensible expectation
of a family with five children, no land and no work. Willy-
nilly the money was used to cover the most pressing
debt or, unfortunately, at times to finance father's evenings in the wineshop.

Since these were "needy" children, the money
should be spent on *practical* clothes—wool underwear,
winter jackets, boots—on vital medicines, on school-
books. *Not* on fripperies. *Not* on white shoes for the
festa. Nor less, as one little boy, who by himself took
care of his invalid mother, so proudly wrote, on a flower
and a *quartino* of wine for her birthday.

Who was to supervise these daily temptations?
Distance excluded Gianna. She could see them several
times a year. She could make suggestions. She could
report to the Fund and the individual sponsors, but . . .
Who was to choose the children in the first place? The
local priest? The teacher, the midwife, the town clerk?
Each had his own clientele. His own feuds to carry on,

his own political sympathies and ambitions to further. Gianna had decided that the young social workers, all northern, all without traditional local ties, who were assigned to UNRRA-CASAS housing units in the villages, would be the most impartial and of necessity the most aware of real need. They were very fair, but they had their problems too, which seeped right back down to Ortona, to London and beyond.

All too soon, in fact just after I had given up thoughts of creativity and reduced my assignment to a neat set of formulas that came rattling out of the typewriter, a classic of childish innocence and treachery rose to the top of my pile of letters.

Dear Godfather,
Thank you for the money you sent us. My mother has paid the rent with it because the Signorina of UNRRA said that once in six months was not enough. She has a new overcoat and is mad at me because I cut down a tree in front of the house. She loves me very much.

My father is in the States and my mother has gone to the Canadians to have her X rays taken again. He says he is making paper flowers for a lot of money and that he goes with the Americans to the bar every morning for breakfast. He says that they have a glass of whiskey every morning so he does too.

I hope to come to stay with you very soon and will pray to Saint Joseph for you. With lots of good wishes from my mother.
Mario

A translator's note was needed, anonymous to be sure, but of such tact and cogency that the sponsor, a retired Canadian gentleman, was pacified. From the file it was clear that he knew Mario's history.* Did that explain or excuse the rent? Not really. Or what, by implication, it had paid for—the social worker's new overcoat? Or the breakfast tastes of American workmen? Perhaps he would dismiss that as merely another oddity of those very odd neighbors: one never quite knew what they might do. And the awful, numbing prospect of the urchin coming to "stay." Permanently? Would the Canadian gentleman know or in his panic remember that, because Mario's mother was tubercular, they were not eligible for immigration? But first, the rent.

The rent, always the rent. Often the sponsorship money was the only cash a family could depend on. Landlords, especially the government, took a dim view of rents paid in wheat or beans or grapes. Did a sponsor, any sponsor, really prefer that a child have new boots and nowhere to live? Assuming that a family so foolishly literal could be found. *If* the sponsor who gave the money also had a right to dictate its use, how, given the distances and the numbers of children, was that right to be administered for him? It was a mechanical problem that had more to do with the nurture and care of sponsors than it did the nurture and care of sponsored children.

There is a fair dose of cynicism in private charity. Many organizations have sponsorship programs. Some limit their work exclusively to them. The reason

*His mother was tubercular. They had been more or less abandoned by the father, who had reached Canada, then, quite illegally, the United States, never sent money and almost never wrote.

is simple: contributors do not relate to a mass of starving children. They can become emotionally entangled with one carefully chosen, sad, scruffy little child whose photograph is sent to them and who writes them innocently recounting the meager joys of a Christmas dinner or the imagined treachery of a social worker's new overcoat. A contented sponsor can be approached for other projects and for unassigned funds. Sponsorships are a fund-raising technique.

Harmless and they do *some* good, the argument goes. Gianna never thought so. How can the choice of ten, twenty children out of a hundred the same age, living in the same village, fighting the same poverty and starvation be justified? To set up an elite, an arbitrary one at that, using criteria that were often positively insulting, in impoverished communities is hardly constructive. Jealousies and backbiting do not need stimulation and all for what is really so very little.*

My skill with the letters varied in direct proportion to the perversity of the children's inspiration. Some afternoons I slogged my way through one verbal bog of explanations and out, straight into the next; others, my fingers rippled along on their own, leaving my mind free to puzzle over the contradictions of the system. Those afternoons I finished with a couple of hours to spare,

*Some agencies sent goods rather than money. Their ads proclaimed that for every hundred dollars, a hundred dollars' worth of goods would go to the sponsored child. *Worth?* In those golden days of government surplus food used for relief, that was a real bonanza. Even with careful buying on the clothes and food markets, quantity discounts could leave an agency with 40 percent of the sponsor's money to cover overhead, jolly inspection trips abroad and presents for friendly secretaries. It was primarily an American vice. The British Save the Children Fund did not indulge.

not that Gianna admitted there could be "spare" time. Even reading, much as she enjoyed it, was a reward for deeds accomplished to be indulged in just as sleep began blurring the mind. To rescue me from temptation— a book, a nap, or worse, both—she found a project for me: I could repair and paint toys in the Baby Hut garden.

Actually, though hardly the point, it was a lovely way to end a long, hot day. Late in the afternoon a breeze drifted up from the sea, soft and coolish. The babies, finished with their naps and their screaming jags at the ritual (and necessary) change of diapers, and restored to good humor by juice and cookies, were out on blankets under the big umbrellas that shaded the sandbox and large tub of water. They were ready for mischief and had a sumptuous supply of equipment for it— bottles, pans, molds, tubes and funnels and scoops.

One look was enough. They wobbled over to fling sand on my newly painted surfaces, pour water into the paint cans and pat their sand cakes with my brushes. I had either to play with them or to paint on a lower level, where they might not see me, or if they did, their approach would be so laborious I had time to prepare my defenses. The larger, stationary toys near the Baby Hut simply had to be done after hours.

The strokes of the brush were hypnotic. Back and forth, back and forth went the hand, while the mind billowed into a cumulus blob that floated on its own somewhere between earth and sun. Suspended in this beatific non-state, I did not at first notice how carefully I was observed. Repetition finally got through to me. Every time I glanced up, Elisa stared at me, eyes narrowed, a slight frown of speculation on her face. *Physical* work, I could guess, was the problem. It demeaned. Gianna was eccentric, the center was, in a sense, hers, but why should *I* stoop to "labor," when I was not forced to by necessity? She must have hoped that my face would somehow betray the secret.

Every hour or so Sorino, skirting Elisa and her obvious desire to question him, wandered down, casually, to observe my progress. The idea of my painting his toys, unsupervised, made him very nervous. He was driven to recommend more linseed oil. Perhaps I did not realize that the secret to shiny paint, to shiny *Italian* paint, he added diplomatically, was linseed oil. No admirer of the mucilage finish achieved with linseed oil, I was of the turpentine school. At least the paint would dry. I could always put on a second coat. No, if I would forgive him, linseed oil was the thing. Gianna had warned we might have this problem. Shaking his head, but not resigned, he carefully skirted Elisa again and escaped the garden to return later for further praise of linseed oil, once more carefully skirting Elisa. He believed in social and professional distinctions and considered himself, in many respects, "middle management," above discussing personalities, especially a confusing one, with the "hired help," most especially female hired help. He was sure neither where to place me nor what to make of me, except that, obviously, I did not understand the finer qualities of linseed oil.

Then there was Ida's more benevolent presence. On her way back from her afternoon rest, shopping and gossip trip to town she always stopped for a whispered conference with Elisa. Every few seconds they popped their heads up to watch me, then bobbed them back down, Ida looking back over her shoulder at me. Did she worry that I disapproved, or was she explaining?

Amused? Agreeing I lowered myself on the gentility scale? She had a few words for me too. Was I having fun? Would I like a cup of tea? Without being too obvious, she also arranged to be near the kitchen door in case I became too involved talking to passersby she judged to be undesirable.

Known and unknown, Pasquale snared them first. His philosophy of gardening—that it was useless to spade beds and trim bushes no one ever saw—kept him conveniently near the fence, available for distraction. Above all else he liked to talk. He was a talented gossip, inventing what he thought would most titillate or shock, in one way or another delay his listeners, and they believed him. How could they not? He was such a mild-seeming little man, a grinning scarecrow with a postage-stamp moustache, a floppy, stained fedora and baggy clothes, which, in spite of the heat, always included someone much larger's discarded suit vest, festooned with an imposing nickel chain.

As a storyteller he was brazenly earnest, almost flirtatious, asking for advice, hinting—just a simple man, he might not understand—but the key to his success was his apparent sharing, the first time ever, of a secret. Only a few feet from him, only half-listening, and not expected to understand or answer, I surprised myself: the dialect he spoke, his private lingua franca, based on the lost Levantine tongue of his native village in Puglia with an overlay of everything he had heard through the years and a binder of superfluous, gluey diphthongs, made perfect sense. So I learned that the baron across the road had *three* mistresses. Think of it—*three!* And, almost as remarkable to Pasquale, they arrived on their own, one by bicycle, two by scooter. Could one man

need three women? Tee-hee! What did he do with them?
and he lowered his voice. Evil little man. He knew, even
I did, that the ladies in question were the maid, sister
and sister-in-law. For Pasquale's purposes Sorino's closest friend was the boss of the Roman black market and
Gianna was "well-connected" at the Vatican, thereby
maintaining delicate social distinctions while endowing
them both with influence and, by insinuation, money,
the world's most intriguing and to him remote blessing.

In the true tradition of the eavesdropper, I heard
no good of myself, though not much ill. At times I was
Gianna's sister, at others boredom overstimulated his
imagination and I was that mythical semi-princess
(fallen), adored in every village, the rich man's daughter who had loved a ne'er-do-well and been exiled from
her father's sight—with a lavish allowance. Pasquale
could not resist that touch. I was a *buon partito*, a good
prospect, for local bachelors. He also suggested a certain willingness on my part without taint of desperation. Unfortunately the passersby he had enlightened
with such twaddle went on, rather more thoughtful than
when they had stopped, and never saw the ambiguous
little ritual of Pasquale, jigging around the bushes,
beating time with his hoe and chortling to himself.

From my side of the bushes I watched, musing
over the renunciation of rigidity and the peculiar benefits thereof, my brush still dutifully going back and forth,
back and forth. It was a lovely way to end a long, hot
day.

Ten

Discovery of a new world is no excuse. Guests are expected to move on: I still had that much sense. Every few days I made plans to go to Florence. Monday on the 1:36 train. Just as regularly on the Wednesday (or Thursday) after my supposed departure there was a festa or a visit or something unusual that Gianna thought I would find interesting, that it would be too bad to miss. Since I was there. I could just as well go on Friday. Then, why arrive on the weekend? And we were back to Monday again.

Not that I objected. I coasted along, quietly, struggling with my letters and the confusions of Italian, understood and not, answered and misanswered to further confusions, and Mirella and Carlo, my painting jobs, and mountains of old clothes. Always those loathsome old clothes. I was determined not to complain. Ever. Secretly I laughed at myself. I might have been five again, consciously "behaving myself," as I had when my mother and father allowed me to go with them on a motor trip through the North Carolina mountains, provided, my mother was very firm, provided I did whatever my father wanted me to do. Never irritated him. Never complained. Never got tired (or never said so). One peep out of me and she would send me home. How exactly she would have managed that, I was too young to wonder, but I wanted desperately to go. I had behaved then, and here I was, twenty years later, "behaving" again, hoping for the same results. I never complained. Not about the lack of water, or the exhaustion that some days reduced me to physical and mental numbness, or food I did not happen to like or sights that shocked me. The stratagem was childish, I knew, but I wanted desperately to stay. I had not yet asked myself why.

The first of the unusual events was Gianna's name day, Saint John the Baptist on June 24, and the first hint of just how unusual it would be came with Ida and my breakfast. She was, she admitted, *vestita da chiesa*, dressed for church. As I dressed in my standard, nonceremonial cotton, I could hear below a clatter of china and footsteps hurrying back and forth to the road. At the kitchen door I almost collided with Sorino, lugging a case of mineral water, in full flight from Ida. She was right behind him, brandishing a broom and shrieking. Out of her kitchen! No one drank mineral water except the signora and the signorina. *She* had seen to us. Just get it out of her way! He meekly took the case around the corner to the back of the house, where there was shade.

One look into the kitchen and I understood Ida's frenzy. Trays of glasses, of coffee cups, on the table.

Bottles of wine and liqueurs under it. Neapolitan coffeepots of varying sizes on the stove. More trays with bat-
talions of serviceable *biscotti*, the kind that would go
with anything, were stacked on the tops of cupboards.
Ida had prepared for an invasion.

From mid-morning until dinner that evening they
marched on the house in delegations—the mayor and
town council, the pensioners, the blood donors, the infant welfare, the Catholic Action, the public health department, the post office employees in the person of the
old man who delivered telegrams, UNRRA-CASAS,
doctors, lawyers and accountants, priests and nuns,
representing a variety of institutions and orders—each
with its bouquet of flowers, its objet d'art in visceral
ceramics to adorn Gianna's shelves (their distribution,
or better yet disposal, seemed a formidable problem until I heard her, admiring a particularly repulsive speci-
men, say she would send it to her mother for safekeeping—a graceful explanation for chronic disappearances).
And, of course, each delegation had a spokesman with
a eulogy he was determined to deliver.

The sitting room was too small for more than one
group at a time. The audiences were private, and we
were the captives of grandiloquence, which, if wearing
and dull, gave me a unique chance to study syntax and
learn, once and for all, that my mistakes were less than
fatal, would probably never be noticed. Gianna's efforts
at solemnity led to a prunes-and-prisms set to her mouth.
She doggedly avoided my eye.

By the end of the day Ida had recycled the vases
so many times that my room was a maze of tomato sauce
tins full of flowers and still Gianna, engulfed in all the
rest, appeared to be lying in state. We called her the

cara defunta, the "dear departed," which she did not appreciate. Another year, she sighed wearily, she must remember to be away.

Next we had Saints Peter and Paul, a national holiday that brought the country to a halt, followed a few days later by Saint Thomas, a local holiday that, twice a year, brought Ortona to a halt. This was the much-reduced warm-up for the real thing, which, in defiance of the Church calendar, would take place in September. Blessedly, this time we were spectators, not attractions.

From all over the district pilgrims gathered to do penance, to give thanks for grace received or beg new miracles of Saint Thomas. They arrived the day before, supposedly on foot, but tradition had given way to chartered buses and piety could be satisfied by getting off a mile or so outside town and trudging the last lap. The old in black, wearing holy medals like service decorations, the newly married, the afflicted on crutches, bandaged, the anxious parents with pale, peevish children, some dressed in monks' habits (a cure granted, a vow kept) and the more cheerful mass of *appassionati*, who, on principle, went to any and every festa they could—hundreds upon hundreds they came, all eager to crawl on their knees from the door of the cathedral to the altar, praying as they went and licking the floor.

This first obeisance accomplished, they scuttled off to establish squatters' rights on whatever unoccupied space they could find. The steps of side altars were highly prized and the subject of constant litigation. For the next twenty-four hours these "pilgrims" would sleep in the cathedral, and eat there, making it at times into a vast indoor picnic ground with children squabbling and playing tag and dogs slinking around in search of scraps. They fell out of ecstasy into feuds, said their beads, made their confessions, mumbled through the Masses, quarreled again over space and snored, all under the haughty, metallic gaze of a Saint Thomas who, incongruously, even in this mid-chest silver bust-reliquary form, displayed the general trappings and disposition of a condottiere, albeit one with a halo. (The fifteen-hundred-year gap Gianna waved aside as a slight discrepancy, typical of such histories and easily explained: he had undoubtedly been fitted out by his Venetian kidnappers.)

Every so often the pilgrims, careful to leave one squatter guardian, escaped his martial sanctity for the more secular amusements offered in the streets. Stalls of a special market sprawled around the center of town. The usual commodities were for sale at prices inflated for the occasion, plus souvenirs, candles and, most popular of all, great towers of slab candy, a sort of taffy-brittle with almonds called *Torrone* that men worked on marble counters, pounding it and pulling and twisting it into shiny hanks until it reached the proper jawbreaker consistency. Processions swayed through the side streets to the wheezes and um-pa-pas of the local band, while in the piazza a "concert orchestra" stretched its ensemble skills in a musical footrace with Rossini and lost, though its heats with "William Tell" were memorable. There were flying chairs and a merry-go-round for the children, who begged for just one ride and, when the moment came, screamed and clung to their fathers' legs. But what I have always remembered about that first festa was people standing, stolidly waiting, hours on end, scarcely moving. Waiting for what? I never knew. The fireworks, perhaps.

We watched them, a poor, little popgun show,
from the garden. To my relief. Those listless crowds
had depressed and finally frightened me. About them
there was a sour pessimism and resentment that I did
not trust. At first I had longed for a reaction, any reaction. On second thought the most probable would be
anger, not a burst of gaiety. Suddenly the status quo
had a grim appeal.

The human mind is treacherous in so many ways.
Mine, having reasoned that far, played an abominable
trick on me. It added together the noisome accumulation of garbage, the casual, sporadic attentions of the
collectors, no water and almost no sewers and, for a
grand total, dragged up from some dormant cell, gave
me Cellini's description of the Black Death. I was well
on my way to becoming the guest Gianna dreaded most,
the "sanitary conditions" bore. No sooner had I vowed
to suppress such qualms than I heard myself stammering about garbage and rats—and, well, so many people!

She was offhand about it, probably recognizing
the symptoms and determined to squash them. Nothing
to worry about. At dawn the mess would be cleaned up,
the people gone. Besides the human body had a way of
developing immunity (But not mine. I hadn't been there
long enough.) to all those minor (Minor? I had in mind
bubonic plague.) intestinal bacteria. Nothing to worry
about on that score. Now typhoid was another matter.
The first bout in the summer cycle was overdue. (The
first?) The worst would be in September, then
Christmas . . .

Following along behind her in the dark, down the
steps and through the garden, I tried to assess this new
threat and to remember if I had been vaccinated against

it. We were on our way to the kitchen for the nightly
bottle of "safe" water, a dubious term, that would allow
us to brush our teeth. She fumbled for the light switch.
I must have been very deep into my intimations of mor-
tality and the early-morning trains I might take. When
she flipped on the light and thousands of *large*, shiny
black beetles skitter-waddled, but with shimmering
speed, across the floor in search of cover, I hardly
flinched.

"What . . . ? What *are* they? Where . . . ?"

"What? Oh, *those*?" Her innocence was studied,
too careful, but that only came to me later. "They're—
uh—a local beetle. The damp climate—everybody has
them. They come in from the garden." She shrugged.
"It's so close. That's why the cupboards are up on feet,
things—you know, like sugar, flour, things like that—
are sealed in tins. At night they come in for a look-see.
Here, of course, they never find anything and, like the
pilgrims, they'll be gone in the morning." She had picked
up the bottle (sealed with a porcelain tap-and-spring
mechanism) and stood by the door, waiting for me to
light our candle and take custody of the bottle so that
she could lock up. "Don't worry. Everybody has them,"
she repeated, smiling, but watching me with a stern eye.
I shivered.

"Revolting, aren't they?" She nodded, busy with
the crow bar, iron sockets and gargantuan key that would
have guaranteed the impregnability of a medieval castle. Satisfied it was in order, she took the candle and
led the way upstairs. She was also satisfied that I had
never before seen a cockroach.

But the next morning the pilgrims and garbage
and beetles—my "ghoulies and ghosties and long-leggety

beasties"—had all disappeared and nothing had gone "bump in the night." I gave up my search for a convenient train and stayed. Logic did not seem to be my great strength. I really wanted to stay, in spite of Ortona, still admitting that it offered every inconvenience, including, now, endemic typhoid, and no saving graces.

Amusements were few and of the kind that should have been simple to enjoy, if one had a mind to, but, somehow, were not. There always seemed to be secret provisos that governed them. Swimming, for instance. My one attempt was abortive. As I approached the water, two Carabinieri appeared from behind a dune, wallowing through the sand toward me, waving their arms and shouting that I was breaking the law. My bathing suit, it seemed—not a bikini, just a chaste two-piece suit that revealed a bit of non-flabby midriff—defied the national code of modesty. They threatened to charge me with Obscene Acts in a Public Place—our indecent exposure—which, with my limited knowledge of strippers and the law, I had always thought a crime exclusive to the male. We reached what they considered a compromise: they would forget the charge—this time—if I put on my robe, got in the car and went home.

An evening at the local cinema had been only slightly more successful. The cashier, uncertain about what sort of tickets she dared sell two women, one a local celebrity, a respectable one, called the manager, who insisted on opening the Prefect's box and would, in his heart of hearts, have felt happier had he been able to lock us inside it.

There had been a small dance, which sounded promising but turned out to be, like most other activi-

ties not specifically forbidden to women or frowned upon,
an official ceremony, this time to inaugurate the new
quarters of the Boy's Club. It had been Gianna's husband's last and favorite project. She, of course, had to
go and I was to play the docile guest. At one time the
building had housed a café and had, off to one side, a
little garden and a minuscule dance floor that was normally crowded with pinball machines. It was there that
we, the Authorities, the committee of sponsors and stray
notabili along with a few of the older boys who could
muster presentable clothes gathered. The bishop opened
the festivities with a prayer and a blessing. The mayor
spoke—at length—and was followed by the head of the
committee, a gallant, portly lawyer with a white moustache, who also spoke at length. Several others showed
symptoms of readiness but were efficiently cut off by a
blast from the public-address system. One of the boys
had come to the end of his patience and put on record.

The mayor led off the dancing with Gianna. The
gallant lawyer chose me. Our dance was not a complete
success. He murmured into my hair long sweeps and
dips and gaspings of words, all in the truest, most oro-
tund tradition of Italian recitation, but all completely
beyond my comprehension. There was a great deal about
l'usignuolo, whatever that was. ("The Nightingale," I
found out later, one of D'Annunzio's most famous poems.)
By the time the record came to an end, we were both
rather sticky and flushed from our various exertions,
and applause from the crowd that had collected outside
the fence to watch only made matters worse.

The bishop was a relief. He did not dance or recite and stumbled instantly into my Chicago–Al Capone dialogue. The mayor danced, but he also asked the

fatal question that took us again to Chicago. I was becoming proficient in its non-gangster delights. The most attractive young man in town was a doctor, whose attentions were what the Victorians would have called "marked" and terribly proper. We discussed the water problem. I was surprised to hear he was no better off than we and had no way to heat water had there been any. I was even more surprised to hear that he lived with, indeed slept in the same room with his mother, who did not allow him to be out after ten. And so it went on, interminably, until Sorino, in an unaccustomed role of duenna-driver, "brought the car around" and drove us home in state.

Such soirées were rare and hardly dazzled. Of more normal evening fare there was little choice. Old westerns, shown on projectors starved for electric current, though funny in their groan-and-gallop, twilight flicker-and-glare fluctuations, did not often tempt us away from the table under the grape arbor. There, for a few hours, Ortona was at one remove, off in the distance, on the headland a fringe of small, geometric shapes, very black and no more real than the silhouette of Bethlehem on a Christmas card. Leaves, ruffling in the soft breeze, dappled the haze of light from the kitchen window. The cats slept, by preference in Gianna's lap. Occasionally the pigeons, alarmed by some imagined predator, gave a few warbling moans—sad, lonely sounds in the night.

We were lulled, perhaps they were too, by the cool, shadowy peace. Through those still evenings our minds meandered. So did our conversations as we gradually grew more comfortable with each other. We talked, we drank some wine, laughed a lot and went to bed late.

By the time my "few days in Ortona" had stretched to a few weeks, I knew a great deal about the facts of Gianna's life, less about her doubts and disappointments, and nothing about her husband. Her references to him were rare and factual, as bleakly factual as the census, and usually came, I noticed, at the end of a long day in the car.

The conversations of two reasonably tactful people, isolated for hours in a car, are not the conversations those same two people would have elsewhere. Time seems to have no limit. The place is an amorphous nowhere between departure and arrival. The generic impersonal slips gently toward the personal, and on, almost imperceptibly, to the regrets, ambitions and bitternesses behind the chronicles. It is easier too because you are not face to face; neither the talker nor the listener feels quite so exposed. We spent many long days in the car. One in particular I remember so clearly. For so many reasons.

We left Ortona at dawn to drop south on the main coast road some seventy-five miles before following a loop inland that would, according to the map, take us to various orphanages Gianna needed to visit. Even the first leg had been slow. Then, in the fifties, paved highways had only two lanes, were crowded, pitted and banked as the donkey ambled rather than as the wheeled vehicle lurched. They did lurch too, in almost continuous lines, cars and clattering trucks, three-wheeled scooter-carts, buses of all shapes and ages, prewar Topolinos converted to drays, bicycles, even motorized Bath chairs, sometimes aided by a dog in harness.

Gianna was a nervous rider, distrusting any driver

as much as she distrusted herself at the wheel. She expected to be copilot, always alert, reading the signs to me, a habit from her years of traveling with Sorino, who was not a quick reader, scanning the road for drivers who, gripped by some raptus of illusionary speed, were about to hop out of their lane and commit mass murder. Her phobia was not unreasonable. Once otherwise rational people possessed a machine capable of motion, they seemed to confuse a trip to the next town with the Mille Miglia, the famous and later infamous thousand-mile race around the peninsula. It was quite futile. No matter how skilled you were and strong of nerve, you would seldom average more than thirty-five miles an hour.

The concatenation of unpredictables was against it. Bridges washed out. Hillsides slithered down onto the road. Accidents, not always serious, but tragedies nonetheless to the participants, became instant traffic jams that could not be unsnarled until the police arrived and took measurements and listened to the accusations of those directly *and* indirectly concerned and wrote up a full report of their fictions.

Then too, every few miles there were railroad crossings with keepers so cautious they trusted neither clocks nor printed schedules. Ten minutes before a train could possibly approach, the barriers were lowered, and no power on earth could move them until the train, however late, had passed. All we could do was wait and watch the truck drivers line up at the side of the road for a round of their favorite sport, seeing who could spray the farthest. They were not in the least shy. After all, women did not travel.

To make up time I was forced to a perilous sla-

lom style—duck out, scud back in, scud out—and to
frantic fumblings of hands: on the wheel, the gearshift,
on the turn signals, lighted flippers that appeared from
and disappeared into slots in the doorposts at far too
leisurely a pace for my maneuvers, and on the horn,
which by law had to be sounded at each curve. With
two hands it was a virtuoso performance. Four would
have been useful. Certainly four eyes, intent on the
swarming permutations of the traffic were better
than two.

Gianna's eyes never left the road, never seemed
even to blink, and her mild comments—that blue truck
is turning in, or the Lancia's going to pass no matter
what—with their suggestion that we had both, of course,
noticed the same thing, were spliced in so neatly that
the ramifications of peasant psychology or the iniquities
of Bourbon rule in the South seemed to roll on undis-
turbed. She mistook my almost catatonic concentration,
which I struggled to present as poise, for suicidal non-
chalance and was determined to keep me ready for
swerves or skip-offs into the ditch that might suddenly
be expedient. Conversation seemed her best hope. Not
constant chatter, but enough to ensure against beguiling daydreams.

From her point of view, Italy, the subject that
never failed us, had one great disadvantage: she talked,
I listened. She led me into dissertations—muddled, I
imagine—on the vagaries of the electoral college and
states' rights. And why my accent, which she thought
curious, was not the Arkansas-Texas twang cum drawl
that she took to be the national standard. I might almost be Canadian, at best a double-edged compliment,
given the English condescension to colonials. In ex-

change, she talked about the charms of Glyndebourne,
the non-charms of clothes rationing, and told me tales
of war that reminded her of other tales of war and youth.
Down near Vasto I "met," as it were, an old school friend
of Gianna's. She had married, had children, was doing
all the "normal" things. After that there was a meditative silence. A few miles farther south the story of another friend who had survived Dunkirk to die years later
in a German prison camp led to another silence.

So, an idle conversation about Faenza and the
corruption of faience china from the subtle color and line
of the past to the crude, garish modern form led us to
a widowed aunt of Gianna's, who still had an old, very
valuable service of the intricate Chinese Chippendale
pattern. Her father's sister. Silence again. Obviously
Gianna was thinking about her aunt.

Her aunt's life did not seem quite real in today's
world, she finally said in a distant, musing voice that
was more to herself than to me, thinking out loud.
Around the turn of the century the aunt had married a
very "suitable" gentleman, somewhat older than she, of
established fortune. They were happy together, but
never had children, which saddened her. Perhaps to
console her or perhaps in the spirit of honesty and certainly with some trepidation, he confessed that he had
had a daughter by a beloved mistress. As a last act before his marriage he had made legal arrangements for
their support and for the child's education. He hoped,
should anything happen to him, that his wife would continue to help them. She did and became very fond of
the daughter, who was herself by then happily married
and the mother of children. It all sounded very Edwardian—and civilized.

She, like many others of her age, felt the war had ruined her. Financially, that is. She had no choice but to economize. She sold the family palazzo, a real one in the center of Milan, and retired with her *governante* and maids to an apartment that she considered slightly déclassé. She also kept a suite of rooms for herself and the governante in a nursing home for those moments when she needed rest. Summers she spent in one of the family villas in one of the five villages she owned outright. She intended leaving them to the Church. Each day, summer and winter, her administrator and her doctor called upon her. An Edwardian story right to the end . . .

That morning, once we turned inland, the road withered to a lane and a half of dirt ruts, for which the highway department apparently considered both maintenance and signposts redundant. In compensation the traffic was minimal. The somnolent old women, who grazed a pig or two on the verges, and the equally somnolent donkeys and their owners, who claimed the center of the road as their own, moved only, and slowly at that, for the odd, hurtling gravel truck. Cars were too quiet to make an impression on them, and our requests for directions, as we sidled by, did not stir any recollection valid for more than a kilometer. We had to find our villages by a terrestrial variation on dead reckoning. If the map were right, *if*, we wanted the third village on the left. They were all perched above us, high on bare mountains veined with promising trails and dry streambeds. But we were in the valley. Every few hundred feet serious, worn ruts beckoned. Which was the one, undoubtedly the only, right track? Nearest the bus-stop sign seemed plausible and led us in relative comfort into an old quarry. Our next choice lumped along through the scrub for five hundred feet and vanished between one boulder and the next.

Eventually, dusty and thoroughly shaken up, we found the first village and our orphanage. A crowd of children collected in the little piazza and stood, gawking at the car in half-frightened amazement—I was inclined to agree with them: our arrival was nothing short of miraculous—while Gianna gave me my instructions. The basic rule was When in doubt copy what she did. Smile often to soften any impression of criticism implied by my silence. Listen hard, never take notes. Time enough later. This was not an official inspection. Swallow my dose of gall and wormwood—the thimble of caustic coffee, the glass of corrosive, homemade liqueur—like a man. *Coraggio!*

The nun who opened the door to us was fat and suspicious. Gianna showed her the mother superior's letter, which earned us a long wait in the cold, dead air of a closet-sized sitting room lighted by a cloudy lunette near the ceiling. A love seat upholstered in green plastic and two matching chairs, instruments of exquisite torture disguised as a suite, hunched over a glass-topped table and its requisite starched doily. A long plastic crucifix hung, off center, on one wall. Whatever the intention, the effect was of a crypt with amenities, the anteroom of a place to which no one wants to go.

A rattle of beads, chains and keys and the mother superior heaved into the room, pushing all before her in the way of fat women, followed by a floating, wraithlike nun, whom she introduced as her alter ego, the bursar. Years of deficit spending and worry had taken their toll on the bursar, creasing her thin, bony face in a perpet-

ual frown of disapproval. Instead of sitting, she fidgeted
around the room, glaring at us from odd angles, over
her shoulder, behind our backs, in nervous speculation.
Just the opposite, the mother superior was all delight.
She collapsed on a chair immediately and patted Gianna's hand, then her arm, then reached over to pinch my
cheek. Gianna did not shrink back. Neither did I. To
smile with any conviction was going to be harder than
I had thought. But I did, until my jaws ached. Through
Gianna's questions and the mother superior's woeful,
whiny complaints and justifications, which alternated with
bouts of flattery and patting. Bravely, as promised,
through the dose of gall and wormwood, which was delivered, like contraband, by a disembodied hand that
slipped stealthily around the doorjamb, waggled, and
darted back out of sight as soon as the bursar gripped
the tray. She was so pleased with this little ruse that
she smiled. It was her supreme effort at affability: to
me it looked like ghoulish delight, suppressed, but with
difficulty.

At last the moment for the tour came. The mother
superior's needs had been discussed at length. The answer was everything, repeated emphatically. *Everything!* Several times Gianna had hinted . . . we must
not intrude on the superior's—and of course the bursar's—busy day . . . indeed, we should be on our way
very soon. The mother superior had demurred. We could
not rob her, so soon, of such delightful company. Such
a treat. Anyway, orphanages and orphans, misbegotten
little waifs, were all the same. Poor, the world's abandoned. Another cup of coffee? Or lunch? And it was not
yet ten in the morning! Finally she sighed, stood up and
with shuffling purpose headed for the door. The bursar
already held it open.

We would see it all. We would realize she had
told the truth; the mother superior's litany began and
accompanied us, a seamless chant, through the entire
network of corridors that were so tortuous and confusing in their pale green sameness. We would realize they
needed everything. *Literally everything!*—food, clothing, blankets. There was never enough of anything to
go around. Now here . . . Another dank, cavernous
room, smelling of sweaty children, acrid disinfectant and
equally acrid tomato sauce, was thrown open for inspection. The dining room. The recreation room, which was
bare except for straight chairs lined up along all four
walls. Schoolrooms with battered wooden desks, attached in pairs by a common narrow-backed bench.

I trailed along behind, and soon two little girls in
stained black smocks and flopping shoes trailed behind
me, whispering and giggling. They were too quick for
me. When I turned they sprinted away to a safe distance and stood, watching me. I went on, never looking
back, until they felt safer and eased up close to me.
Without warning I reached around and snagged one by
the back of her smock. The other one pounded back down
the corridor in terror. I squatted by my prisoner and,
putting an arm around her shoulders, I parted, very
gently, the not very clean brown hair that had fallen
over her face. She stared resolutely at the floor.

"What's your name?" Silence and a shake of the
head. "Don't be afraid. Just whisper it in my ear." For
one brief instant huge brown eyes, deep set and with
gray-purple smudges underneath, inspected my face. The
lids drooped again.

"Maria Grazia," she half-whispered in a surprisingly deep croak. And how old was she? Ten. She was
not whispering. That splintered baritone was her voice.

The other little girl had edged up closer. She had impetigo sores around her mouth and short, blondish hair made bristly by dust. I put my other arm out and drew her into our huddle. What was her name? Rita, she mouthed. No sound came out. Did they like it at the orphanage? Eyes flashed at me and away again. Maria Grazia shrugged. Did they have enough to eat? Long pause. Both little girls hung their heads. Maria Grazia leaned still closer to my ear. "No," came the rumble. Rita shook her head. Had they wanted to ask me something? Nods. What was it? They exchanged sidelong glances, their eyes still well hidden from me. Maria Grazia took a deep breath, and a second.

"Did you drive the car?" She gulped. "Somebody said you drove it." It was my turn to nod. Rita nodded too. Apparently her role in this adventure was limited to seconding whatever her friend said. "Is the—the car yours?"

"No, it belongs to that other signora down there with the mother superior. She lets me drive it." I turned toward the end of the hall and there was no one there. Still, they understood. They had seen Gianna.

"Would you take us for a ride?" Maria Grazia asked, now brave enough to look at me with pleading eyes that were already shadowed by the disappointment she expected. I explained, as she knew I would, that I couldn't, that time. If we came again, I would. I promised. Was that all right? She nodded unhappily. Rita nodded too. I hugged them both and sent them off, giggling. Now to catch up with Gianna and the mother superior.

My pale green corridor came to a dead end at another pale green corridor. No one was in sight. To the left I heard voices—excited, little girl voices. Three-quarters of the way along, a door was open. At least I could ask directions. If I could get anyone's attention. In a long, narrow dormitory, jammed with beds and a curtained-off cubicle just inside the door, a frantic evacuation was under way. Beds were stripped, sheets and blankets everywhere. Little girls struggled along the aisle, their arms bulging with wadded sheets. Older girls folded blankets. A young nun, red faced and perspiring, popped out from behind a lopsided pile of blankets she was carrying toward the bed nearest the door, where there were other piles. Her mouth formed a silent "Oh." Her flush deepened, and she motioned me toward the hall. She dumped the blankets and joined me.

"A little spring cleaning," she panted. In July? "Airing mattresses, putting away blankets." I wondered why. That high in the mountains it was cold at night. "Can I help you? Are you lost?" I explained. She smiled. I should have gone to my right at the end of the corridor. They would be in the workroom just down there. Look for the sign on the door.

I found the *"Laboratorio."* It was empty except for four knitting machines and half a dozen trestle tables with bundles of gloves and glove linings scattered on them. At either end cardboard cartons held other bundles of gloves and glove linings. The shipping labels were from a company near Florence. Five or six doors down the hall I again heard voices, somber voices this time, and found another Laboratorio sign. Gianna, flanked by the mother superior and the bursar, was admiring the needlework of the "older girls." There were eight or nine of them around another trestle table earnestly and rather awkwardly hemstitching sheets. They were older only in the sense that they had finished fifth grade, so did not have classes and were available for "commissions," in this case a trousseau.

We were paraded through the organized bustle of the kitchen, with its derricks and steaming caldrons. One thin, tired-looking girl sat on a stool surrounded by galvanized tubs, washing salad. The pantries were next, then finally, on the last leg, the dormitories, the first actually the one I had wandered into earlier, and the mother superior's begging turned shrill: sheets and blankets, she *would* have them.

The young, red-faced nun stood off to the side, listening, her hands twitching nervously with her rosary. Once she almost interrupted, but at that moment the mother superior threw back the white cotton cover on the nearest bed. There! We could see for ourselves! They had only scraps of blankets and ragged sheets. Just as she said, those beds were now made up with scraps, frayed at that, of blankets and sheets that were crazy quilts of patches. She threw back another bed, seemingly at random, on the opposite side of the room. More patches, only one sheet, a square of stiff military blanketing.

My expression must have been doltish, which was as well. The young nun watched me anxiously. I looked around idly, doing my best to mime boredom, and wandered back into the corridor to wait. We saw another dormitory, another with cullings from a ragbag for bed linen, and Gianna eased into the delicate formalities of extricating us.

Once more back in the car, bumping down the track to the valley, Gianna and I compared notes. My discoveries confirmed her suspicions. The mother superior, it seemed, was susceptible to compliments and, once properly appreciated, had waxed confidential. Life, even in an orphanage, must be decorous. Gianna sympathized. An example must be set for the girls, no? Certainly. A larger reception room, real chairs and sofas. Decent china for visitors—and then—it would take awhile, but she was set on having dark uniforms, Sunday uniforms with little capes, for the girls. There were so many ceremonies, and they could walk behind important funerals (which, though she did not mention it, was a pious service that invited healthy contributions). Think of the *figura* they would cut! And someday she would have a car. So undignified, traveling by bus . . .

Gianna had reached the Yes, but . . . stage. What about food? The everyday things that . . . that, she thought to herself, you were begging for just moments ago. The mother superior waved all that aside, her wiliness clouded by the pleasures of boasting. She was a special "favorite" of the Prefect. Anything she wanted— why, he had already promised "modern" furniture, Formica and metal tubing—greatly admired because it was new—and a television set. His largesse did not stop there.

For all her laments the storerooms bulged with supplies—edible, tradable and salable. Obviously she had a market for sheets and blankets. Why not food too? And that other unmentionable (child labor, captive at that, could not in the most expansive humor be admitted), her well-organized commerce in glove "finishing." No doubt it produced a steady income and had the considerable virtue of keeping the girls busy afternoons and evenings.

The mother superior was a shrewd old harridan, her means not too different from the Silesians'. Her ends, however, were. For her, more and better food for the

girls, training that would help them later, a more normal, active life were not in the scheme of things. No, it
was not a place, we decided, that screamed of neglect
and need, but rather of exploitation. Nothing Gianna
could do would change the desolate lives of those little
girls; so, sadly, a line was drawn through the name of
that orphanage.

By mid-afternoon we had visited three others,
avoided lunch at all three, and, encouraged by Gianna,
I had become expert at wandering off on unofficial re-
connaissance tours. My initial success was not repeated.
I found nothing more incriminating than stray ragamuf-
fins with harassed nuns in pursuit. The fifth orphanage,
the last on our list, was in a village which, even by the
standards of our ordinance map, was minute, no more
than a cluster of houses, and something of a phantom.
The roads we tried to follow no longer existed. No one
actually knew the place; a few had heard of it, they
thought. In one town the tobacconist insisted on calling
the music teacher. The *maestro* traveled. He would understand our map. He studied it intently—upside down—
and finally advised us to turn right once we reached the
valley again, then, after a bit, left. That's what he always did, and it took him everywhere he wanted to go.

With such lucid directions the odds were against
our ever finding the settlement, but after further wrong
turns and inconclusive interviews, we wandered out of
a scrub wood into a rudimentary piazzetta—a church, a
fountain and along one side a row of tall, narrow houses,
all attached, sharing walls. Two of them, according to a
plaque, were the orphanage. The doors were locked, the
shutters closed and the bells went unanswered. Orphanages, unlike businesses, do not go bankrupt or move
to new premises. A woman, who must have been

watching us through her shutters, stuck her head out
and suggested, rather ambiguously, that we try the
cemetery. Down the lane there, near that row of cypress.

We met them just outside the gate—ten little
girls, stairsteps, the youngest five or six, the eldest
twelve or thirteen, and three nuns, two young, pink
cheeked, and a much older mother superior, who was
small and fragile and already out of breath. The children crowded around us, asking questions as though we
were a half-expected surprise they had been promised.
Would we stay for supper? Spend the night? Had we
brought bags? They could loan us nightgowns. The young
nuns shushed them. The mother superior frowned and
shook her head, but kindly. She was still short of breath.
I suggested I get the car. No, no, that was not necessary. She was all right. Behind her the younger nuns
nodded emphatically and pointed to their hearts.

The mother superior sighed as she settled in the
back seat. Soon, she supposed, even this little walk would
be too much for her. At one of their front doors she
produced from somewhere in the folds of her habit an
iron key the size and weight of a hammer and let us into
a sepulchral kitchen that ran the depth of that house
and must originally have been stalls. Two square windows, very small, very high in the walls, and the tran-
som over the door provided the only daylight. In a wide
and disproportionately tall fireplace, more baronial than
the room seemed to warrant, embers of a fire glowed,
and beside it sat a shapeless, still more or less upholstered armchair, which—it was easy to guess from the
embroidery hoop, a sewing box, a breviary, pads of paper and a scattering of letters—was the mother superior's general headquarters. The center of the room was

taken up by a long, raw wood table with benches at the
sides and stools at the ends. All that was utilitarian—
cupboards, one with a two-eyed gas burner, a bread box,
a stone sink with above it a wooden rack for drying
dishes—stood well back against the walls.

The mother superior, more sure-footed indoors,
skimmed along with quick, tiny steps, filling a kettle,
putting it on to heat, getting out cups and napkins, and
finally, before allowing herself to sink, again with a little sigh, into her own chair, pulling out the stools, so
they faced her. She was sorry she could offer us nothing
more comfortable. We would think this a very odd place,
and it was in some ways. Perhaps she should explain.

The two houses were the bequest of the parish
priest, who had died very young. Indeed, it was undoubtedly his mother who had directed us to the cemetery. She made everything that had to do with the orphanage, however minor, her business and on principle
disapproved. She was inclined to demand explanations
in a noisy, aggressive way, but could cause no real trouble. Her son had left only the houses. The nuns had to
supply all else through their order or the authorities or,
when they were lucky, gifts. We would see they prac-
ticed simple little economies, like cooking as much as
possible over the fire. Gas was expensive. Kindly disposed peasants kept them in wood. They managed—
sometimes not so well. We would see. The children were
happy. She worried that now she was far from well there
was too much for the young nuns to do. We would see
for ourselves, it was far from perfect, more like a dis-
orderly family than a proper institution, but for children who had no families, maybe that was not all bad.
Maybe . . .

The children stampeded into the room, and she stopped, turning to smile at them, as much as to say, You see? Several rushed to the back of the room and disappeared through a door that, to judge from the thumping and scraping that followed, gave onto a stairway. Two were reminded that it was their turn to put away the lunch dishes. They volunteered to make camomile tea for the mother superior—and for us too, if we would have it. The rest crowded around the mother superior to stare at us. She scolded them. It was impolite to stare. If they wanted to ask questions, speak up. They hung their heads.

Our tea was served by earnest, wobbly little girls and included a plate of dry cookies, six dry cookies, that were watched by six pairs of longing eyes. Gianna refused. So did I. The mother superior took one. The silence was broken by a gurgling cascade of water down some nearby pipe and the thunder of footsteps on the stairs. Ten pairs of eyes now watched the plate, and the young nuns, leaning against the end of the table, watched the children with gentle, sibylline smiles. The mother superior drank her tea slowly and talked of their problems and needs. Food, anything warm—sweaters, coats, blankets—no matter how old. Material, if we had some. Their project for this summer was dressmaking. They were learning to make their own clothes. Those ten pairs of eyes never left the cookies. Finally the mother superior handed her cup to one of the nuns, her cookie still on her saucer, and suggested we be shown the house—while she refereed the division, the equal and peaceful division, of the cookies, half for each girl. And no quarreling. To a babble of happy voices, we left for our trip through the maze.

The houses were totally unmatched. The stairs were not adjoining, the levels of the rooms were not equal. Doors opened from rooms of one to meet the stairs of the other in mid-flight. Each floor had one small room, or two tiny ones. The mate to the kitchen, up three stairs from the little entrance hall, had been divided in two, the front half serving as the mother superior's room, the back as a storeroom-pantry. It held pathetic little stock. On the other two floors beds were wedged in everywhere, each with white metal tubing, head and foot, which served as clothes and towel racks. The sheets and blankets were only slightly less ragged than those used by the first orphanage for "show." Two cubicles without doors had been contrived for the young nuns. That way they could keep an eye on the girls, they explained. As we clambered up and down the treacherous stairways, the inconveniences and the ingenious compromises became more and more obvious, but most impressive was the nuns' unshakable good humor about them.

In teams—an older with a younger one—the girls took turns at chores, so that all learned how to cook and clean and wash dishes without martyrdom in one dread service. That said, the nuns admitted they themselves did the laundry. After school the mother superior taught the older girls to embroider and hoped to start them soon on sheets for their trousseaus. We were taken to admire the lavatory, the source of the earlier gushings. I stepped back out of the way and stumbled into a large zinced tub that sent awesome clangs and clatters screeching through the houses. Baths were also taken in teams, of four this time, three evenings a week— Thursday, Friday and Saturday. The mother superior was odd man out and was allowed, I imagined, to bathe when and as she chose. Seniority must have its privileges. This was a bath night, so the tub had been left close to the kitchen, yet out of sight.

We were feeling our way back down into the kitchen, when the nun in the lead stopped and turned to whisper back to us. She was so worried. She had this on her conscience and hadn't dared tell the mother superior, but sometimes in the winter they—they got the littlest ones hot-water bottles. Poor little things were so cold. But she wasn't sure. Maybe it was spoiling them, leading them into evil habits, into . . . She could not quite bring herself to say it, but she feared there might be something sexual, or at the very least hedonistic, about a hot-water bottle for half-frozen, lonely little girls. Gianna teased her, gently. What could possibly be wrong about saving a child from pneumonia? Or chilblains? Or simply from being cold and scared in the night?

Our departure was almost as exciting to the little girls as our sudden appearance at the cemetery gate. They crawled through the car, inspecting it. They directed traffic, what traffic they could find, mostly chickens and dogs. They laughed and shouted and waved, oblivious to the priest's mother, who scowled down on the scene from her observation post. Aware, but not intimidated, the three nuns stood by their kitchen door, laughing too and waving. Before we were out of the little square, Gianna vowed she would send them a dozen hot-water bottles, if she had to buy them herself. Beyond the staple blankets and food (that night supper was to be broth and bread), there were so many things we could send. For ten it was much easier than for a hundred: lengths of material, sweaters, socks, even

combs to replace what had to be *the* communal one—
half of one, broken off and snaggle toothed—we had seen
on a shelf in the lavatory. Our enthusiastic plans petered out to silence. We were tired and we still had a
long drive. Gianna seemed pensive and sad. Probably
something about the day had reminded her of other days,
I decided, and concentrated on my curves and ruts.

Just as the sun disappeared below the horizon,
we wiggled out of the mountains onto a bare, rocky mesa.
Gianna motioned me to stop. Spread out before us, in
this light red, shadowed with deeper red and here and
there on the edge of a bluff, the pink beading of a town,
were the scorched, eroded tablelands of Puglia.

"My husband thought the Holy Land must look
like this," she said finally. "This sort of place, in this
light—he'd stop the car and just sit, looking at it. I always wondered what he was thinking. He seemed so
far away." She gave a little half shrug. I stared out at
the landscape, motionless and silent, waiting. For long
seconds she did not go on, then, when I did not expect
it, she added, "If I asked, he'd smile and say, 'Oh, the
Bible, I suppose. Man's woes that never change. *Man*
who never changes. It's all there.' He'd drive on, talking about something else, as though we had never
stopped."

I took that as my cue and drove on, still silent.
She stared out the window. Without warning, when the
red world had almost faded into anonymous darkness,
she started talking about her husband, Ernest Thompson. I never heard her pronounce the name of this man
she had loved. He was always "my husband," as though,
unnamed, he were a figure of fable, an eerie fable of
long ago, she could treat with a certain detachment.

Eleven

Gianna had liked all The Boys, especially, even from the beginning, Ernest Thompson, who was the informal leader of the group inasmuch as the Friends expected him to plan and report on their activities, those he dared mention. He was a tall, slender, young Englishman with even features, fine, sandy brown hair and horn-rimmed glasses that gave him a serious, rather owlish look. At the beginning of the war he had been almost through his medical training. He was also a conscientious objector, a category the British military found suspect and treated accordingly. Ernest Thompson's abhorrence was killing. He refused to carry a gun, but he served as a medical corpsman through the African campaign, the landings in Italy and on north through Europe. A long war. He could not forget what he had seen in Italy: the desolate faces of the people who had watched their houses, their villages being systematically mined and blown up and who were then shoved out in no-man's-land toward the Allied lines; or the stumps of masonry that had been their villages; or the hunger and fear. He came back to Italy.

By the time Gianna met him, unlike the others, who used a handy patois of dialect, army jargon and Italianized English, he spoke fluent Italian with a pronounced English accent and an even more pronounced English mental bias. He despised the professional beggars and whiners who thought foreigners were naive enough to believe any tale, no matter how absurd. He cut them off with withering sarcasm that did not quite wither because, convinced of the gullibility of their intended victim, they took it literally. On the other hand, he was endlessly patient and gentle with the sick and the old, particularly old women. Soon enough they discovered his medical ability and adopted him, against his will, as *their* doctor. Wherever they thought they might find him, they waited. Morning and night at the palace door, at the Autopark, in the squares of mountain villages. He cleaned and bandaged their sores. He bound their sprains and stitched their cuts and explained what he thought was wrong, what they must do, and they believed him. He urged them to go back to the local doctors, about whom they complained so justly. They nodded, they smiled, but that was all. They knew better. He was *their* doctor, the real *medico dei poveri.*

He was also a stubborn persuader. He spent long hours in the dingy back rooms of cafés or at kitchen tables, surrounded by wives and mothers and children, talking to discouraged men who had no faith in the goodwill or intentions of their neighbors. They trusted him. If he said that *all* the men, even those whose houses were finished, would work, then, well—against their better judgment—they guessed they would go along with him. Maybe this time . . . if he said so . . .

Which he did, with oracular calm and grave reservations that he kept to himself. He was never sure. He temporized, he juggled and prayed that of all the dozens of plates he set spinning, one would not wobble to a halt and bring the rest down with it. Collapse, sooner or later, seemed inevitable, if for no other reason because the men would recognize the contradiction of the double personality they had invented for him. They insisted on believing him an honest man, something rare in their experience, one who a priori suffered from an almost Franciscan innocence. At the same time they boasted to each other of his shrewdness: he always caught them out, could not be tricked. For them honesty without innocence was impossible. He could see that. But shrewdness without intent to swindle was for them just as impossible. It made him uneasy, this ambiguous position. He came to see himself a manipulator, and a manipulator, however honorable the cause, is something of a Fascist, the higher being who forces the lower orders to accept what, according to him, is best for them. It made him very uneasy and there was no one he dared talk to.

His schedule was often different from the others'. He was not always with the trucks or the building teams. He had to see to the official formalities in Chieti, the endless paperwork without which there would be no supplies. Houses might be going up in several villages. He tried to see each. There were always problems. His zigzags along the valley seemed more and more to match Gianna's, and when they did she could do twice as much in a day. Early he dropped her near a village, arranged to meet her around noon at a crossroads and take her on to the next on her round. She might come back with him, or, if he planned to go farther on, she climbed into one of the trucks. Soon she started bringing picnics. It was a quick, practical way to have lunch; that was the excuse anyway: otherwise they would have had nothing.

There was plenty of time for talk. About The Boys, the villages, the foibles of the officials they both knew or those of the ones she should meet. He told her hilarious stories of the things patients confided to their "doctor." Could they be true? Many were, it seemed. Gianna's store of improbable, bawdy secrets was growing. The women whispered them to her, sure that she would "understand." Sometimes she did, sometimes she did not until she had told Ernest, who roared with amusement. She blushed and tried to ignore him.

Eventually more serious questions, among them manipulation, could be explored. They did not rush into discussion. They sidled, I suspect, and being the relentlessly idealistic people they were, set up a serial pattern that repeated itself over the years, like the plot of a soap opera, a purely intellectual one, with its peaks and promises, and its resolutions hinted at, but never quite attained. The problem was semantic. They agreed in every important way. Only their labels were different: they trailed wisps of doubt. A fatal tolerance, perhaps? An inclination to theorize, when action . . . ? What Ernest took as Fascist arrogance, Gianna saw as a phase in the Fabian process of Socialization. His slow, necessary steps to reform were her political sops.

They were not political zealots. It was all theory,

very Anglo-Saxon theory at that, and a relief from the insistent, gritty problems of how to feed children, how to build houses for them, how to force a mayor to pipe water or consider an even more revolutionary installation, sewers. They enjoyed their chiding, teasing tussles with the Perfect World and soon, long before they would admit it, there was something less arcane between them. It was unplanned, unprofessional and unseemly: they were falling in love.

Spring played its part. Days were warmer. Gianna could finally shed the layers of sweaters and coats that had not kept her warm and the mountain boots. She was not vain, but it was a relief to know her nose was not bright red. The work was going almost too well. The nurseries were slowly turning into nurseries, not just feeding way stations. Others were planned. In the summer she would have a course, the first of many she ran for her own teachers and later for teachers of a number of Italian agencies. The bank had finally conceded that it did seem to have money for her. Even the supplies arrived regularly—at Ortona—and Ernest furnished the magic carpet that brought them on to her. Storage and distribution were still challenges, and La Pontificia was still eager to relieve her of the trouble. Polite evasions brought outright demands and accusations.

La Pontificia was disgruntled about many things she dared not mention, but one she could allowed her flights of moral indignation: Gianna's "conduct" with The Boys. How riding in trucks and jeeps with them could be "conduct," moral or immoral, Gianna never understood. La Pontificia was not prepared to explain. In lieu of hard facts she preferred insinuations. People won-

dered. People saw. The good name of her daughters . . .
The strange hours. The rumor was . . . She made her
stand public by coming each morning to the window and
scowling down into the street as Gianna loaded her purse,
coat, parcels and picnic into whatever transport had come
to pick her up. The Boys paid no attention. They helped
her. But Ernest, freshly shaved, in clean khakis and
heavy, polished brown shoes, always nodded and wished
her good morning. To her intense irritation.

When Gianna told him about this latest campaign, she could almost hear him say to himself,
"Women!" He certainly did not take it seriously until he
realized how much it upset her. Then he had a suggestion. He and one of the others, preferably a conven-
tional-looking type, no beards, no monkeys, should call
one Sunday afternoon and explain the work they did
and how it dovetailed with Gianna's. They would present a united, respectable foreign front, working for The
Good of Mankind and the Succor of Harmless Innocents
Battered by War—flourishes to be added (or sub-
tracted) to suit their hostess's emotional temperature.

It might work. La Pontificia agreed to receive
them; she even aired the parlor for the occasion. They
arrived on time, scrubbed and pressed, with new hair-
cuts and clean fingernails and a display of good manners
and compliments that so impressed La Pontificia she began to simper flirtatiously at Ernest. He eased up to
the business at hand by talking about her vast influence
on the welfare of the valley. She simpered. Both financial and moral. Since he knew she seldom had the time
to travel—actually she hated cars: they made her sick—
he had brought some pictures of the Friends' work and
also Gianna's, in which she, La Pontificia, had been so
instrumental.

Ernest was a very good photographer. I had seen
many of his pictures. Later I went through boxes and
boxes of them, divided into categories. He had a series
of people carrying things—women carrying long boards
with loaves of bread on their heads, a woman balancing
an aged Singer sewing machine, complete to its wrought-
iron, curlicued base, on her head, a priest wrestling the
plaster statue of a saint along the road. Another series
was of people in repose, many of them apparently waiting, the old withdrawn, into either a private serenity or
a just as private and bitter resignation. Which was it?
The question could haunt. There was another of feet.
With shoes, some that did not match, without shoes,
bound in rags. It was surprising what feet could suggest about the invisible person attached to them. The
pictures he showed La Pontificia were in the "business"
category, before and after pictures of the houses, meetings with the men and Gianna's nurseries in evolution,
with mothers and children on the rampage.

La Pontificia was impressed. Her daughters, who
had stared into space with rather waxen neutrality, decided it was safe to nod. Once started, they seemed unable to stop bobbling and pecking like distressed chickens. By the time they were sent off to get refreshments,
Ernest's partner had fallen under their spell and was
nodding too, and Gianna was very nervous. If things
got out of hand, this could be a debacle. There was a
terrible gleam in Ernest's eyes that his glasses only
partially disguised, but he pressed on solemnly to the
fame and respectability of the Friends Service Committee, forgetting to mention *any* religious connection,
Protestant or otherwise.

The daughters returned bearing thimbles of coffee and plates of hard, musty cookies, which they passed

around, still bobbling and nodding and now smiling. La
Pontificia murmured about the need for cooperation and
coordination. Ernest agreed. It was vital. His partner
fidgeted. The daughters' smiles may have seemed pred-
atory. There was so much Ernest would see that she,
tied to her official duties, would not. Perhaps he could
keep her up to date on any surprising . . . Oh yes, he
understood. So she would be better prepared . . . They
kept up this conspiratorial duet, until Ernest offered
flowery thanks, vows of information to come, and took
himself and his friend off, only just in time to judge by
the grumblings of inexplicable mirth that floated up from
the stairwell.

La Pontificia was charmed. Such serious, respectful young men. She no longer presented herself at
the window in the morning, nor did she scold Gianna
about The Boys. She found other grudges to huff about
that were as satisfactory. Once or twice Ernest called
on her, for the sake of courtesy; he had no information
to offer. The incident was dismissed, or so Gianna
thought, as a funny story, until several weeks later The
Boys asked her, very formally, to come for supper and
put it to her that her living arrangements were miserable.

They had found a solution. Two of the young men
were leaving and would not be replaced. There was already less work, and gradually over the next two years
the project would wind down altogether. Would she join
them instead? No, she must not object until she had
heard their offer. She could have two rooms, one for a
bedroom, one for an office, on the floor with the dining
room, kitchen and drawing room—common room. The
Boys all slept above. She would, it was true, have to

share the shower with them, but they had devised a new system of baffles that absolutely guaranteed . . . Even La Pontificia would be satisfied. The luxury of their transportation facilities, she already knew. If the Fund supplied a jeep, as had been suggested, there was room in the Autopark. (That was the jeep cannibalized on the Naples docks.) They could also provide limited storage for supplies. Should she need more, space in Ortona could be found. Obviously her receiving and shipping problems would be simplified. She would be expected to pay her share of the expenses, which came to little more than the Fund paid La Pontificia, and—if she didn't mind—maybe she could do something about their menus. They had run out of ideas beyond the mounds of spaghetti that were their staple filler.

As enthusiastic as they were, and autonomous in their own arrangements, they were disappointed when she said she could not give them an immediate answer. She had no doubts. She knew what she *wanted* to do. But—the Fund had to approve the move, and whatever expenses were involved, and then an official explanation, not simply Gianna's, must be given La Pontificia. Although she did not mention it, there was also the problem of an acceptable explanation to her mother, whose devotion to free thinking and mild revolt did not stretch to include the casual ways of modern young women, most especially not of her own daughter.

The Fund approved, and Gianna's mother announced her imminent arrival in Ortona, to be delayed only long enough for her to arrange the care of her cat and garden. If the prospect of her visit churned up a fair panic and complex rearrangement of schedules at the busiest time of the year, it also gave Gianna an excuse for a general turnout of the house. The Boys were pernickety about clean clothes and blind to dust and grime. The cook, who, anyway, had been wary of this new presence in *her* house, took offense, then reversed her stand and helped Gianna in a last-minute sewing bee to make curtains from sheeting. The Boys were surprised to find themselves rigging makeshift rods.

Their visitor arrived, exhilarated by the trip, as slight and wiry and curious as ever, and, contrary to everyone's expectations, particularly her own, was delighted with all she surveyed. Not that it could not have done with a bit of reorganization, but she would see to that. Give the house a good turnout, make more efficient arrangements for the laundry (in that she was defeated by the scarcity of water. Later she admitted it was miraculous how much was clean, where at first she had seen only how much was dirty.) and balance their disgraceful diet. What in the general flurry had been forgotten by all with the possible exception of Gianna was that she spoke runaway Italian with a pronounced Lombardy accent and a tendency in moments of stress to piquant phrases in dialect. Unlike other visitors, she was *not* in limbo without a language. She could carry out her threats, and no one doubted she would, with tact or, if opposed, by force. She resisted the shower. Quite impossible. Time took care of that. She found the local accent ugly, mushy and incomprehensible. Time took care of that too. Everyone was *so* nice to her.

Gianna bundled her off to see nurseries. Mother was always ready for an excursion. She only needed her hat and gloves. No, a lady wore a hat and gloves. She did in England and she would in Italy, even rattling through the Sangro Valley. The Boys were sweet to her,

positively courted her. When, after she had been allowed several days' rest "at home" and the cook was
threatening mutiny, they insisted she should come with
them to see their projects, she fitted herself out once
more in hat and gloves and clambered up into the cab
of the truck as though it were her favorite form of
transport. The Boys were her footmen. They brought
coffees to her. They stopped to let her admire the view.
They found and policed latrines for her. They even
managed a sort of lunch for her, but when she demanded they get down and order a peasant to stop
beating his donkey, they balked. For one thing, he was
not exactly beating him. He was slapping him on the
rump with the broad side of his billhook, which was a
local way of keeping a sleepy, reluctant donkey on the
move. She could not abide cruelty to animals. How would
they feel if someone slapped them constantly on their
rear ends—with a billhook? They were timid. She was
not. They must let her down at once. They dared not
refuse. They sat, dumbfounded, and watched as she
stalked up to the man, grabbed the billhook, flung it out
into the ravine, treated him to some ripe Lombardy in-
vective to the effect that he should be ashamed of himself and flounced back to the truck. She was now ready
to go home, she declared. She had seen enough of these
barbarous people for one day.

For Gianna's mother, a sortie in defense of the
rights of donkeys, like her polemic with the cook about
how to wash a tomato-sauce pot, added zest to a visit
she was enjoying enormously, so much that Gianna
worried she might settle in as matron pro tem. The young
men were charming to her, protective of Gianna and
omnipresent auto-chaperones, she decided. A bit of quiet

observation and she had identified Ernest as the shadowy presence in Gianna's recent letters. She saw a lot of him and was neither alarmed nor displeased. Gianna was happy, that much she would admit and nothing more. Her mother recognized stubbornness—who better?—and if she must wait in silence for them to make up their minds, then, thank you, she preferred to do so in her own garden with her own cat. She had stayed quite long enough. It was time she went home, she insisted, but she was so delighted by the protests, proposed delays and celebrations that she actually left happy. The visit had been a success for all.

Now, before the nurseries opened, Gianna had to make up for lost time. Her new stores had to be set up and plans made for the fall. Ernest suggested she hire a man to help her with the hauling and lifting. He knew someone very dependable. He worked part-time, as assistant to the local dentist, a veterinary, who after the war decided to expand his practice to humans. He had never kept an office. He did not need one. Just as he made stall calls on cows and mules, he made house calls on humans, and his assistant, for this special service, rode pillion behind him on his scooter, clutching the tool kit, mostly pliers of varying sizes. On arrival it was his duty to place the patient on a sturdy table, drape him in sheets and then hang on to him for dear life while the "doctor" went about the only treatment he knew—extraction. The young man was always free in the afternoons and hung around the Autopark, hoping for work. He needed money. He was ingenious, a good mechanic and strong. He was Sorino.

Soon, with his demented willingness to work, however long the hours, and to please, he was indispensable. He wanted desperately to have a "real" job, and he worshiped Ernest, would protect anything or anyone that was his, which he quickly perceived as including Gianna. She had hired a navvy and got, instead, a man of all work and a bodyguard. That may have been Ernest's plan. He was a man who did plan, and now he had an extra element that complicated the already complicated decisions he must make about the future. The wheres, whats and hows of his life—their lives, if they were to marry—had to be clear. Given the growth of Gianna's projects and the Fund's support and the slow, entirely reasonable dismantling of his work, there were what must have seemed irreconcilable problems. However it was, and Gianna said very little about it, they drifted along for another year, these two people who were not drifters by inclination.

In many ways they were happy. They were doing work they liked and believed useful in a country they loved. Each day was still an adventure. They shared the messes and amusements and they shared what free time was left over, but . . . What finally tipped the scales—a sense of time running out as one by one The Boys left, or the sudden realization that between the Fund and the Friends there was more work than they could do, or both—I never knew. They decided. There were no more doubts, no what-ifs, and no one could make them change their minds: they were going to be married as soon as possible. Of course in Italy it was not quite that simple. The whole bureaucratic opera buffa had to be played out first.

Certificates. Nothing could be done without certificates. Of birth, baptism, of *stato libero*, that is, proof neither was married to someone else, of citizenship and residence. All to be on government franked paper, one of the fiscal convolutions of Mediterranean countries that does not have a British counterpart. Gianna and Ernest wrote pleading letters to registry offices and town clerks and friendly rectors, and one by one certificates began to arrive. None, however, that bluntly, unequivocally declared them non-bigamous. Stato libero had no British counterpart either. Helpful friends at the consulate in Rome suggested a consular statement attesting to the non-existence of such a certificate under the British civil code, but then gave it up as useless: in Italy the applicant, or the accused, is assumed guilty unless and until *he* proves otherwise. The same friends went to work with His Majesty's stationery and sealing wax and concocted impressive documents that declared the aforementioned nubile in the name of God, King and the powers invested, et cetera. They also warned that every sheet of this double dossier not written in Italian would have to go to the Ministry of Foreign Affairs for translation, notarization and registration. Only Gianna's birth certificate was excluded.

Gianna and Ernest had planned to be married in the spring. Ultimately they considered it a victory to be married in September. Some of the certificates reappeared immediately, decorated with rivets and ribbons and blurred purple stamps. Others seemed to have vanished without trace. The explanation was always the same—vacations, short staff. Fall would see everything right. Indeed! Obviously to win a place at the ministry one had to be a sophist or a eunuch, or preferably both. Meanwhile the certificates that had been returned were sliding inevitably toward the expiration of their validity, and a diligent scribe, who was not at the beach with his in-laws, noted that, as Gianna had joint citizenship, although she used a British passport, an Italian certificate of stato libero might be in order. At this point, had they been able to get their papers back, they would have gone to England to be married.

Twice during the summer there seemed a chance—which came to nothing. They had wanted a week or so off for a trip, maybe some swimming, but, as fall approached and the opening of the nurseries, that too had to be abandoned. There was one last hope. Gianna had agreed to visit the centers of two Italian agencies in Calabria and discuss possible collaboration—nurseries, courses for teachers and social workers, feeding centers. She and Ernest might have a few days alone—in the car—or maybe even a weekend along the way.

Each month she sent a rough schedule of her plans for the next month to the London office. By August she had stopped mentioning that she might be married. Early in September it was official. They were notified to present themselves at Rome's baroque marriage hall, where gilt thrones and stewards in swallow-tailed coats and galloon awaited them. They were also notified by the Fund to present themselves, the morning after the wedding, at the airport, where an official visitor awaited them. All unknowing he would share their honeymoon. Gianna and Ernest never really did have a holiday alone together, which is not to say they did not travel a lot, especially after the Fund provided the station wagon and the work started its southward sprawl.

Almost immediately Gianna found there were, in summer, minor complications to a trip with Ernest. Hotels were few, and private baths, sometimes even private rooms, were non-existent. The "next" could be hours

away. You took what was available, which did not bother
Ernest. He was game for anything. But—when it was
hot, he refused to wear undershorts: he wanted a clean
pair of khaki trousers and nothing else, beyond a shirt.
Also he never wore pajamas. That he did not pack any
did not occur to Gianna until one fateful night in Cas-
trovillari, when the last room at the hotel had three beds
(and no window) and their current guest was a representative of the Swiss Red Cross, a lady of impeccable
modesty. Their solution is recorded in a shaky photograph of Ernest, laughing, propped up in bed, wearing
a frilly nightgown with flounces of embroidery at the
neck and sleeves. After that Gianna carefully included
shorts and pajamas in *her* luggage.

Certainly in the next two years they traveled—
Gianna almost constantly, accompanied by either Ernest or Sorino. There never seemed to be quite enough
time. The nurseries, the courses, the sponsored children and a new challenge—the huge and tragic govern-
ment-run orphanages and infant welfare centers, where,
if she found a receptive director, and occasionally she
did, who was desperate enough over the endless wards
of withdrawn, perpetually sick children to try anything,
she was allowed a small experimental section. Even in
Ortona itself, where nothing flourished that was not force-
fed and prodded daily, she had a nursery. Ernest had
organized an association of pensioners, and the nucleus
of the boys' club was begging him for help. Sorino had
negotiated the marriage of what had been left on the
docks of an English Land-Rover to what had been left,
after the African and Italian campaigns, of an American
jeep, creating a useful, if temperamental vehicle. Not
satisfied with that, he had collected wheels and bits of

truck bodies and springs and miscellaneous metal shanks until he had enough debris to construct a small flatbed trailer. The arrival of the station wagon seemed both a reward and a confirmation of permanence in which none of them had ever quite believed. The next impossibility that might be possible was the Baby Hut. They schemed.

Ernest and Gianna had moved into a small peasant house, not far from the one I knew, high above the road, overlooking the sea and that pitted, scorched triangle of land the town council deeded to the Fund. The first step was accomplished. The second, a building, could mean years perhaps of begging—still. That endless stream of guests, the trips, the honeymoon with them, explanations, repetitions of explanations, attention to diets, dinners and prejudices, suddenly it all seemed worth it: the answer to their very first pleas for help was a prefabricated building from one group, money for foundations and tile roof from another, and from yet another, money for equipment. Ernest and Sorino set up as small-scale contractors.

Until the Baby Hut was finished, really finished, with the building inaugurated and functioning and the landfill and rubble on their way to being a garden, Ernest refused to pay much attention, but he was not feeling well. There was no one, single thing. He just did not feel well. He slept badly, his appetite came and went, his temper was uncertain. Nothing to worry about, but he did not feel well. The Friends wanted him to have a complete medical examination. He promised Gianna that early in the summer he would go to England. When the time came, he put it off. In the fall, if they weren't too busy. By September he was no better, even he would admit that. He decided to go at the end of the month.

Late one hot afternoon—it happened to be their second anniversary—he came to Gianna and told her he and Sorino were taking the boys down for a swim. Wouldn't she come with them? No, that would give her time to finish up all the messes on her desk. He should go on without her. He kissed her lightly on the cheek and said he had a lovely surprise for her—for their anniversary—she'd see later, and off he went.

The beach they used was more a sand spit than a beach, directly below the house at the foot of the steep cliff, and could be reached from a little track that led off the coast highway. The jeep (and its trailer) was an ideal charabanc for boys, wet or dry. Ernest had taught most of them to swim and at the same time had insisted on certain rules, which however obstreperous, wrestling and shouting, they might be in the jeep, they obeyed. They were to stick together. They were not to go beyond the depth set by the older person with them, they were not to stay in the water too long, all those commonsense prohibitions that seem so logical to adults and so odious to children. In compensation both Ernest and Sorino played tricks on them. They dove underwater to come up in unexpected places, often grabbing a boy's legs and lifting him out of the water on their shoulders. To be dumped over backward into the water, naturally. They boys loved it and tried to catch them or come up under them, without much success. Ernest was very quick, diving, ducking, reappearing at amazing distance to surprise a boy who was totally unprepared. That afternoon he was everywhere. He lifted boys, he wove in and out, up and down under again. No one could tell where he might surface next.

Sorino organized races. Ernest helped two young

boys with their underwater swimming. They all splashed around after a ball in a free-for-all version of water polo. And then, once more, Ernest wove in and out, up and down under again, lifting boys, dunking them, pulling others down with him. No one could tell where he might surface next. Suddenly they realized that he had not. He had disappeared. They searched the beach. He was not by the towels. Back in the water. No one had seen him. They called. They waded down the coast a way. Nothing. Sorino went for help.

For two nights and a day Gianna sat by a window, looking at the sea, while Sorino, his friends and the local fishing fleet trolled for Ernest's body. At dawn of the second day, they found him.

Twelve

August and that inviolate, almost mystical Italian rite, summer holidays, were upon us. The Baby Hut and nursery would be closed. The nurses and teachers would rush for home and I, inevitably, would depart on the 1:36 train for Florence. About that I had no time to think. I was too busy. We all were. Inventories had to be taken of *everything*—of the stores, of supplies in the Baby Hut and nursery, right down to the last diaper and pasta pot. The quarterly sponsorship money had arrived. Dozens of money orders had to be written and sent. Gianna was determined to visit the sponsored children in the Sangro Valley, whom she had not seen since late the fall before, and, too, there were my two little charges, Mirella and Carlo.

They, if not the rosy, sleek-haired babies of diaper ads, were obviously stronger and healthier. He had become an explorer and sly. One minute he would be playing in the sandbox, and the next, unnoticed, he had nipped off at his speediest lurch and sprint to the far reaches of the garden, where he vanished into the bushes or behind the laundry, intent on putting every (to him) strange object he came across in his mouth. Once tracked down, he came back amiably, *if* he was allowed to bring his treasures with him. So worms and snails shriveled in the sun, stones attempted fusion and clothespins warped under his watchful eye, until no one was looking and off he went on his travels again.

Mirella was less adventurous but just as curious. She prowled from the shade of a large umbrella to the sandbox and back, lugging her vital equipment behind her—a pail, a scoop, plastic tubes of all sizes, odd bottles and cups. She liked to fit things together, fill things up, not always with results that pleased her. Or pleased Elisa, who caught her once shoveling sand into a baby's diapers. It could have been water, her other passion. She controlled the traffic around the big tub where the children played. No one could draw near without her approval. She was very determined, very select. Such industry and vigilance were tiring. When she was cranky, the first sign of trouble, she whimpered quietly to herself. Somehow she understood no one wanted her to cry. No one who had ever seen her gasping attacks—with the first flush, then the deepening cynanotic grayness—wanted to see another. She would wobble to the closest familiar adult and stick out her hands. Up, please, in your lap. Cradled and comfortable, she dozed for a few minutes. Soon she was off again on her projects, a determined frown on her face. In her six months she had gained weight and strength. Her resistance was greater. But her heart was the same. What is now, even in Southern Italy, a common operation was then unknown.

More time, more food, more care would have done so much for both Mirella and Carlo. Instead, they had to be entrusted again to the care of their mothers. Not that their mothers were unkind. They were poor. They were ignorant. They were convinced that bread's and pasta's ability to fill a child meant that they were just as good for him as vegetables and fruit and meat and eggs and milk—and far cheaper. That five children in one bed could get the rest they needed; there was only one bed available. That the simplest, most basic rules of hygiene were fancy foolishness. They had no water, no sets of diapers or plates, glasses and spoons to go around and still thought, if the truth were known, that babies grew stronger and healthier in rigid swaddling. All this in spite of the pointed advice Elisa would have bestowed on them twice daily—in the morning, when mothers brought their babies, again in the late afternoon, when they took them home. Of course neither Mirella's mother nor Carlo's had even been exposed to her lectures. They lived too far away.

Mirella's departure turned into a celebration. Her mother had come down once, a memorable day all agreed, to visit Mirella. She had begged to come back at the end of the term. After all, the Comune paid for her bus ticket, so she wasn't wasting money. Perhaps that should have warned me, that and her nickname—La Zumparella— the Little Jumper. Any reference to her produced gales of laughter from Elisa, Vanda, the cook, even from Gianna, and no explanations. No, no it was impossible. When I met her, I would understand, they promised. Then, early one morning, right after her unannounced arrival, they fed me to her, like an hors d'oeuvre before the serious business of the feast. I understood almost at once that it really was impossible to describe a two-legged tornado.

Elisa had met me at the door, making signs to be quiet, which, given the screeching, squawking conversation that echoed through the rooms, hardly seemed necessary. No one could be asleep. She had a surprise for me, a visitor. She led me to the kitchen, where a woman bounded about, thumping Mirella up and down on one arm, gesticulating wildly with the other to emphasize the already dramatic details of the story she was telling the cook. Mirella, jounced around, always off balance, had wild, startled eyes. She flung her arms out to us, and Elisa took her, at the same time introducing me to, of course, Mirella's mother, who was for the moment struck dumb, as though I were an awesome, majestic power. Perhaps Queen Victoria.

Her looks were innocent. She was tiny, both ageless and shapeless though thin, in a clean, lavender wool dress that was white along the seams from repeated scrubbings with lye soap and stones. She had added what I assumed were decorations, curious ones—two patches of a much deeper lavender over each breast. (The reason, which, along with a plethora of other facts, came out later, was practical, not frivolous. They were mends: mother's milk may be good for babies, but not for clothes.) Her hair was non-descript brown, neatly combed back. Her features were non-descript too, or at least were reduced to such by snapping brown eyes that missed nothing and flashed back instantaneous judgments, amusement, fears or doubts. Her tongue lagged only slightly behind, creating an impression of compulsive emotional and intellectual greed. At any given mo-

ment she desperately wanted to see, understand, tell
and hear *everything*. It was easy to understand why the
Comune would pay her bus fare or anything else rather
than have her pestering, complaining around the village, threatening. Hers was a formidable and exhaust-
ing personality.

The cook, who had been about to serve the trav-
eler's therapeutic coffee, judged that I too would need
bolstering and added a second cup to her tray. There
was no escape. Mirella's mother and I were put down,
facing each other, at the kitchen table. Everyone else
crowded around to listen, to prompt and finally, when
she spun off into impenetrable dialect, to interpret. First
they had her tell me about her other visit.

"*Ohooo, signoree*, if you only knew—the excitement, the jostling. That bus, *signoree* . . ." *Signoree*,
her form for *signorina*, was also her exclamation point.
"*Ohooo, signoree*, I was so excited. And the bus made
me *so* sick and then I saw the sea. *Ohooo, signoree*, the
sea!" Although she had lived all her life just twenty-five
miles from it, she had never before seen the sea. She
opened her eyes very wide. "*Ohooo, signoree*, just
imagine. It goes on forever, doesn't it? It must. I never
could see the other side." She had talked to the bus
driver. He promised to let her off at the Baby Hut gate.
He knew right where it was, which impressed her. And
there everyone was so good to her and Mirella was so
well. Mirella laughed all the time. "*Ohooo, signoree*, she
was hungry all the time too. She'd never been like that."
They had had a good time, laughing, she telling all about
her trip down, that horrible bus. And could I imagine
that she had had fish for lunch! Fish? She had never
eaten fish in her whole life! When she left, she told them

she'd come back every day, if only they'd invite her. Even that awful bus ride was worth it.

Maybe coming to Ortona had some magic influence on her life. Just the day before they'd heard that her husband, who was a shoemaker without land, had been given a place on a road construction crew. It was the first work he had had in a year. And, *"Ohooo, signoree. . . ."* She had forgotten the best part of her visit—the trip home. She was so tired and so excited and the bus swayed around so much and she was so sick that, when she finally got home, she aborted. Lost her baby. *"Ohooo, signoree*, it was a perfect day! Just perfect!"* That had been her twenty-second pregnancy. She had nine living children.

On that second visit she had meat for lunch, which was not quite so exciting as fish. Still, she had a second helping and listened to every word Gianna and Elisa told her about how to take care of Mirella. First of all to be quiet with her. Before long Mirella crawled up in *her* lap and nuzzled down against her neck and both smiled.

Late that afternoon we stood out on the road with them waiting for the bus, Mirella looking anxious, but in her mother's arms, clinging to her collar, and her mother saying over and over again, *"Ohooo, signoree,* I've had such a beautiful day. I'd come every day, if you'd invite me."*

Carlo's departure was not a celebration. We took him home, and it was a great deal farther than anyone had thought: the family had moved—several times, we discovered. No one knew just where. We tacked back and forth across a wide, seared valley, stopping to ask at settlements of two or three houses huddled together, following the vague, I-seem-to-remember directions until tracks petered out in a nowhere of stubble. On Celestina's back seat Carlo sat in my lap, posting to the bumps and gabbling happily. For him it was a lovely adventure. For us, a puzzle. A registry office? In which of the toy villages high on the ridge? Or the police? Again, in which village? The search could take days, weeks, given the schedules of government offices. What if we did not find his parents? Who would take care of him? Maybe Ida, or the assistant in the Baby Hut. For how long? Surely, sooner or later, someone would remember and come for him. Although—with no work and families too large—children were abandoned every day.

Between the heat and the wind in the back seat, I felt singed around the edges. Carlo wanted water. The novelty of it all was wearing off. Every so often Sorino stopped to look around, and we were enveloped in the cloud of dust Celestina normally churned out behind us. Gianna had said one last try. It was more than lunchtime. The offices that might help us were closed. All sensible people were hiding in darkened rooms. One last try, then home. Now that we were standing still, the checked, dun-colored clay hissed in the heat, the stubble rattled at us.

Sorino saw something he interpreted as the ground floor of a house without a roof or a second story. One day it would grow another, and perhaps another. It was a common sight after the war: even three-quarters of a house—the ground floor and half the second, waiting for its other half. As money was collected such houses grew. Meanwhile they sat in their own prairie of weeds, builders' shards and the flotsam from work-

men's lunches. Sometimes a family, or in the later stages
several families, camped in them. Without light or water:
those were the very last capital investments. We must
at least look.

It was there, somehow sharing four small rooms
with two other families of relatives, that we finally found
Carlo's mother. She was a thin, young woman with a
bony, lined face and the distraught look of someone who
never quite caught up. At the moment her problem was
tomato paste. There were tomatoes in various stages of
done- and undoneness everywhere—on the floor, on the
dirty, bare wood table, in pots on chairs, and the puree
itself, spread on trays, drying outside in the sun, each
attended by its own swarm of lazy files. Several dirty
children, looking quite murderous with tomato goo
smeared up to their elbows, watched us suspiciously.
No one seemed very interested in Carlo. Surprised
rather. The woman cleared off two knock-kneed chairs
and pointed at them. We both declined: we could not
stay. (Gianna had impressed on me that rush bottoms
are the favorite haunts of lice.)

Could Carlo have some water? His mother dipped
a filthy glass in a tub of water on the floor and handed
it to me. I still held him. Gianna explained his diet without much conviction. What he needed, in detail. What
his frail intestinal system did not tolerate. His mother
nodded, her face expressionless, bewildered, as though
she had not understood. She repeated the last phrase in
each set of suggestions with numb, questioning wonder.
No peppers. Rice and grated apple. Liquids. Weak tea.
No peppers. At the threat of starting da capo, to dis-
tract her I asked how she stored the tomato paste. In
bottles, I had thought.

She tugged the table drawer open and pulled out what looked like a gnawed slab of red rubber. You can keep them anywhere, she told me, tossing it back into the drawer, where it landed on top of a much used, gummy towel. We left soon after. The trip back to Ortona was hot and silent. No one wanted to admit the obvious: poor little Carlo would not have been missed.

Finally, one morning just before dawn, we set out with Sorino and the jeep on the round of sponsorship visits. I still have a partial account of that day, started, I imagine, one quiet Sunday afternoon, for what purpose I no longer know. The facts can be trusted: though I seem to offer them as my own wisdom, they were stolen straight from Gianna.

At the Sangro River we turned inland. . . . Mountains still veined with snow faced us. Across wide fields of wheat until quite suddenly the valley narrowed and the road became a little track skirting precariously around steep, rocky hills. Every mile or so were scooped-out holes on the valley side, where the shoulder and much of the road itself has wilted away. By hugging the stone cliff we could pass, always with that awful moment of doubt, and Sorino would again plant his foot on the accelerator, his hand on the horn and away we flew, challenging any oncoming traffic. What would have happened had we met a car is still a mystery.

Without warning we plunged into a village that ran up and down the mountainside like crocheted edging, its yellow houses bright in the sun. As always the north walls were black with mildew. Donkeys, loaded with logs, meandered down the middle of the street on their way home from predawn trips to the woods. Their owners, half asleep, followed behind them in heavy mountain boots and long, black cartwheel capes that have fur collars and clasps at the neck of silver bosses with a chain. Women, carrying baskets on their heads, strutted along in front of us to turn off abruptly and disappear up stairways that are the streets.

Sorino stopped at a doorway guarded by chains of bright-colored, noisy aluminum beads. The last café of the day, the last chance for coffee and "comforts." Italy is not, I've decided, a country for women: few loos, no bushes. Through a corridor-room with the counter and coffee machine and into a back room where four men played cards by the hazy light from a French door that opened into space. Far, far below in the mist we could make out the stony river bed. A silver ribbon of water glistened, twisting off to some hidden source. Opposite, in the early-morning sun, the hillsides, their clay furrowed by centuries of rain, were giant flutings of light and shadow. Behind them, frosted mountains, where villages cling in crevices, like the last plants in a blighted rock garden. The view from a funicular that for some unknown, terrifying reason had stopped midway in its journey.

The proprietor immediately turned on the coffee machine. Gianna insisted I would like to use the lavatory, which, for once, was not true. Nevertheless, I was led downstairs to what would be a basement had the building not been built into a mountain, and out through a French door, this one obviously with a balcony, and left in front of another, smaller door. Inside was a stone ledge, rather thronelike, with a hole worked in the center and around it a golden raffia doughnut. Two inches or so below I could see dark, murky green liquid. Who discovered this flume? It cannot be manmade. Who figured out the hydraulics, what level the proposed mixture would seek? We couldn't exactly ask, but it is both flushless and odorless, and the scenery, once you can control your lurching, vertiginous tendency to fall forward into it, is unique.

The valley choked in like a funnel until the neck was just wide enough for our road, twisting along one steep hillside, for a stream and across the way towering ribs of rock, a great fan of them, each slanted, overlapping its neighbor. Behind nestled a village that seemed to be a haven for old men and children naked from the waist down. The women were working in the fields (where are they, I wonder?) because their husbands are away for the "season" being cooks and waiters, the village profession. The bare bottoms had just as practical an explanation. So, unfortunately, did the potbellies. Gianna had me guess the children's ages: in every case I was two or three years under. They are very small, their heads large and their faces, old. Some had been entrusted to their grandmothers, who led the family pig or a pair of sheep on ropes along the road, searching for greens. Their shoes, the grandmothers' that is, were strips of rubber tire, pinched together at the front, mashed down and tacked in a heel cup at the back and bound around the ankles with cord. A modern variation on the old goatskin *chiocche*.

After the village, the road settled down to hairpin turns from which the vital switchbacks had washed away in last spring's rains. Sorino had to pick his way through the holes and around the humps. We passed a sign pointing the way to Mirella's village, but it was too

high, straight above us, to see. Just beyond, where there
was no sign at all, Sorino wheeled off to the left, up a
slope, over boulders and along a wash that he admitted
was a streambed, not a road. This is the shortest way
to Rosello! As the spider crawls. In saddles of land no
larger than dips that are protected and trap topsoil as
it slides down were patches of wheat. The rest is rocks,
clay and dry bunchgrass. Traditionally this was summer
pasture for the herds of sheep that wintered on the Roman plain and is connected to it by a network of rocky
lanes, known only to shepherds and called *tratture*. Now
there are no herds—the war again—but there is talk of
restocking. From the looks of the rubble piled high in
Rosello's piazza, it will be awhile before herds will fit
the budget.

That is about all we did see of Rosello too—we
arrived in the middle of the festa. Men, shaved and in
their wedding suits, women, scrubbed, combed and self-
conscious in their best shapeless cottons, milled around
the stalls of a makeshift market. When the vendor would
accept it, especially for produce, the women paid in
wheat. Red and blue rugs, even bedspreads, hung from
balconies and windows, a peculiar way to honor the
saint's statue as it passes underneath in procession. Festa
or not, we made our calls.

For the first one we twisted around and around
up stairway alleys until finally at a corner there was a
steep, narrow little house with four steep, narrow stairs
leading into it. A toothless old woman in a rusty black
dress and head scarf to match opened the door and motioned us into a dark, smoky room with an uneven brick
floor and walls that had, sometime in the past, seen
whitewash, but are now oily brown. On a stone slab,

barely raised from the floor, a fire of sticks spluttered, giving off smoke that drifted into the room well before it could rise as high as the hood. The only furniture was a table and five chairs.

From a stairway almost hidden at the back of the room came a younger, black-garbed woman with a gaunt face. She shook hands and collapsed on a chair, saying, *"Beh, signoree . . . ,"* which sounded like the introduction to some comment and must not have been. She stared at us in silence. Steps again at the back of the room, and a young man and two girls, dressed for the festa, appeared. He was quite the dandy in a blue cotton suit, white shoes and a carefully arranged pompadour that reeked of brilliantine. He was not shy either. He took the floor, telling us that he had been in Naples, had just come back, he supposed for good, he added with a sneer, but he would not work in the fields. No indeed, that was too much to expect of a man of his tastes. He would try to find work of an appropriate nature. What, exactly, that might be he did not say. He would have, if two children had not come pounding in through the front door. A little boy, very thin with puffy, dark bags under his large brown eyes, was dragged along by a slightly larger little girl with stringy hair. The boy, Pierluigi, was the sponsored child, and was wearing, we were told, clothes bought with the sponsor's gift. They were festa fancies that would not have pleased the sponsor.

Pierluigi had a hard time fathoming who we might be. He stood, looking at us with his eyes half closed, breathing audibly through his mouth. Gianna had a long discussion with his mother, the younger of the two women, about having his tonsils out, which I hope includes his adenoids. There was a lot of resistance to the idea. No doctor. (The doctor in Quadri is supposed to look after Rosello too.) Well, but the trip would be so upsetting. He had just had another cold. They could not afford it. (The sponsorship is ideal.) At that point our dapper young man put in that they had other uses for the money. His dreams of celebrating the festa in high style were short-lived. Gianna said she would keep the money, add it to the next installment and pay the doctor's fees—if the operation had been done.

I had been trying to work out the household arrangements. Was this the whole family? I asked. No, Pierluigi's father and another son were still in the fields, picking beans. That means nine people—the grandmother, the mother, father, the boy in the fields with him, the two grown daughters, Pierluigi, the sister near his age, and the arrogant young man—manage somehow to sleep in the kitchen where we sat and the bedroom of the same size upstairs. They are the only rooms in the house. Gianna asked if they were going to the festa.

"The men are," the dandy specified. Behind his back the girls simpered. They had plans too. "And the old women are in the procession. The band from Vasto is coming. There'll be fireworks too. Couldn't we have a thousand lire to pin on the Madonna's skirt?" Gianna was firm, which brought the civilities to an end. We left.

Traffic had picked up. Donkeys clopped slowly upward, followed by their solemn-faced owners, who yipped occasionally to keep them moving. Women hurried home with their shopping bags. Down in the piazza Sorino had picked up the children of our next visit. Could they . . . ? Could they ride in the jeep as far as their house? Elvira, a sturdy little girl of perhaps six with the rosy cheeks of mountain children and wide, wondering, cornflower blue eyes, sat on my lap, perspiring happily under the double stress of excitement and two dresses. Apparently she had rushed home for her best dress, a coarse cotton plaid, which, unless it had two collars, one brown, one blue, she had put on over her everyday garment. She had not changed her shoes; they were scuffed mountain boots caked with mud and manure. Her little brother, Franco, who looked exactly like her with a touch of demon added, sat on Gianna's lap, muttering, "Francuccio isn't going to the nursery. He won't. Not Francuccio!" Later his mother explained that he had a fixation about the nursery. The few times they had succeeded in getting him there, he had stayed an hour or so, sitting perfectly still like the sixty other children, and had then run off to play by himself in one of the stair streets. He meant it: Francuccio would *not* go to the nursery.

The house where they live with their mother, father and two older sisters is a two-story, two-room house with a dirt floor. It is part of a Fascist housing development, twelve units built before the war, and has one great merit: no one is sure to whom it belongs now, so the rent is not collected. Some of the houses are without doors. The Canadians burned them to keep warm, Elvira told me. Many of the windowpanes are missing, and the plaster has come away in large hunks. Elvira assured me the roof is good. She also told me that she is nine (not six, as I had guessed). She ran inside. We could hear her urging her mother to come out.

She met us at the door, rubbing her hands clean

on her dress. A sturdy, weather-beaten woman, she was a replica of Elvira, prematurely aged and slightly hunched as though to avoid pain. Those same blue, blue eyes were curious, but not innocent. Even when she smiled, they looked tired. Behind her stood a tall, slender girl with curly blonde hair and those same eyes. Giovanna, her mother explained with a rush of awkwardness, was to be married. The girl blushed furiously, dived back inside and began pulling chairs together in a semicircle around a kettle of beans, simmering over another smoky twig fire. Such formality made Elvira shy. She kept her eyes on the floor. At our questions she blushed, then stammered a few words in answer. Finally we released her to play in the jeep with Sorino and Francuccio. Giovanna ducked out with her. Their mother sighed.

"I don't know what we're to do. This summer—well, this summer has been about the end. If I work in the fields, I bleed all night, great gushings of blood. Three times it's happened. What am I to do?" She shook her head, weary and discouraged. "I'm getting so weak. And there's Anna. We do what the doctor tells us, but she's no better. We do what he says. We really do. I need an operation—he said that too—but with Anna to care for there's no money." She leaned over to stir the beans, then sat staring at them. "There won't be many beans this year. The fields are so dry. Seems God deserted us this summer." Giovanna slipped back in, panting. She had a small packet wrapped in heavy brown paper. Very quietly she filled a coffee pot with water and settled it on the fire. Next she got out cups, saucers and a tray. Her mother waited until she came and sat down behind us. "Giovà, show them your trousseau." Blushing again, she hurried off upstairs to return with a large cardboard box that she put on the table.

We gathered around for the show—cotton flannel nightgowns, slips and bloomers she had made, a length of heavy cotton for a dress, coarse wool for a sweater (she liked the color, a sort of mulberry), a pair of sheets, one rather unevenly embroidered, cases, a few towels. A layer of things at the bottom she did not show us until I asked about them. More blushes. Linen sanitary towels. The undershirts, handkerchiefs and shorts for her fiancé that custom requires be part of her trousseau. While these were brought out, shown and carefully put back in the box, her mother told us about the young man.

Giovanna had described him simply as nice and kind. Her mother agreed, but there are problems. He has no land. His father does. There are only two other children, so—someday—there will be land for each of them, not a lot, just some. They will have to live with his family. Maybe in a year they can marry, that is, if the father is satisfied with the dowry. He is not now. Says there are not enough sheets and there have to be blankets. Giovanna is saving, but it is hard and there is little work for her. After she took the box back upstairs, she gave us coffee. Gianna asked about Anna, the mysterious, invisible Anna.

The Fever is always the same. The doctor says to give her broth, meat broth. She will not eat it. Takes nothing. Water, maybe a cup of tea, the vitamins. The Fever is like that. She has seen others. Always tired, always asleep. Eight months Anna has been in bed. The Fever is like that. That insistently The Fever, The Fever, can only be one fever—tuberculosis.

We went up the twisting ladder-stairway with high risers to see her in the general bedroom. It was very bare, very clean. Two double beds, a crucifix, a framed dollar bill and a small window, tightly closed. In the bed near the door was a thin girl of twelve (fifteen?) with wide, reddish lavender rings around blue eyes and matted blonde hair that clung to her head. Her mother explained who we were. She closed her eyes again and smiled. Gianna asked how she felt. "Tired," was all she said in a whisper.

Downstairs, we hunched again over the bean pot and Gianna talked of food and air, light exercise, but signora Appugliese was noncommittal. The doctor had said . . . The doctor didn't . . . There was no meat. Just the few links of sausage that hung from the hook in the ceiling above us. All that was left from last winter's pig. There would not be one this year. They had not been able to buy a piglet. Her husband's pension, three thousand lire a month (about five dollars), had not stretched that far. A pension? "He fell in the top of a machine and is *invalido* now," she told us, a statement that did more to confuse than to explain. In my mind's eye legs stuck out of a concrete mixer, flailing as they turned. Later Gianna told me that, vague as the accident is, there is no doubt that his right arm is useless.

It was hard getting away. She wanted us to stay for some beans, the ones bubbling in the pot that would be ready at noon. It was 8:00! We promised we would come again before Christmas. We would eat beans then. She was not convinced, but did finally let us leave.

"It helps to talk, I don't know why. And really, if God will send us a little rain, everything will be all right." She asks so little of the world and her God, but,

even if it rains, she will still have the hemorrhages and
Anna and the long hungry winter.

An unexpected visitor, a power failure, something made
me stop there. I know that we went on that day, churn-
ing around mountains and through river beds, into villages with dual personalities—one part, a graveyard of
masonry stumps and rubble, the other, a surrealist no-
man's-land of harlequin walls, crazily angled roofs and
here and there stone huts put up in defiance of the master plan. We saw most of the forty sponsored children
in the area. We missed a few who were off, working in
the fields.

   We also met that mythical woman, cited by all
opponents of public housing, the one who stored potatoes in the tub of her spanking new bathroom, which
was also, naturally, the first she had ever had. She was
more of an entrepreneur than we are led to believe such
types are. A war widow, she had no income and no
prospects beyond a small pension whenever the government clerks got around to her file. Her only asset was
the new apartment, and she made the most of it. She
had sublet one bedroom to a family, the kitchen to another. She and her two children lived in the second bedroom. They shared the bath and cooked in their own
rooms. The sitting room, now reduced to a communal
hall, served as storeroom, toolshed with bicycles hung
on spikes driven in the walls and most importantly as
the stall for her tenants' donkeys. As to the tub: why
shouldn't she keep potatoes there? The Comune had not
piped water into the housing development, probably
never would.

   By twilight we had done a loop through two val-

leys and were on our way down to Ortona with the sun
setting behind us. In that light even the Bailey bridges
were dramatic. The mountains had the absolute definition of triangles of colored paper—red, purple, a few
green—pasted on an improbable midnight sky. Dark
seemed, literally, to fall, as an eclipse. More improbable
still, I remember seeing Ortona, a series of bright dots
strung out below us, and feeling we had come back to
civilization, come back from a cruel world I had thought
long banished to history books. We were very tired. We
must have been to equate Ortona to civilization.

In the next few days, while I wrote a report on
each of the children we had seen, their thank-you letters piled up by my typewriter. Late one hot afternoon
I came to Pierluigi's, written, predictably enough, by
his officious brother.

Dear Godmother,

*I am coming to write you these few lines
for my little brother Pierluigi, who is in bed
with his maidens and does not feel up to writing right now. Thank you for the money you
sent him. The English ladies brought it the day
of the festa of the Madonna and suggested that
we take Pierluigi's maidens out with it. My
mother doesn't think that would be possible because it will be very expensive and you never
know how those things are going to turn out.
It might be worse.*

*The day of the festa we spent the whole
day in church praying. Pierluigi said a prayer
for you and asked the Blessed Virgin to bring
wealth and all good things to you and yours.*

*When he has recovered from this last bout I
am sure he will write you.*
      With best wishes to you and your family,
                              Giuseppe

A stunning attack of satyriasis for a ten-year-old
boy, all wrought by faulty phonetics: brother Giuseppe
had confused *donzelle* (maidens) with *tonsille* (tonsils).
Fortunately the condition was reversible, an appropriate final service for his translator, I thought. His
sponsor, a maiden lady in Bury St. Edmunds, would not
have approved of Pierluigi, the Rake of Rosello.

Thirteen

Final days, busy with final deeds, were gloomy, I had to admit, but only to myself. Gianna was hardly more cheerful. She was to spend much of August in southern Austria, visiting the Fund's work there. With each mail she hoped to hear that the Swedish SCF would give the prefabricated nursery building; instead came announcements of official visitors who expected to be picked up in Rome or Florence or Venice and had three days in which to see sponsored children in central Sicily or nurseries in Calabria, before they needed to be delivered back to Rome or Florence or Venice. Italy was, after all, a very small country—to those who had never driven the length of it. She resented their nibbling away at her time for "real" work. She was worrying, trying to splice together a schedule she could survive. Several nights I had awakened to find her light on. Better to read, she said, than lie in the dark, listening to the mosquitoes buzz.

One morning, still in her robe, she appeared at my bedroom door, peeked in at the piles of oddments, mine, that I had collected in the last few days from the office, the back seats of cars, the Baby Hut, and made a face. I knew what she meant. Propped up in bed with my second cup of tea, I had been wondering how, each time a suitcase was unpacked, its contents expanded never to contract again.

"Don't forget the 'stores,' " she teased. "No contribution is too small." She sat on the end of the bed and thought for a moment. "I'm exhausted. I made two decisions last night. Not one. *Two!* Like to hear them?" I suppose I nodded. I know I was surprised. She seemed to want my approval. "Well, first—maybe not in order of importance—"

"First" would be last. Gianna's approach to compromise was carefully oblique. She staged a formal debate. With herself. She presented both sides, she rebutted both sides, after which she could declare herself the loser to temptation, always against her better judgment. The rationale, for what, still obscure, had to be explored. She was neither a Stoic nor a Spartan, she specified, and she did *not* believe in endurance for endurance's sake, no matter what I thought. There were certain aspects of the situation I had not taken into account. The house was not hers. She had no idea how long she would be in it, or in Italy. The Fund could not be expected to provide luxuries. Theoretically, of course, I was right. She had a salary and there were alternatives to faltering electricity. Ah, now I knew where we were, and I laughed. She lowered her head, offended, and then started laughing too.

"Sounds like a presentation to the Foreign Relief Committee, doesn't it? Well, anyway, *I* decided—against my better judgment—to buy a water heater for the bathroom." She paused for a second. "Sorino can probably get it at that plumbing place in Pescara. Oh dear!" She laughed again. "I forgot Pasquale. He'll never forgive me. His flowers! His poor flowers! Now, the second decision. Want to hear it?"

Second would be last too, but this time the exposition was easier to follow. She had thought long and hard about this, and felt, actually, it was quite unfair to suggest it. Against her better judgment again. Unfair to tempt me from the pleasures of a more conventional Italian interlude. (For all my good intentions, there was apparently no doubt that I could be tempted.) She did need the help and she enjoyed having the company. We got on surprisingly well, perhaps partly because we were both only children and respected the withdrawals and reticences of that solitary breed.

At that point she bogged down, I think because she wanted to leave us both room for graceful retreat. The rest came out in an embarrassed rush. The Fund had told her that the car and driver would be needed in Austria. Sorino was not happy about being away so long. She found it awkward to travel with him for so long. He was very tactful, but hotel staffs always assumed—Well, never mind about that. The point was—Would I like to take his place? When we came back, I could stay, helping her, until the University of Rome opened. Or— I could finally go to Florence, which was fast becoming a joke.

Without the slightest hesitation I chose Austria.

Sorino may not have wanted to make the trip, but he did not take kindly to being deposed. I must be trained for my new office. He chose the Autopark in the early

morning and late afternoon, when the Quonset hut provided a modicum of shade. He drilled me in tire changing and general maintenance. He assembled a bundle of
tools, wrapped in useful rags, and a metal box—a mechanical survival kit, jammed with the parts I might
need and would not find easily in Italy or Austria: spark
plugs, a full set of belts, points, assorted springs, wash-
ers, nuts and bolts. He demonstrated slowly, carefully
how and where these could be installed, then lit a cigarette and leaned back to watch me struggle. The points
I always got in either upside down or backward, and I
was never sure how to judge the tension of the belts. A
matter of feel, he said. Couldn't I tell? My progress must
have been satisfactory. At least, after a careful preamble, he confided in me—about the car's secret vices—
and I began to doubt my qualifications for my new
profession.

Impressive mileage over the variety of rumpled
surfaces that were Italian roads had brought on premature mechanical fatigue. Nothing *probably* would
happen. Then again, one never knew. A new oil pump
had been ordered. However—when the oil pressure
suddenly dropped to zero, all I had to do was bang the
gauge with the heel of my hand and usually the needle
would slide slowly back toward normal, so it was hard
to tell whether it was the pump or the gauge that had
hiccups. Now about the *boccoli* that rattled against the
steering column . . . The dictionary gave "bushings,"
but did not explain why they should be noisy or why, if
tightened, they tended to lock. On balance Sorino thought
it better they should thud. Again, not a serious worry.
He did want to warn me that with warm weather any
prolonged idling, such as a traffic jam or waiting at a

railroad crossing, and the radiator boiled. Never remove the radiator cap until all the spewing had stopped,
and never add water unless the motor was running.

He was either pulling my leg or trying to frighten
me off. At least I knew a bit about radiators. What's
wrong with the thermostat? Uh, nothing. Well . . . ?
Another thing, the starter . . . No. What's wrong with
the thermostat? Uh, nothing. Works very well in winter. Why not in summer? Needs a different adjustment,
different temperature. Well . . . ? Sorino, who enjoyed
a full dose of Italian male infallibility, especially in "his"
fields (and some others where he expected no challenge), also had several habits that betrayed him as a
meek and honest man. Whenever he saw the highway
police, he slowed to a crawl, never realizing that attracted their attention more than his speed ever would.
And always if he had to tell a lie, even just a white lie,
he shuffled his feet and looked away. He could not meet
your eye. He stuttered and stumbled, avoiding the lie.
He stuttered and stumbled about the thermostat too,
until, reluctantly, he admitted he had removed it. Just
for the summer. He was sure it slowed the car down.
Faster, but given to boiling, made no sense. Would he
at least *try* the thermostat? He could not refuse. He
never admitted that it worked, neither did he take
it out.

We went back to the starter. It enjoyed an intermittent disgruntlement. Without warning it managed to
throw a spring or a spring and retracting arm and refused to turn over. Not even a willing whir. There were
two possibilities: a hand crank, one of the world's dead-
liest weapons, which was supplied with the car and suggested that the manufacturer knew much about his

product he did not care to divulge, or a complex manipulation that was good for one crank only. If it failed to
catch, the entire operation had to be repeated. Sorino
was patient and insistent. I must learn the trick. I had
to reach deep down, work my hand through wires and
belts, into the innards of the motor and slip off three
rings that fit snugly, one over the other on a shaft. When
I had managed to snake them out on my little finger, I
was to separate them and put them together again.
Getting them back onto the shaft, together, in the proper
way, was the difficult part, or so it seemed in dress re-
hearsal. When I made my debut unexpectedly one warm
September evening (again I had not gone to Florence),
I discovered that, yes, manual dexterity and luck were
important, but the sine qua non, if the operation were
to succeed in Matera at the height of the height of the
Sunday promenade, was indomitable poise.

Beyond my startling speed at changing tires, Sorino was not impressed by my mechanical skills. Neither was I. I had to hope Sorino was right: nothing,
probably, would happen. So, Gianna and I set out for
Austria, each with her own complement of professional
worries.

The rest of that summer until very late fall is in my
memory like a magic-lantern show. The machine is fractious, given to grinding. Sometimes slides are trium-
phantly presented upside down. Sometimes only half a
slide. No amount of coddling, nor even a good kick, will
expose more. Next slide. An inexplicably crepuscular
scene hints at shapes, but refuses details. The next, just
as inexplicably, is translucent. Mind and memory in collusion are capricious editors, by turns sentimental,

starkly factual, or macabre. A fractious machine, indeed, yet I prefer its glimpses, however flawed, to the log of our peregrinations, which could be culled from the postcards, dozens of them, that I sent my parents, assuring them I was alive, somewhere.

True, we drove an appalling number of miles, about six thousand in eight weeks, and everything that possibly could go wrong with the car did. Not on the Austrian trip. It waited for the next one, south this time, to play its tricks on an innocent and now far too relaxed driver. First an accelerator spring popped off, the gas pedal slammed to the floor and the car bolted, like a livery horse determined to get rid of its rider. We surged into, and almost through, the first garage, jarring the owner from his siesta. He ambled sleepily around his customers' cars that were up on jacks or over oil pits, poking in and under their engines, until he found a spring that, if not a perfect fit, would do. I did not ask how he would replace it. I had an idea.

A two-day truce and then, out in the sizzling wastelands between Matera and the coast road to Calabria, we blew a gasket and a great many other things, the names of which I did not even know. We burped and shuddered and prayed our way into Taranto, it being the closest city that was also downhill. Several more days were lost in futile attempts at repair before we returned ignominiously to Ortona by train, Gianna and I in a compartment, the station wagon on a flatcar. According to Sorino, *I* had melted the motor.

As an interim car, we rented a minute, elderly Fiat. It went up in smoke at the gates of L'Aquila. Sorino would have said *I* melted the electrical system. We did have one bit of luck. The guest we were to meet in

Rome was tired and more than content to sit in the garden, drinking white wine.

Taranto was not yet behind us. The real souvenir of our visit arrived two weeks later: we both came down with paratyphoid. By then we were in Zagreb, at an international congress of social agencies. As it was we arrived late. This time cartographic rather than mechanical problems. The maps supplied by the Yugoslav tourist bureau were, at best, statements of intent. The highway, so straight and broad and red on paper, was in reality a network of cow paths that ran from farmyard to farmyard. To change three tires in one day only took brawn. To get three inner tubes patched took ingenuity. At the deluxe hotel the mattresses, stuffed with vegetable fiber, harbored colonies of voracious fleas. Tito did give an elaborate reception for us and, as we drove the head of the Fund to Belgrade for his next series of meetings, the oil pressure gauge twitched one last time and died. The pump—well, I was not quite sure.

All we could do was press on toward Italy. We made it in one long, silent, powerless glide down the mountain into Trieste. A generator brush had burned out. A mechanic promised a handmade replacement in twenty-four hours. Not that we cared. In the grips of another of the tertian, quartan and octan bouts of fever, headaches, nausea, ague and general misery that would plague us for weeks, we did not care about anything except bed.

But on and on we went, sticking to Gianna's relentless schedule, through breakdowns and fevers, to the very end, which naturally was the most important of the visitations and the most difficult. We were to pick up the head of a British charity and his assistant in

Venice, take them to Ortona for half a day, on to Matera for most of another day* and deposit them, dead or alive, in Rome by noon on the fourth.

A thousand miles with two extended stops and a car bent on betrayal. It boiled at every railroad crossing. I drove with a two-liter bottle of water wedged between my hip and the door, until the fan belt, a new one, broke, identifying the problem. At night in the rain somewhere in Puglia. I had Sorino's spare, of course, and between his training and a strong surge of adrenaline got it on, the pressure not perfect, but close enough until the next morning, when a garage would be open. Then the starter collapsed. After each stop I took it apart and reassembled it, sometimes more than once. The two visitors watched me anxiously and with some wonder. I never dared admit the bushings were slowly locking around the steering column. They were already nervous enough about hairpin curves. When, the last night, we arrived at the hotel in Salerno, they were so exhausted they left me to carry their bags.

Several days later a cable arrived at our pension in Rome and I forgave them. On their safe return home, and probably out of gratitude to a higher power, they

---

*Matera was a constant on the itinerary because of a complex experiment in progress there. A consortium of government ministries and agencies was slowly evacuating fifteen thousand people from caves, *I Sassi*, to new housing, high-rise apartments and planned agricultural villages, with all the cultural and social upheaval inherent in such programs. An archaic society was to be broken up. A modern and more civilized one should replace it. In conjunction with it were massive programs for land reclamation and consolidation of small holdings, for health care, for schools and social centers. The Fund, again collaborating with UNRRA-CASAS, was involved in all aspects of child care.

had presented the Fund with a check: the "Italian team" must have a new car immediately. In the meantime we had bought, with our own money and very cheaply because it had British plates, a much-used Morris Minor. A stodgy, visiting-nurse sort of car, we thought. We soon discovered it had a surprising character: it never balked, went anywhere, like a jeep with springs and leather upholstery. There *was* one problem. In our enthusiasm for a whole, healthy car, we had glossed over how we were eventually to divide it. Week by week? Month by month? Longitudinally?

The car was one symptom of the euphoria that hit Gianna like a benign virus. There were others. She ordered clothes and bought books and squeezed the latest films in between elaborately complicated plans to meet friends she had not seen in months. She was decidedly "off duty," and for once the question of with or without leave did not bother her. Just a reaction, she assured me, a celebration of her own, private autumnal equinox. Summer was over.

Professionally hers had been a great success. A foreign agency cannot demand or command. It must be invited to perform, and preferably, if it is a private agency, the expenses should be paid by someone else. The position is awkward and ridiculous at the same time, but those endless miles and the endless meetings, each a tiny, diplomatic step toward a secret end, had been worth it: Gianna's dance card was more than full.

Would she help organize a conference on institutionalized children and the effects of emotional privation, which was a pernicious problem, hardly recognized yet, in Italy? The government would be delighted to play host in exchange for the right to send the directors of provincial orphanages. Would she expand her experiment for the Infant Welfare—a project one courageous pediatrician had taken a chance on—of moving ten children of different ages out of an orphanage and settling them with a couple in a normal apartment? The results had been impressive: the children were healthier, more alert intellectually, more stable, less withdrawn emotionally, all at a slightly lower cost per child simply because they had not needed the staggering quantities of antibiotics common to institutionalized children. Would she devise some form of prekindergarten unit within the institution that would tend to stimulate the same kind of mental, social and motor development in the children? Would she come to the two training courses planned for the teachers of 350 nurseries that one government agency ran in the South? Please. These young girls, who knew little enough, and mostly antiquated theory at that, needed to learn the *practical* ways to solve common nursery problems in lost mountain villages.

This, of course, was Gianna's forte. For this she had wanted the new nursery—to have enough space for small groups of teachers to see that simple solutions work, to show them how and why they work. She could offer proof, not more theory. And then came the prize of the summer, a query really, only an announcement by implication: the Swedish SCF wanted to know when she could have a foundation ready and if she could have the nursery erected and functioning by spring.

Even as she dashed around Rome, catching up on normal life, freight dispatchers shunted Swedish flatcars, laden with wall panels, partitions, windows, shutters, rafters and ridgepoles for a house of seven rooms

(one of them large enough for thirty children, their tables, chairs, cupboards and toys) from one freight division to another, obeying a basic railroad tenet that motion in and of itself, to wherever, is good. In this case
it was at least encouraging, especially to the dispatchers who got rid of them, because the measurements of
Swedish rolling stock were not compatible with those of
the older sections of the overpass-underpass-tunnel system, which had, perforce, been reactivated after the war.
Our cars were wandering in haphazard search for an
exit from the labyrinth. They were reported in the most
unlikely places on their way to still more unlikely places
and would continue to zigzag about the country, all at
the expense of the government, for several weeks before they finally came to rest in Ortona. There a foundation, just slightly out of plumb, not quite horizontal
either, rose each day a bit higher. Our last, most exhausted guests, the donors not only of the new car but
of the foundation and roof, had actually huddled under
an umbrella in a driving rainstorm to lay the corner-
stone, an unimpressive column of tufa blocks at one corner of a shallow excavation that looked like nothing so
much as an Olympic wading pool. Gianna's summer had
been a great success, but she had a lot to do before she
could succumb to her own, private vernal equinox.

As for *my* summer, "professionally," with its
succession of inglorious, mechanical improvisations, it
rated only negative praise: it could, presumably, have
been worse. In every other sense my summer, roaming,
sometimes coursing between Venice and the Strait of
Messina was the fantasy of a timid tourist, enamored of
Italy and overburdened with luggage, come true.

Fourteen

And then there was Rome. Always Rome, with its dazzling beauty and its maddening bureaucracy, where so many of our trips began and ended, our reward for good behavior. Of course the Rome of 1954 was not today's. It was still a very provincial city, shabby genteel, comfortable, however improbable that sounds now, a wonderland of surprises and good-humored chaos.

Illogically, the first day or so of each visit seemed a return to the familiar, to a place where gravity worked and vertical was vertical and the unknowns were, in a sense, known—except the traffic, which, though light, was uniquely, suicidally Roman, a round-the-clock drag race, punctuated at each intersection by fender-to-fender tournaments of chicken.

In my free time I explored. I crawled through excavations. I spent hours trying to convince the surly "ushers" who guarded the doors of the university's administration buildings that I must be allowed inside to talk to someone about my status, only to be told and told again that nothing could be done until after All Souls'. Come back November 8 or 9. Not sooner! I lingered at sidewalk cafés, blatantly eavesdropping on my neighbors' conversations. I took sedate rides on the rattly little tram that plied a circular route through and around the walls of the old city, and in my more practical moments I even looked for a place to live. I found an infinite variety of attics without windows and apartments overlooking air shafts—grandly referred to as "inner courtyards," with delicious views of bathrooms across the way, afterthoughts cantilevered into the void and glazed like miniature solaria—and was depressed. But the magic of Roman evenings blurred my doubts as the mists blurred and softened the forums. Fountains sprayed in deserted piazzas. Streets were shadowy, romantic; in the ruins of Largo Argentina the squatter still received midnight callers and allowed them to feed "his" cats. We were young, and friends were easily made. Day or night, Rome was a deceptive city, a beguiling one.

But by the third morning in the pale, aqueous light before colors and shadows claimed their saturated brilliance, my doubts would again be with me and I half-realized I was playing hide-and-seek with myself. Here there was something of fantasy, a place of escape. It was no longer quite the real world to me; somehow *that* was much farther east now, across those bare, desolate mountains in the Abruzzo, and I had to admit, unwillingly at first and only to myself, that I wanted to stay there.

* * *

About Ortona, in three months of being there—and not
being there, which aided the digestion—I had learned a
lot. Gianna had been right. The house, though charming, had its flaws. In the way of miniature fauna, the
cockroaches on their nightly tours of inspection were
minor inconveniences. More deadly were the gluttonous
moths that ate any form of woven goods, wool by preference, but silk, cotton and synthetics would do. Fleas
found me scrumptious. No one wanted to encourage col-
onization, so I had strict orders from Ida to dump *all*
my clothes out on the stairs as I went to take my bath.
She then spirited them off to the garden, where she
shook them, brushed them or put them in a zinc tub to
soak, depending on her estimate of contamination. The
stray louse, left behind by thoughtless guests, excited
her to cyclonic housecleaning. She would not tolerate
vermin.

The flora thrived too. Mildew antiqued the books
with freckles, while it perfumed. There were two kinds
of mold. One sprouted dark patches on the walls, like a
three-day beard, the other spun cotton-candy blobs and
had a penchant for shoes, which, if we were away for a
few days, it modeled into fluffy, surrealistic sculptures.

Even "improvements" had a way of developing
equivocal personalities. An electric iron should have been
handier than the old flatiron, but, except in mid-afternoon, when the Ortonesi were napping, not enough
electricity seeped through to heat it. The radio suffered
from the same malaise: sound was available at midnight
and dawn. Appliances were unknown. Refrigerators, for
which Italy would be famous all over the world, had not
reached the provinces. They too needed to be encour-

aged with electricity. Coffee was ground by hand, so was laundry with the aid of a deadly bleach, which, more efficiently than any washing machine, reduced the stoutest cloth to islets and archipelagos. Gianna, dreaming of cakes and roast chickens, had allowed herself one luxury, a small gas stove with an extremely small oven. For all its tantalizing promise, it had a basic problem, and clairvoyance and luck were capricious substitutes: it had no thermostat. Food carbonized with amazing speed. Cakes turned to concrete, or the bottled gas ran out midway in the operation. Considering the general reluctance of mechanisms to work as they should in that house, we could not pretend perfection of the new water heater.

It was a simple contraption—a small firebox, topped by a slender metal cylinder with a smoke pipe and a gooseneck steam vent that exited on the roof. No water ran into the tub unless water from the holding tanks replaced it in the boiler, ergo no explosions. The manufacturer boasted of these extraordinary safety features. Before Ida left on her afternoon jaunt to town, she lit it, so that Gianna and I could each have a bath before dinner, assuming there was water. Once it started to draw, she instructed Pasquale, who at that hour was always hoeing along the fence, to put in a few more sticks of wood later. If he was not involved entertaining passersby, he remembered. He was not too conscientious. He still resented the terrible waste of water.

The little heater functioned nobly, belching out water so hot that we could dilute it enough with cold to have good, full baths, if any bath in a sitz tub qualifies as such. Until one evening some vagary of the famous safety devices had left the boiler partially empty. Com-

ing along from the office, at the very moment we saw
the gate and the Baby Hut, we also saw a billowing,
tufty cloud of steam that shrouded the roof. The house
faded and reappeared dramatically in swirls of mist, like
the *Queen Elizabeth* plowing along through a stormy
sea. To Pasquale's delight. From his flower bed he
watched the show, laughing, at times bending double to
relieve the strain on his stomach muscles, tears rolling
down his cheeks. If we *would* insist on bathing . . . !

Pasquale enjoyed calamities, those of others, but
he had suffered too many himself not to know it was
impolitic to gloat openly. At the sight of us, he hunched
over his hoe and set up the mumbled chant that he
claimed soothed his plants. Once more he had taken up
his pose of docile plodding. And it was a pose. Life had
rigid rules and limitations. In public he kept within them,
seeing himself as one of the governed, not one of the
governors. He was cautious, even a bit afraid of Authorities, a category from which only illiterate peasants, his own kind, were excluded. He placated Them
with little bows, a touch of his hat. When the occasion
called for it, he could back away from the presence with
courtly respect. If, as it often did, his sly sense of humor led him into transgressions, he pretended they were
secrets that had slipped out, not to be shared.

Outwardly his life was normal to his age and caste.
He had a small pension, a respectable job with a token
salary, which for his friends he inflated to monthly opulence, and what he considered "light hours," from six
to six with an hour out for lunch. Best of all, he had
that middle-class premium, half-day Saturday, still called
sabato inglese, English Saturday, and a status symbol
before such things were so common. Sunday morn-

ings—dressed in the black wedding suit, which served
for best and would eventually see him to his grave, a
white shirt, buttoned at the neck without a tie, and an
undented black fedora—he went to the barber for his
weekly shave. When he joined the men standing in the
piazza, his chin was clean and his upper lip sported a
sparse postage-stamp moustache that for much of the
week was lost in general stubble. There would be pasta
for lunch and afterward a good lie down. His Sundays
were relentlessly middle class. Toward dusk, if he felt
like splurging and there was a "revue," he went to the
cinema. Otherwise he lounged around the cathedral piazza, watching the younger men line up for the local
house of prostitution. Already that morning he had as-
sessed the young ladies' charms as they paraded to
church behind their portly madam. His wife was neat,
quiet and at home, invisible, as she should be.

Indeed, all was exactly as it should be, except
that Pasquale himself had a secret he tried to disguise:
he was a closet anarchist, a resigned, absolutely inac-
tive one until the war had, perversely, given him new
hope.

In 1943, when the shelling began, Pasquale and his wife
did not pack their valuables and trail into the fields with
their neighbors, partly because they did not own a shed
or even a cave in a hillside where they could hide, partly
because their "valuables"—one large, old-fashioned radio and their *padrona*'s silver—were not really porta-
ble. He would not leave them to looters. And there would
be looters. If the padrona's silver were stolen . . . ? So
they stayed and kept watch over their treasures, alone
in their one-room masonry hut on an unpaved street,

really a sandy corridor lined with one-room, one-story masonry huts, Via della Speranza, Street of Hope.

They were terrified. The explosions, the thuds, the creaking and snapping of beams, the cascade of tiles, some near, some distant though nonetheless grim, and then the slow silting of their own roof as it began to buckle. Pasquale shored it with what he could find on darting expeditions into the street. Their treasures were safe under the bed. The light had gone. Water too. Then days of bursts from machine guns and hand grenades. Stumbling footsteps, shouts in strange languages. Blasts. And when finally the Germans retreated north and calm should have returned, came the Sikh patrols that enforced the curfews.

To Pasquale they were uniquely terrifying and fascinating. He still talked about them with pale, shaky wonder. Here they were, he and his wife, trying to clear out the rubble, patch their roof, find food, and here, too, from twilight to dawn, were the Sikhs, stealing silently through the streets, at the slightest sound—the tinkle of a tile, the clawing of a rat—slashing out with their broadswords. *Chouf!* was his imitation of the sound. *Chouf!* Anyone in the way was cut in half. No questions asked. Each morning, fully as remarkable to Pasquale, who had not had a bath since 1938, when friends threw him into the sea as a joke, the Sikhs commandeered any fountain that was running and took down their hair, washed it, combed it, rewound it and their turbans and wandered casually off through the crowd that had gathered to watch them and now stumbled and lurched to get out of their way. Pasquale claimed they had brought lice to Ortona, where none had been before(!), but the truth was that they were more frightening than the noisy mechanical war itself. They were also probably the only force that, simply by their presence, could have kept peace in a dark, destroyed town full of hungry, desperate people.

Soon enough the troops, Sikhs and all, were needed elsewhere, and the Ortonesi were left to clean up, prop up and try to avoid starvation. The Allies appointed a new mayor, a much-respected non-Fascist shopkeeper, bureaucracy began to function again after a fashion, a very Byzantine fashion, and Pasquale perceived dimly at the end of his faded rainbow what might be his pot of gold—*Danni di Guerra*—war reparations.

He was not alone. His neighbors to a man were doing their alchemic best to convert rubble into rubies. According to their claims, every old flour bin had been of solid walnut, every bedstead inlaid with ebony and ivory, just as every chicken that had roosted underneath (anywhere from ten to fifty by their conservative estimates) was a prized layer. Prewar, peacetime Ortona, if the bereaved residents were to be believed, had been an antiques bazaar camouflaged as a vast chicken yard. After these flights of fancy all they needed were recommendations from the mighty and near-mighty, or so they thought and were often right. And, too, each family whose house had been destroyed or damaged had a right to a new one or compensation for the old.

In the fullness of time and at the pleasure of the Authorities, Pasquale did have a new house, a small apartment in public housing, but that phrase, "compensation for the old," stuck in his mind. Compensation for the old! It had a promising ring. He had discovered, he was sure he had, a way to get rich *and* bring the Authorities to their fiscal knees. He would be a man of substance and then . . .

Gianna had told me that sooner or later I would be honored with an improbable tale. I should listen very closely. I would recognize it, she promised, because Pasquale always began it the same way: "You see, nobody knew it, but I was the owner of the castle." One day, when I was painting toys and Pasquale had not found anyone entertaining to talk to, he came over and sat on a stump near me and started talking. Did I know he might have been a very rich man? I nodded. No satisfaction in that. All because of the war, he added. Pause. "You see, nobody knew it . . ." and there was the fateful sentence.

Long before the war a woman, L'Americana, not that she was a "real" American, according to Pasquale, because she had been born in the Abruzzo and "taken down there to America" as a girl, had bought the castle of Ortona, a fifteen-century souvenir from Aragon's rule over the Kingdom of Naples, that stood on a promontory jutting into the sea just north of town. She remodeled it and then filled it with splendors hard to imagine—"towering mirrors and big, shiny furniture that glittered with gold"—thus realizing her dream to return to Italy conspicuously more affluent than when she had departed.

Naturally she needed a "staff." Pasquale and his wife were hired and given quarters in the castle. He was to be a gardener and gatekeeper, she, "lady's maid" to the signora, though judging from his stories, her duties often declined into the realm of maid-of-all-work. Pasquale's were elastic too. One of his regular morning chores was to take the signora's coffee to her in her bath. Occasionally he was even handed a long brush and told to scrub her back, which he thoroughly enjoyed, at least in retrospect. These were heady times. For the signora's parties, when her Italo-American friends dashed over from Rome in their flashy cars and flashier clothes, Pasquale doubled as butler and sommelier. He probably made up in enthusiasm what he lacked in polish, although the guests, from his description, would not have been critical. They were a rowdy bunch, especially the women, who were no better than they should be. (They drank!) He was too prim to offer details, but was obviously both impressed and shocked by them.

Suddenly, when "those people" started the war, the signora wanted to leave Ortona, go back to America. Mussolini would not allow her to (so ran Pasquale's version) because once an Italian always an Italian: those who returned were to stay.

She had other problems too. Her cousins, as relatives and *true* Italians, claimed an inalienable right, a pseudo-dower right several times removed, to equal equity in the castle. She summoned lawyers from Rome, and they all screamed and squabbled. Then one day she had a long talk with Pasquale. She had a plan. She had decided to deed the castle to him. With him she knew it would be safe. He could not read the paper, a failing he would never admit, and he did not believe her, but only the foolhardy contradict an employer. He stuffed the supposed deed in his pocket and promised to protect the castle. She disappeared to Rome, and perhaps beyond, never to be seen again.

When, a few days later, the cousins heard the news, they came, raging, to the castle. The gate was closed. Pasquale refused to open it, nor would he open it for the Carabinieri. He did not trust them. Men they took into custody for no reason vanished without trace. He passed the "deed" through the gate to them. And he could hardly believe it—*they* said he was the padrone of the castle now and went away.

He and his wife stayed on there until the Germans came and ordered them out. They could take their possessions with them. But where? They found the little one-room house, packed it with the signora's big wardrobe, her brass double bed, her linens, her silver and the precious radio. The rest they had to leave behind, knowing that, piece by piece, it would disappear. All they could do was watch. What they saw was puzzling. The Germans were tunneling under the castle. Then trains began stopping right below it and soldiers marched out, lined up along the freight cars and slowly moved past the open doors, where each was given a wooden crate to carry into the tunnel. Back and forth like ants, until the train pulled away on down the line. Some days there were three or four trains.

Unknown to Pasquale and beyond his imagination, the Germans had made a munitions depot of his castle. They also effectively, if unintentionally, mined it. In 1954 several squat, slope-shouldered towers, bits of ramparts here and there, and odd lengths of wall, the incongruous dentils added by some Victorian fanatic still intact, were all that remained. Allied bombs and artillery shells had sent the rest spewing up, over the cliff, down and across the railway line and off into the sea in what must have been a spectacular display of fireworks. The grandeur that had been Pasquale's castle was a shell, abandoned by all save those in search of an outdoor latrine and two horses and one mule whose owners stabled them there on the sly.

The phrase "compensation for the old" had stuck in his mind, but he was duty bound to await the signora's return. Instead her cousins came. In her place, they said. At her instruction. They brought papers for him to sign. He had a right to war reparations. After all, the Germans and the Allies between them had ruined *his* castle. They would take care of the formalities. He would be a rich man. All he had to do was sign. The signora wanted him to sign. She also wanted him to keep the linen and silver and whatever else he had been able to save. He had been a good and loyal servant. Now he would be rich too. He made his wavery *X's* on each of the lines they pointed to and settled back, confident that soon he would be a man of substance and then . . .

And then, nothing went quite as it should. First he had been served with a packet of official-looking papers, which he could not read. He assumed it was good news, *the* long-awaited good news. Next he had the humbling experience of consulting a lawyer, who, not too illogically, did not believe his story. Investigations were in order. However, he did inform Pasquale that the papers were a suit for payment of war damages, filed against him by the National Railways. The disruption of the main Adriatic north-south line, caused by the explosion of *his* castle and the subsequent avalanche of debris across the right-of-way, was described in graphic detail, as were the costs of clearing, repairs, fines and interest, to be paid immediately.

Nor did the lawyer's investigations offer much comfort. They confirmed that Pasquale was, indeed, the owner of the castle. They also brought to light what he should have suspected and had not: the cousins had tricked him. He had renounced any claims, rights or pretensions whatsoever to war reparations in their favor. Meanwhile with each cloudburst and blizzard another clump of Pasquale's castle slithered over the bluff, down onto the tracks, mangling whatever it could not drag out to sea, and another suit was filed against him by the National Railways, outlining his negligence, his latest disruption of the right-of-way, public property after all, the damages thereto, the costs for clearing and repairs with the threat of compound interest to follow. Somehow, being a man of property was not quite as he had envisioned.

In 1954 Pasquale's prospects had only just recently vanished, or worse, done an about-face. Authority had snatched back its capital *A*, and he was more circumspect. He no longer allowed himself gleeful celebrations of others' mishaps. He still celebrated, but quietly, to himself. No more than a smirk and a twinkle gave him away. Again he was the docile peasant, the pose in place. It masked the sly mini-swindles that gave him almost as much pleasure as his big coup might have, had it come off. Not all were, strictly speaking, illegal.

One of his hoaxes relieved us for a while of the feature Gianna most disliked about the house—the lack of privacy. I had come to agree with her. Week in, week out the constant stream of people was wearing. It was never safe to wash your hair or sit in a bathrobe, reading a book, or put the sewing machine up in the sitting room and make curtains. People came at all hours, Sundays, whenever it suited them. People who had not kept appointments, because it was raining, came three days later at lunchtime. Social workers turned up as dinner was put on the table. The Vice-Prefect, who was charged with Public Security, a category that included control of foreigners' activities, liked to drop in after 8:30 P.M., knowing Ida was gone. His assumptions were well out-side the precincts of Public Security. Early Sunday afternoons priests appeared at the gates. "We know you don't take naps." Holidays for no specific or predictable reason brought delegations from the Old People's As-sociation, the Boys' Club and the Blood Donors' Asso-ciation, all groups Gianna and her husband had helped found. They could not be turned away. We were strangely ineffectual at warding off these invasions. Even when we barricaded ourselves in the house, pretending to be away, we were caught sneaking up or down the outside stairway. There was no escape.

Pasquale found one. The tracks of his hose in the dust had given him the idea, and the discovery, one dark night on an empty back street, of an unattended red-and-white striped sawhorse gave him the chance to try it. Outside the gate in the lane, where it was visible from both ends, there appeared the sawhorse, support-ing a very official sign, painted by a friend, perhaps So-rino (he never admitted it). ATTENTION! DANGEROUS PASSAGE! POISONOUS SNAKES! The evidence was there to be seen, an intricate tracery that wiggled around in the dirt and off under the bushes of the hedge. It could, of course, have been a veiled reference to us, which would double the fun for Pasquale.

No one came at night. By day people stopped at the top of the lane and shouted for Ida, who told them we were busy or away. Try during office hours. When we actually were away, sawhorse and sign were re-moved. For our return they were brought back out of hiding and positioned complete with new "snake" trails. Weeks, peaceful weeks, passed before the town Works Department identified and repossessed the sawhorse. By then Pasquale's attention had shifted to piles of gravel, thoughtfully dumped at even distances on both sides of the road, in preparation for patching. Mornings now, just after dawn, he sauntered in, pushing a wheelbarrow loaded with gravel, which he solemnly spread over bare spots only he could see on the playground. Gravel, he commented, was almost impossible to identify.

Gianna was right. The peculiarities of the house, at times accentuated by Pasquale and company, were many and varied. But then in a Southern town, devastated by war, the peculiarities of daily life, some tragic, others amusing or puzzling, were legion. I had learned, slowly, about them too.

Instant democracy had brought its confusions. It kept the Fascist laws of public security and still promised equality and the benefits of the complete welfare state to every man—*if* he were formally, in all senses of the law, employed. In Ortona almost no one was. There was little work, and no employer wanted to hire, officially, someone whom, should there be no more work, he was virtually forbidden to fire. On the other hand, the men were frozen in place by the public security laws. They could not get work elsewhere without a certificate of residence: said certificate was issued only to men who *had* work. And almost worse, while they searched in this unfriendly "elsewhere," they risked being picked up by the police and charged with vagrancy—or held on generic suspicion without charge indefinitely, or shipped home with an obligatory *foglio di via*. Whichever, they were still unemployed and now had police records. One of the requisites for a job was a certificate from the police attesting to "good conduct."

Italians are pragmatic, especially about survival. Making do, as the expression *l'arte di arrangiarsi* implies, is an art. Laws that suit the politicians who write them do not necessarily suit all who are subject to them. But Italians like to tinker. A slight adjustment here, a slight twist of interpretation there, nothing that an enforcement agency would notice in the general, handwritten confusion of those long-ago days before computers and identification numbers issued with birth certificates, and *Ecco!* a compromise that allowed small employers and would-be employees to survive. Men were hired by the day without medical insurance or pension contributions, or were permanently "on trial" and so not eligible. They were the lucky ones. If they complained or caused trouble, men more obliging were eager to take their places. The others "made do" on the odd jobs they could find, unloading trucks, digging foundations, whitewashing houses. One man, whose scrawny, pigeon-breasted children succeeded each other year after year at the nursery, even made his "living" as crucifer in funerals. He seemed to enjoy the power of his office, smiling gently as his approach brought shop shutters clanging to the ground in a noisy show of respect, but for his fee of one hundred lire (sixteen cents) he did not feel duty bound to wear a clean cassock or take off the grubby wool cap he wore in all seasons.

The wives also had duties in this fraudulent modus operandi. They maneuvered the family onto the rolls of the poor, which provided them with the free services of a government-paid doctor, the *medico condotto*, and some medicines, plus textbooks and a black smock for their school-aged children and a ludicrously low monthly bread subsidy, a remnant of a different time and a drastically different lire. Competition for such desirable status was savage, and any technique for attaining it—from courtship and bribery to outright blackmail—was valid. The women spent a lot of time keeping their benefactors happy—or anxious. Spare moments were for their own jobs, usually domestic chores for the gentry. They hauled their stove wood and their water from the fountain. They did their laundry. They made their spaghetti sauce and washed their dishes. Their pay was a few pennies or a meal or even promises of future largesse, perhaps a recommendation. No one complained. Every little bit helped. The average income was three hundred dollars a year.

Children had their uses too, which in those early years made obligatory schooling (five, then later eight years) and child-labor regulations (no employment under fifteen) unpopular. What better source for bar boys, barbers' helpers, tailors' apprentices? Little girls could deliver messages and carry packages for women who did not yet have maids to establish their social distinction. (Ida was ashamed of Gianna, who would not let her trail around the shops with her, a respectful three steps behind, collecting paper twists of elastic and buttons or a ream of typing paper.) One man, who stalled his horse and cart in Pasquale's castle, was more enterprising. He looked beyond the local situation. Each morning the weather was good, he took his two children on the bus to Pescara, the nearest pseudo-city of any prosperity. They got off at the station. He went to his favorite café to wait while they "worked" the main streets, up one side, down the other, begging. As Pescara grew, which it did in a feverish sprawl, so did their routes and his bank account.

If he had one. Such an account was not very useful. No one believed in bank secrecy, or for that matter in banks. They were symbols of the greater world, their real function seemingly limited to the collection of promissory notes. Savings accounts that earned 1½ percent interest were hardly a hedge against inflation, and checks, other than cashier's, suspect. Local tradesmen were loathe to accept them (if a customer had the money, he would have paid cash, no?) and should a check—even one written on a branch of a national bank such as the Fund's—escape the territorial boundaries of Ortona, it had about as much value as a laundry list. Such "foreign" transactions were best accomplished by postal money orders.

A truly "foreign" transaction set off all safety systems except the actual alarm on the vaults. To deposit money that had been legally exported (with Bank of England approval) through the London office of the Italian bank, money that had been legally imported into Italy and so noted at the bank's main offices, Gianna had to sign twelve times, relieving everyone who had, willingly or unwillingly, come in contact with it of any responsibility, for the money, her actions or her probity.

One clerk was deputized for this major procedure, a pudgy, little man whose face, above a never quite clean collar, was an amorphous blur of stubble and tinted glasses. He was beset by problems, among them a liver, a mother-in-law and an ailing father. Before any business was broached, their health or perfidy must be inquired after. Otherwise he vanished into the offices at the back of the bank and sulked. Either Gianna could be a stickler for Anglo-Saxon detachment and efficiency and lose hours waiting out his fits of displeasure, or she could cultivate his good will, which at its peak guaranteed no more than moderate speed. Since his initials were needed on a form simply to cash a check (after he had posted the amount on the account record and incidentally seen that the balance covered it) and since, at the end of the month, a statement of the month's debits and credits was also needed, something Italian banks are required to supply only at six-month intervals and then without canceled checks, Gianna, and now I as her runner, cultivated his good will.

Even so, one month the statement had a mistake of over a million lire (over $1,600). When, after a three-day struggle, we discovered it was *his* mistake, not ours in the accounts, and raged at him, he accused us of being inconsiderate. That day he had had a terrible headache. How could we expect him to be accurate, knowing how he suffered with his liver? He placed his right hand, open, fingers splayed out and down, roughly over his heart and rolled his eyes up toward the ceiling. Indeed, how could we scold a martyr? There was next month and another statement to anticipate.

However inconvenient to the conduct of business, delicate sensibilities were one proof of gentility. Our banker was merely loyal to the conventions of local Society. They were not to be ignored. If they were, reprisals were in order, the more public the better. The evening promenade (where he had little chance of finding us) was the favored arena. Snubs were graded according to offense. *Sostenuto* was a distance of manner and a nod. *Togliere il saluto* was the withdrawal of any greeting. Neither by word nor by glance was the victim acknowledged: the boor was invisible. Watching the permutations of snubs and slights and the rapprochements that would gradually be accomplished was the most satisfactory amusement of the town's bourgeoisie. It had a number of attractions. It was free. There were eight performances a week, once on weekdays, twice on Sundays, and it was, besides, one of the few activities couples enjoyed together, she busy about her cycle of huffs, he about his, both alert to the nuances of others' feuds.

There were not many couples without some quibble to exploit, but should two such meet, they followed a concordat of admissible topics. It was hoped that dinner had been good. On parting the same would be hoped of supper. Health with all its ramifications came next and required use of a special glossary. A very refined, euphemistic one. The body, along with most everything else in the world, was vulgar. So, for some reason, were pigs and pork, although they could be mentioned as long as the rider *con rispetto parlando* (respectfully speaking) was added. Women were always *in stato interessante*, never pregnant. Shoulders were a constant embarrassment, forever facing the wrong direction, being rude to the person behind. In the front seat of a car, going through a doorway, in a theater. Apologies for them—*Scusate le spalle*—peppered the day, as though there were feasible alternatives. Feet did not exist. They were extremities. They were appendages. In the early stages of building the nursery, but only after bewildering conversations that seemed pure gibberish to us, we discovered feet could be more obviously inanimate objects, such as foundations. "This rain is ruining our foundations," became an intimate, almost racy statement.

We seldom joined the evening promenade. By the time we left the office at 6:30 or 7:00, the idea of dress-

ing in acceptable finery to pace sedately along a street
we saw all too often did not appeal, especially with loud-
speakers bleating at every corner *"Trieste à noi! Trieste à noi!"* an uneasy reminder of the parroting, mind-
less bombast of the too recent past. If, however, letters
were urgent or Ida had the evening off and we planned
to have dinner in town, we could not avoid it.

Even our arrival was a spectacle. I was the only
woman in town who drove. Furthermore, I was the only
woman the children had *ever* seen drive a car. The sight
frightened and fascinated them. And shocked them. They
gaped, then they gasped, *"Guarda la femmina che porta
la macchina!"* usually followed, after another gulp of
surprise, by *"E fuma pure!"* Look at the female driving
the car! And she smokes too! We could not sneak into
town, we were piped in with these singsong phrases.

By comparison the *struscio*, beyond the lovely
onomatopoeia of its name, was a letdown. Each time,
Gianna found that she had inspired a new set of animos-
ities, as evidenced by the sostenuto treatment—a teacher
whose child had not been taken at the nursery (for the
obvious reason that he was not poor), a doctor's wife
whose full-time maid had not been given an overcoat
(for the same reason)—and, almost as disconcerting,
found that the old ones had warmed up to tepid bows
and simpers. As with most games, unless you played all
the time, you lost the touch. Gianna may never have
had it, and I, for my part, was always too distracted by
little scenes played out quietly around the fringes to follow the main event. I liked to watch the barber's boy
shuffle and skip through the crowd on his endless trips
to the café with jugs of water to be heated at the coffee
machine's steam nozzle, or the scrubbed-up workmen

who ducked into the stationery store and paid ten lire for a squirt of brilliantine from the two-liter bottle that sat on the counter near the cash register. And there were the pantomimes performed in the draper's window for the benefit of the passing public: customers elaborately undecided about lengths of cloth they and the shopkeeper knew they had no intention of buying, indeed, could not afford.

I also had a project I was obstinately devoted to, though it was hopeless. I stopped regularly at the two pharmacies to ask if they had received any sanitary napkins. The reactions were always the same. The pharmacist fixed me with glazed eyes and shook his head. I knew what was in his mind: Will this silly woman never stop asking? When I failed to vanish meekly from his sight, and he realized that I expected some verbal expression, he resorted to the Olympian pomposity that defies contradiction. "That item is unfortunately not available at this time." I chose to understand that meant it would be at some future time.

In fairness, I already knew from an uncomfortable morning spent in the customs section of the Florence post office that there was a general vagueness about the "item." At the time I had assumed it was willful. The problem was a box my mother had sent me, containing what she considered the essentials for my Italian spring—several evening dresses, the silk shoes that matched, some silk dresses, a suit and my calling cards. She had padded them and cushioned them with an amazing number of sanitary napkins. The inspector was dubious about the calling cards, but did concede no one else would have any use for them. And what exactly were these? He held up a napkin, letting it rock gently to and fro in front of my face. The box could not be released without a satisfactory explanation. What, exactly, were *these*? Bandages, I offered. That is, a type of bandage, I mumbled.

People had turned to watch us. Again the inspector waggled the napkin in my face, then went off and conferred with an older man. Together they came back to my box and began dismantling one of the offending objects. With each layer their expressions were more puzzled, their questions gruffer, and all I could do was mutter "Bandages." We were headed for an impasse when a young man, who had come along behind the counter, so must have been a customs official too, called them away for another whispered conference. He was very emphatic in word and deed, batting his forehead with the side of his hand in case his opinion of his colleagues' intelligence remained in doubt. Predictably they passed his wrath on to me, shoving the box, which by then was semi-collapsed and with each movement dribbled its contents about, across the counter and ordered me to remove myself and my mess. Immediately! I did in some disarray, wondering if the lowly sanitary napkin could really be such a novelty.

In Ortona for the first time I saw the women's magazines. They were long on dressmaking, romantic stories, etiquette and personal hints, such as the desirability of shaving your legs and under your arms, advice that Elisa dismissed instantly because it would "weaken" her sexual powers—a daunting idea that left me speechless. There were advertisements too of intriguing ambiguity. Even good old Camay had a new personality. We were promised it "Seduces, seduces, seduces three times!" Others extolled the latest hygienic wonders—deodorants and sanitary napkins—in prose so coyly obscure the exact use of the product could not be identified.

I told Gianna I wanted to try buying sanitary napkins in Ortona, now that they were nationally advertised. "Oh do!" she said with a patient, Mona Lisa smile. There would be no help from her. The embarrassment and the failure prophesied by the smile would be mine. Alone, I persisted, too stubborn to give up, and when success unexpectedly came, of course Gianna was away. There was no one to share my elation.

One evening at dusk, as I came out of the post office, the lights in the pharmacy across the way flashed on, revealing an entire window taken up by a display of sanitary napkins, great Dolomitic peaks of them, in bundles wrapped with white-and-blue paper that suggested a recondite surgical secret within. People crowded around the counter, mostly women who did not mind in the least waiting for the pharmacist. Not for Il Bello, as he was known. His looks, his great height, his Roman nose and sleeked-back silver hair impressed them. His pachydermal dignity impressed them. He even seemed to deliberate over the questions he asked, the same ones repeated dozens of times a day in the same sad, reluctant voice. These very qualities that might have convinced them he had a sluggish mind had instead established that he was a grand seigneur. They waited, patiently admiring, to be served, and even his habit of taking those judged of more elevated station first did not upset them. Usually it irritated me, but that evening I was willing to accept the honor.

My request was received with a bewildered questioning stare. There was a whole window display of them, I reminded him. He nodded, turned and with the slow, blind gait of a sleepwalker disappeared through a curtain of beads into his inner sanctum at the back of the shop. It seemed a long time before he plodded back through the beads with a package wrapped in lavender tissue paper. Very tactful, I thought, getting out my money. He took it, then leaned stiffly over the counter, beckoning me to do the same. "Forgive me for asking," he said, his voice softened to a tête-à-tête whisper. "But what do you use them for?"

Our forays into the *struscio* climaxed with dinner at the town's only restaurant. It offered few surprises. At our arrival neon bars would blink and splutter on in the one room, revealing the antiseptic splendor of a dozen tables with white cloths and whitewashed walls, unsullied except for four brown, molded plaques of elfin creatures in their workshops frantically busy about something. I never quite made out what, though I had plenty of chances: every Southern *trattoria* had a set. The boy-waiter with the frog face would come skidding out of the kitchen, wearing his basic uniform—a white shirt, very, very short black shorts, black anklets and black, scuffed shoes—and struggling to get his black bow tie snapped in place. Behind him came the fat, chinless proprietor, Don Ciccio, and behind him, just sticking her head out of the kitchen door, the cook.

Evenings were quiet. Midday brought the crowd of traveling men and teachers and government clerks, who had been assigned posts away from home and so lived in rooms and had a "subscription" with Don Ciccio; twenty meals a month for eight thousand lire (thirteen dollars). At supper there would be a few strays and the other pharmacist, who did what he called "eating light" before going to bed. He always had the same delectable dish. Plain boiled spaghetti, over which he poured cod-liver oil.

With a great, grinning flourish the waiter would seat us at a corner table and then, flicking at the table-cloth with his all-purpose napkin, would recite the menu, which never changed, but in his deep, deep voice sounded impressive. Pasta, dry or wet—with sauce, or in broth. Meat *al piacere*, that was some part of a cow we nick-named Gertrude, who supplied untold yards of tough, grainy, gray meat, never steaks or chops. Or fried eggs. Vegetables were scarce; salad, dangerous. There was no fish; the best of the local catch went to Rome. Fruit would be bananas that set your teeth on edge. Choosing was a formality. Before the waiter skidded back into the kitchen, the cook had our order well started.

Don Ciccio moved in to entertain us with the day's problems, usually about water. The Turkish toilet, just off the kitchen in the alcove with the wash-up sink, was clogged. There was no water. Plates from lunch were still soaking in big galvanized tubs. Ah, here was our first course. *Buon appetito!* The napkins were always wet and steamed herringbone patterns on our skirts. By the time the pharmacist reached for his carafe of cod-liver oil, we were ready for our check. We were home never later than nine, tired and depressed.

This was life in Ortona. Nothing of fantasy and no escape.

Fifteen

The last two weeks of October, Gianna was in Bologna for a course, so even such somber delights as dinner at Don Ciccio's were taboo. *Serietà* again. A few days in Ortona and the world always warped, slightly. Alone there it seemed positively atilt. Or was some delicate gyroscopic mechanism in my brain out of kilter? It was hard to be absolutely sure, harder still to cling to the idea that everything and everyone else was atilt, not I.

Gianna's train had barely left the station when the Baby Hut assistant scampered off to Campobasso, or maybe Avellino, one of those towns not exactly prominent on the beauty-contest circuit, in pursuit of her manife destiny as the next Gina Lollobrigida. The judges not agree, but that was five days later.

Every morning a man lurked on the office st clutching a large, leather, patchwork shopping bag, which came yowls and hisses of rage. He wanted to discuss a simple proposition. His wife thought their cat was ugly. The only time I allowed him to open the bag I had to agree: it was not just ugly, it was the meanest-looking old tom I had ever seen. She fancied one of Gianna's, therefore they were prepared to swap their tom for Gianna's pretty cat. I was not. Selfish! Outrageous! Inconsiderate, he blustered, but the next morning and the next and the next he was back, on the stairs, with his cat in the shopping bag and a new argument.

Was it reasonable to pay a water bill for the *fifth* quarter of the year? Plus a huge charge for "overconsumption"? Bearing in mind there was seldom enough pressure to fill the holding tanks. Futile speculations. The water company offered two choices: pay or be disconnected. I was also advised that no protest of the bill would be entertained until *after* payment in full had been received.

Not to be outdone in the field of imaginative administration, the telephone company demanded a $250 deposit for long-distance calls, which might, sometime, in the future, be made from the telephone.

Sorino, having missed half a dozen perfect chances, decided it was now or never if the house were to be whitewashed before the rains came. Two days, he promised, no more, of complete upheaval. Downstairs one day, upstairs the next. Furniture out in the garden, books under the rosebushes, chaos, only surpassed by the messy, mizzling business of getting the whitewash on the walls, which was accomplished by Pasquale, manning a hand pump submerged in one of the many buckets dotted around the floor ready to use or be tumbled over, and Sorino, wafting around a long noz-

zle-wand. Pressure and aim were both erratic, but in
two days, as promised, every surface was covered—
floors, windows, doors and incidentally walls. Scraping
off the undesired quantities took much longer.

A sponsor's package had to be divided into two
packages to meet Italian measurement regulations. At
the post office the package clerk refused to accept both
at the same time. Not two addressed to the same person. Regulations. He's a little boy. These are toys,
clothes. No. But why? That's what the regulations said
. . . They were Holy Writ, not to be questioned. That
I did seemed to imply an element of subversion in my
character, which may have prompted the one excuse he
offered. Did I realize that guns could be broken down?
That the individual parts would be within the weight
and size limits set by the ministry? I argued that I could
take my packages to two different post offices or mail
them, "them" now tacitly established as gun parts, on
two consecutive days. Thereafter in the post office or
on the street, in the café, he watched me with sullen,
wary eyes. Was I dangerous? Or had I been making fun
of him? Authority must not be questioned. Dignity must
be maintained.

One morning, very early, Pasquale discovered that
his prize stand of bamboo, which shielded the playground from people who stopped in the lane to gape at
the babies, had vanished overnight. Gone, every stalk
of it. I heard him stomping, whooping and cursing around
the garden. I peeked out the door, watched his war dance
for a minute, then crept back to bed, clinging to the
temporary safety of ignorance. With my breakfast came
Ida's report of the affair. Pasquale had hinted that my
failure to sound the alarm was possibly collusion. "Don't

worry," she added with a grin. "Every year about this time someone steals his bamboo. He suspects all of us, even the signora."

Afternoons, after the Baby Hut and nursery were closed, Elisa, the nursery teacher and I set out together to visit the children and their families, four or five in the two hours before dinner. The round was continuous through the year, but more concentrated at the beginning of terms and always started with those children who had been absent, which eliminated any systematic approach to it. We had to cut back and forth all over town.

A few lived in public housing, up staircases that were already gouged and smeared, the steps chipped, and the window glass out. The apartments were small with small rooms: two bedrooms, a bath, kitchen and an all-purpose room, usually empty, that was designated a dining room as a symbol of future aspirations. Cots, straight chairs and a cupboard in the kitchen were shadowy lumps in the light from the twenty-watt bulbs that were used to avoid exceeding the allowed free minimum of electricity. How many people actually lived in each apartment was a family secret. Behind a door or in a corner by the cupboard a grandmother, wrapped in shawls, always dozed, her head drooping toward her knees. The brashest young mothers in public, at home were subdued. There was no one to deceive, no expectations, maybe bread and oil for supper. The children sensed it too. The chatterers of a few hours before clung now to their mothers' knees and stared with big, dulled eyes at nothing.

Many more of our children lived in one-story, one-room houses that lined the sandy back streets, like Pasquale's Street of Hope. Every activity, except eating

and sleeping, spilled out into those streets, creating between the small fountain, waterless for the most part,
at one end and the grate to the sewer at the other, a
neighborhood sitting room–playground–battlefield–latrine. Women sat on chairs outside their doors, knitting
and keeping an eye on the fountain for a chance trickle
of water. Women stood in knots, screaming at one another, the daily engagement in an ongoing feud. Children crawled around in the dust with mangy dogs and
furtive cats. There was always a ball that a bully had
to kick full force, always a baby who fell, howling. Down
by the drain another group of women, emptying their
slop pots, recited their parts in another marathon feud:
whose turn it was to sweep and clean up around the
drain. Except for the old, men were invisible. They spent
their days in the piazza, came home only at night. Those
streets and houses were crowded, noisy, certainly squalid
and unsanitary, but life was there too, greedy and aggressive. Each day the people scrabbled to keep what
they had, steal what could be stolen. The competition
was too fierce here for the gloomy resignation that
seemed built into the very walls of public housing, where
should have been hope.

But by far the largest number of children lived,
again one room to a family, however mixed the generations, in the maze of a multi-storied, collapsing mill,
below the main road, near the clearing where the buses
congregated. Between children who were sick and families we should see, we were there almost every evening. I dreaded it. I tried not to think about it, pretend
I was not going, not really, not today. The girls would
have accepted any excuse. I always went, but it was an
act of will.

The mill was a large, unadorned block of brick,

much neglected, battered by the war and now a derelict that shivered ominously with each truck that passed. Whoever owned it—and I no longer remember, if I ever knew—undoubtedly had collected war damages in excess of any conceivable value and abandoned it with a sign warning the structure was unsafe, trespassers entered at their own risk. The homeless, who invaded it, could not read and would not have cared.

The entrance was off a courtyard, a sinister place at any time of day, strewn with garbage that was continuously worked over by cats, dogs and other less appealing scavengers, alive with brawling children and shrieking women. The arguments that went on day and night and often developed into slugfests were always about water. There was one faucet—next to the one foul toilet that might have served a few of the tenants had it not been perpetually full of stones.

Only the foolhardy ventured inside, into the total blackness, without a flashlight. The floors were wood planks, rotten and treacherous in what would have been the normal lanes of traffic. Habitués knew the detours. Jagged ladder-stairways, rotten and at points missing one or two steps entirely, led upward three flights. When we appeared in the halls, women who had been screeching in fierce, animalesque rage, stopped, offered help, directions. They even batted their brooms around in the dark corners to drive off scratching, scuttling creatures we could all suddenly hear. It seemed a measure of their mutual distrust that each family we visited escorted us to the next and abandoned us only when that door had been answered.

The rooms were alike in every dismal dimension, large and bare with raw plank flooring, unevenly spaced,

and one window that was nailed shut and covered, glazed
would not be the word, with heavy, oiled brown paper.
In summer it was ripped out, but summer and winter a
miasmal smudge, colder or warmer and better not ana-
lyzed, clogged the air. A black, tarry syrup dribbled
down the walls. From ropes strung in cat's cradles back
and forth across the rooms hung discouraging assort-
ments of damp rags, underwear and sometimes a diaper
or two, "borrowed" from the nursery, and behind it all,
in the gloom, the one standard piece of furniture, a double bed. Everything else had been scrounged from
bombed-out buildings and trash heaps: low cupboards,
their doors torn off their hinges, provided surfaces for
gas rings; splintered bench-chests, upended fruit crates,
backless chairs become stools; rusty tin tubs that stored
water, leaking it, drop by drop, down onto the neighbors below. Some cracked plates and a misshapen pot
or two without handles were shoved out of the way on
the floor by the cupboards. Single strands of twine, fixed
to the walls with nails, served as slings for lids and hooks
for dented ladles. Children slept on the bed, nesting in
tangles of sheets, rags and clothes not in use at the moment. Others scuffled under the bed or crawled around
their mother's feet as she tried to sweep up or, when
they got in her way, crouched in the middle of the floor
and screamed. Old women, who were immune to chaos
or in a state of withdrawal from it, sat near the window, always with their backs to it, staring apathetically
at the floor.

Our arrival brought an instant reversal of roles.
The sleepers woke up, the scufflers turned peaceful,
peeking out at us, the crawlers sat still, their eyes huge
and curious, the mothers leaned on their brooms and

the old women bustled about, scraping off crates and
stools with calloused hands until they found three that
offered some stability and a minimum of nails and snags.

Elisa and the young teacher knew the children
and their families. They talked. I was the silent partner
soon forgotten, left free to watch and wonder always at
the same things. Where and how did so many people
sleep? Eat? What did they do about bladders and bow-
els in such a place? Or conceiving children? Obviously
they did—somehow. And always, without quite realizing it, I found myself staring through wide gaps in the
floor boards, watching another woman with a broom or
a child or an old man waving his arms in the room below. They were slatted scenes—a knife hacking at bread,
a baby kicked away from its mother's skirt. Lean slightly
forward and I saw a woman's face contorted in rage.
Lean slightly back and through another gap I saw the
man whose hands held the knife. He hacked at the bread,
ignoring the woman. A pause in our conversation and
their voices growled up around us. On to the next visit.
Another room, another family and, through wide gaps
in the floorboards, other slatted scenes, life theoretically, being acted out in the room below.

The mill. I could not shake it off. It fascinated
and revolted me. It infuriated me. It jarred most of the
assumptions I never knew I had made, about civilization and progress, how people, rich and poor, acted and
why, and rearranged them, as the slight twitch of a kaleidoscope leaves the same pieces in a dramatically different pattern. Two thousand years later and the mill
was a replica of those teeming, stinking, sinister tene-
ments that once crowded up to the backsides of the Roman Empire's glittering white marble monuments to it-

self—with two differences: the mill was of brick and those people were alive today. Archaeology seemed a dead subject, an evasion, an intellectual lie.

My evenings I spent in soporific study of the blueprints and the building instructions for the new nursery. The flatcars had found their way to Ortona, finally, and the panels were now carefully propped around the perimeter of a rotten floor, the only floor left, in a huge abandoned warehouse. The blueprints and instructions had arrived too—all in Swedish, which brought on embarrassed confessions. No one, not Sorino, not Gianna, not the contractor, had any idea how to mount the house, where even to start. I was the resident expert, an honor bestowed on me simply for having lived in a country where wooden houses are common. I objected that I had *looked at* thousands of wooden houses, but never from a structural point of view. No, at least for a brief while longer, I was their expert. My task was to reason my way through the blueprints, step by step, numbering pieces in the order, I hoped, they would be needed *and* at the same time to put together a trilingual lexicon—from Swedish to English to, where the dictionary helped me, Italian—for mortise joints, purlins and rafters, joists, panels, gable walls and such.

It seemed a useful, yet harmless way to spend my evenings, but again, I had forgotten that nagging question of *serietà*. Mine, I realized, must be very fragile, very fragile indeed. After dinner, when Ida was through clearing up, she had me follow her to the door, then stood in the garden, listening to be sure I turned the key in the lock. Twice Sorino arrived about nine-thirty, banging and shouting not to be afraid, he just wanted to see that I was all right. I let him in, and he looked at the blueprints and the dictionaries and papers spread over the big table, nodding as though relieved. The third time he made me cross. I asked if he did house checks on Gianna.

"Oh no. She's a widow!" was his answer, a statement of fact that suddenly was open to a variety of interpretations, most of them unflattering. And did he distrust me or the Ortonesi? (Both, was Gianna's reaction later.) The next morning, in a better humor, I was ready to have some fun with this boring business of *serietà*. Whatever Sorino suspected me of, it was not, thanks to the distracting innocence Latins read in blue eyes, guile, so casually, in passing, I mentioned to Ida that his visits were, after all, as compromising as anyone else's. Good heavens, even his wife might think . . .

Ida cocked her head to one side and stared at me thoughtfully, skeptically. Women seldom base innocence on looks. She also knew me better. Slowly that big jack-o'-lantern smile, flashing with aluminum teeth, spread over her face and she began to laugh. She had a hoarse laugh, more of a rumbly giggle that swelled up from somewhere deep inside her and always brought with it a special childish delight. Still laughing, she clopped back downstairs. In a few minutes I heard the jeep stop outside the gate, followed by a hissed, emphatic conference. I had been right. She would not keep it to herself. Sorino was very subdued that day, silently apologetic. That evening he switched to surveillance by telephone.

All was quiet again, and I was alone with my deciphering. Of blueprints and vocabularies, as long as I could concentrate, of my own thoughts, when they be-

came too intrusive to be ignored. Phrases I had heard,
or half-heard, bubbled through my mind in Jack-be-nim-
ble jingles

> *Southerners are dirty*
> *Southerners are thieves*
> *Southerners refuse to roll up their sleeves*
> *Southerners are lousy*
> *Southerners are drifters*
> *Southerners are willing to sell their sisters.*

Why such scorn from people who did not know them?
"What this country needs is a zipper across it, right below Florence (Florentine version)/ right below Rome
(Roman version), and let the rest float out to sea." "Af-
rica begins at 'La Portella' (the gateway to the Kingdom of Naples)." Had they ever been there? Known any
Southerners, those seers? No.

   The bourgeois Ortonesi, few in number and suspicious of change, it being always for the worse, were
little better. They were afraid of the poor. Shopkeepers
watched the men in the piazza as though they were offensive, physically distasteful. Look at them. Never had
it so good. There were mumblings, too, about the cas-
tor-oil treatment. Mussolini knew what he was doing:
that was the way to keep them in line.

   Landowners grumbled about the waste, tragic
waste, of money on housing. For people who had always lived like animals. What would they demand next?
This was the problem.

   Even the attractive doctor, whose mother would
not allow him to stay out after ten, said "they," that

ragged, unemployed blob of humanity, had never had such fine medical care. (Maybe, but . . . The hospital was halfway between bombed out and rebuilt. There was a surgeon one day a week, no ambulance, no water to wash patients or bedpans. Syringes were, supposedly, boiled. Blood transfusions were dumped from open beakers into funnels that had used filter paper in them. Illiterate midwives held sway over the obstetrics ward. Tonsils were removed in doctors' offices without benefit of anesthetic and the child sent home with a sheet, his own, wrapped around his head. Pasteur and Lister might never have been.)

Teachers blustered about ignorance and superstition and earnestly advocated five years' schooling, no more, for minds too simple, too blunted for intellectual niceties.

I resented the condescension and the true, willful ignorance, so smug and gratuitous, that could dismiss millions of people as unfit for a chance at life. But why should *I* resent how Southern Italians were treated? By other Italians? I was no reformer. I knew I could change nothing, improve little. I might even do harm. Why, then?

In those long, quiet evenings alone, deciphering, I never really understood. I was too upset by the specific examples to see that what actually offended me was the unfairness of it all. Now, so many years later, when all those basic assumptions, thoughtless ones that I never knew I had made, have been shattered into different patterns, it seems naive. Even then to me justice was an imperfect concept, a structure to be administered, wisely, perhaps at times, too often unwisely. To me fairness was separate, a moral obligation of the individ-

ual. I suppose I wanted it to be absolute. So many years
ago! I had not found out about absolutes, but fairness
. . . And if no one fought . . . ? The charms of ancient
Rome and the Romans evaporated, leaving questions
without answers—and more decisions. Exhausted, I went
to bed only to dream of structures collapsing, crumbling, crashing around me. In the morning, still exhausted, I awoke to dissect yet again the conundrum of
the mill, which was really the conundrum of Ortona itself. With each twitch the patterns of my kaleidoscope
shifted.

The morning of the day Gianna was to return, Sorino
insisted I meet him at the cemetery. Against my objections and excuses, he insisted. He wanted my permission, but before he could tell me for what, he had to
explain. In situ. I chose noon, an hour when most people would be thinking of lunch. Sorino, and, to my surprise, Pasquale stood waiting for me at the gate. This
was a joint project, a species of verbal rondo with "custom" as the central theme.

    Each year, as All Souls' approached, they worked
to put Ernest Thompson's grave in order. They cleaned
the headstone, blacked the letters, pulled up the weeds
and put out new gravel. They also banked the grave in
flowers at terrible expense. Once the funeral was over,
Gianna had never been back to the cemetery. Never—
as far as they knew. She was always carefully away for
All Saints' and All Souls'. Each year, this was the third,
they, Sorino and Pasquale, had taken the place of the
family. What in the world did they mean? Neither really
wanted to go into that. It was customary. People would
talk, if . . . If what? Well, it was *usanza* . . . What?

Signora Gianna would not approve, they knew that, but
. . . But *what*?

From a pocket Sorino pulled out a box and handed
it to me. Inside were yellowish deckled cards with a
photograph of Ernest Thompson, looking very young and
solemn and slightly out of focus, over the dates of his
birth and death and a maudlin, pseudo-pious reevoca-
tion of his premature demise. I was appalled. They knew
Gianna would not approve, but Sorino and Pasquale took
turns, standing by the grave, talking to people who
stopped, and giving each a card, a *ricordino*. They knew
Gianna would not approve, but it was custom. Also, the
night before All Souls', custom again, in front of the
grave they set out a table with linen, plates, silver and
eventually food. This was to welcome the soul, to as-
sure him he was cared for and expected. What happened to the food? I asked, but they were beyond the
reach of sarcasm. Oh, it was all gone the next morning.
No doubt one of the cemetery keeper's prerogatives of
office. That seemed to bring us to the end of another
difficult subject. I waited.

This year they had thought, well, it seemed time
to do it. There had been comment about its omission.
Again, from his pocket Sorino brought out a box. Inside
was an oval, porcelain medallion with the same photograph of Ernest Thompson printed in sepia. They wanted
my permission to have it attached to the headstone. Like
all the other headstones, Sorino added, hesitantly. Pasquale nodded.

I could neither give nor withhold permission. They
seemed to have taken over the grave as their own. They
knew, they admitted they knew, that Gianna wanted
none of this. She had tried to avoid it. Why, then . . . ?

People thought she did not care.

Sorino and Pasquale knew better, I objected. She would never come, dressed in dourest black and veils, to wail at the grave. Not even to satisfy custom. She had tried to do what Ernest Thompson would have wanted. The authorities, ecclesiastical and civil, had blocked his cremation. A scandalous idea in Italy then. She had done the next best thing. She had him buried in a winding sheet, in a plain pine coffin, the grave marked by the simplest, most factual headstone. They knew her wishes. If they chose to ignore them, that was up to them, but they could never say *I* gave them permission to do what we all knew she found pagan.

That was that. I had not been very diplomatic about it. I did not feel diplomatic about it and would have stormed away, leaving them to struggle with their consciences, except that they both seemed stricken. I had told them the truth. I had not meant to shame them. What they had done and wanted to do was not shameful. It was an invasion of that privacy Gianna held so dear, but not with any malice. So I stood with them, waiting.

By then it was a difficult story to tell me and it took awhile. After the shock of Ernest's disappearance and Sorino's finding his body, there had been a short delay for the coroner's examination and the issuance of the death certificate. Gianna had given Sorino precise instructions for the undertaker. He thought, well, shock. A temporary failure of reason. Well, whatever he thought, he changed Gianna's instructions. He had the coffin lined in zinc, for which he paid himself, and, with Ida's help, he smuggled a suit, shirt and all the trimmings out of the house. Ernest Thompson had been buried with proper dignity, as Ortona required he be buried.

When Sorino finished, I said nothing. What was there to say? Silence made Pasquale nervous. He started several times—"We thought . . ." "The signora didn't seem to . . ." "What would others . . .?"—then gave up and stared at the ground. We all stared at the ground, until Sorino asked very quietly that I not tell Gianna. She need never know. I promised I would tell her nothing. Of that he could be very sure.

I left them there by the grave and went home, loathing Ortona, railing at Ortona and the Ortonesi, who would allow nothing, not even grief, the grief of others, to take its own form. *This* was the place where for the first time in my life I woke up each morning consciously happy, consciously looking forward to the unknowns of that day, to the absurd, puzzling or horrifying discoveries of that day. This dreary, cruel, bigoted place!

As I left to meet Gianna's train in Pescara, Ida gave me a message from Sorino: he would be late, but would be at the house before we got back. In other words, the medallion was to be put on the headstone.

Return had its ritual that seldom changed: a visit to the nursery, to the Baby Hut and now the new nursery, which was still just a foundation, threatening to founder before the nursery floor that would cover it could be poured; Sorino reported; Ida, as usual, made the household catastrophes sound funny; and the mail was sorted, not a great deal this time because I had kept up to date with all but "policy matters." Gianna unpacked and had a cup of tea. She looked over my pile of construction notes and settled down to filling the gaps in my Italian synonyms as though they were the captions of a crossword puzzle.

Dinner came and Ida left. We dragged the tall-backed chairs over in front of the clay stove and opened the door of the firebox, which made it *almost* like having a fireplace. Ortona was a place of almosts. Gianna had some sewing in her lap, but already heavy-eyed and sleepy, she stared at the flames. I had a book open on my knees, only as a stage prop. My mind seemed to have turned into a centrifuge. It had been that way all afternoon, flinging out ideas, unrelated, wild ideas. I grabbed at one, lunged for the next, tangled them both to find myself chasing a third. I had not thought Gianna was paying any attention, but she broke into my merry-go-round confusion.

"Did it depress you that much—being here, I mean?"

So I explained my predicament: that I wanted to stay. She stared at me for what seemed a very long time. At me, but obviously she was not seeing me. She was far away in her own thoughts.

"Yes. Yes, stay if you like. I'd be delighted," she finally said. "But I should warn you of *one* thing." She paused to be sure I realized how serious she was. "No one who stays in the South is ever quite the same person again."

She was right, of course. Still, I never regretted the decision and now I know *that* is where it all really began.

Afterword

Thirty-five years, to the month, after I first saw Ortona and the Sangro Valley, I went back. It seemed only fair. Other than fly-over glimpses from the thruway I had seen neither in twenty years.

Ortona is still an amoeboid town, sprawling, dusty, noisy, but it sprawls in a very confident, modern manner. No more rubble and tatters. Apartment buildings spill out in all directions, contained, for the moment, by the towering tanks of a wine cooperative on the south, by hangarlike sheds, offering goods and services (two proclaimed themselves *zapettificios*, a local semantic invention, meaning a factory that makes *small* hoes, as to the Ortonesi "foundry" must lack elegance), by the usual number of service stations and on the west by the huge new hospital, gray concrete in pure contemporary-medieval-fortress style. What is old has been replastered, repainted and embellished with gaudy plastic to match the new.

Squashed, almost invisible in all this splendor, the nursery crouches under a jungly wilderness of acacias and rose brambles. Sea air and twenty years of neglect have brought on the molting and melting stages of collapse. Several coats of paint would be therapeutic, but the prognosis is not hopeful. From the floor rags hung out to dry on the windowsills and the sounds of piping voices within, the nursery was in session. I did not go inside.

Down the lane, paved now, really a street, Gianna's house has a spurious air of sophistication: the stairway is enclosed in glass and brushed metal; the front door of mahogany-esque wood, worthy of an investment banking establishment, sparkles with varnish and hardware.

In town there are several comfortable, if not luxurious hotels (hot water at three in the afternoon!); two, possibly more, excellent restaurants; and cafés with waiters in smart jackets who serve *aperitivi and* hors d'oeuvres that would put Doney's to shame. True, the "new" post office, circa 1960, still appears to be under siege, all its window and door grills down except one. Cars and trucks and scooters and people, well-dressed people mill around at all hours. Not "doing" anything exactly, just there. By eight in the evening movement is reduced to a shuffle in place.

Where does the prosperity come from? No one seems to know.

The Sangro Valley is the bucolic reflection of the same. Small dams have made small lakes. A four-lane highway does not go very far or to any place in particular. Clean, modern villages, hillsides with scatterings of small Alpine villas. BMWs (local licenses) charging back and forth, but not a donkey or peasant in sight.

People say there is no work. The highway deviated the "tourist" trade. And the BMWs stream by.

One morning Ida, her magic smile flashing, but porcelain now, had coffee with us. She would not come out for dinner. She has not been well—must keep to a diet, must either lie down or wear a heavy back brace. There was an unusual look of gravity about her too that for a moment I could not place: ah, the glasses! I had never seen her in glasses. They did not affect her mind or her tongue. Her memories seemed to have a comic twist, even the sad ones part, somehow, of a happier time. I teased her that now as a lady of leisure with her house and her pension, she had time for the evening promenade.

"Who me, *signo*?" she laughed. "Who'd want to in the summer with all these kids? In winter you don't dare show yourself unless you have a fur coat." Which reminded me. Where did she think all this money came from? "Nobody knows, but people always find a way to steal," was her answer. The *arte di arrangiarsi* moved to a higher plane? Cynical and yet . . .

As we left Ortona for the last time, we became entangled in a traffic jam and a maze of one-way streets, unknown to me, a new neighborhood of detached houses and low apartment buildings. Suddenly on our left were the gates of the cemetery, like the nursery, semi-engulfed by progress. We stopped. Sorino's sepia medallion still marks Ernest Thompson's grave. He is forever very young and solemn and slightly out of focus. I wondered what he would have made of the change. Even more I wonder what Gianna, that astute judge of all things Ortonese, would think, but I will never know. She died in October of 1986.